A TREASURY OF THE
KINGDOM

A TREASURY OF THE KINGDOM

An Anthology

compiled by

E. A. BLACKBURN

and others

The Kingdom of God is within you.
ST. LUKE xvii. 21

1954

OXFORD UNIVERSITY PRESS

NEW YORK AND LONDON

Printed in the United States of America

FOREWORD

THERE is a need, increasingly felt, for an anthology of readings that would serve to bring home the eternal nature of the Christian message, which is not confined to the Bible alone, but is expressed in the lives and writings of countless Servants of the Kingdom. This anthology is an attempt to meet this need.

E. A. B.

SEVENOAKS
October 1953

NOTE

THE introductory notes have been written, not merely for the private reader, but to provide announcements which may be required when passages are read aloud.

ACKNOWLEDGEMENTS

For permission to include extracts from the undermentioned works grateful acknowledgement is made to the following copyright-owners and publishers:

St. Augustine, *Confessions*, translated by F. J. Sheed: Messrs. Sheed & Ward, Ltd.

Iulia de Beausobre, *Flame in the Snow*: Mme de Beausobre and Messrs. Constable & Co., Ltd.

E. Moberly Bell, *Octavia Hill*: Messrs. Constable & Co., Ltd.

G. P. Bidder: *The Times* and Dr. G. P. Bidder.

Margaret Bondfield, *What Life Has Taught Me*: Odhams Press, Ltd., and the late Margaret Bondfield.

A. C. Bouquet, *Lectionary of Christian Prose*: the Rev. A. C. Bouquet and Messrs. Longmans, Green & Co., Ltd.

J. A. Bouquet, *A Book of Saints*: the Rev. J. A. Bouquet and Messrs. Longmans, Green & Co., Ltd.

J. H. Burn, *A Day Book from the Saints and Fathers*: Messrs. Methuen & Co., Ltd.

Caesarius of Heisterbach, *Dialogue on Miracles*, translated by H. von E. Scott and C. C. S. Bland: Messrs. Routledge & Kegan Paul, Ltd.

R. M. and A. G. Carlyle, *Leaders of Religion*: Messrs. Methuen & Co., Ltd.

Carmina Gadelica, edited by Alex Carmichael: the trustees of Alex Carmichael.

St. Catherine of Siena as seen in her letters, by V. D. Scudder: Messrs. J. M. Dent & Sons, Ltd., and E. P. Dutton & Co., Inc.

G. K. Chesterton, *The Everlasting Man*: Miss Collins and Messrs. Hodder & Stoughton, Ltd., and Dodd Mead & Co. (U.S. copyright 1925 by Dodd Mead & Co., Inc.); 'A Christmas Carol' (from *The Wild Knight*, J. M. Dent & Sons): Miss Collins and E. P. Dutton & Co., Inc.

The Christian News-Letter: the Christian Frontier Council.

Joseph Cottler, *Man With Wings*: the author and Messrs. George G. Harrap & Co., Ltd.

Sir Stafford Cripps, *God in Our Work*: Mr. John Cripps and Messrs. Thomas Nelson & Sons, Ltd.

Dostoevsky, *The Brothers Karamazov*, translated extracts in Robert Bridges's *The Spirit of Man*: Messrs. Longmans, Green & Co., Ltd.

T. S. Eliot, *Murder in the Cathedral, The Rock*, and *The Journey of the Magi*: Mr. T. S. Eliot and Messrs. Faber & Faber, Ltd., and Harcourt, Brace and Co., New York.

E. B. Emmott, *The Story of Quakerism*: the Literature Committee of the Society of Friends.

Epictetus, *Manual and Discourses*, translated by P. E. Matheson: the translator and the Delegates of the Clarendon Press.

Erasmus, *The Education of a Christian Prince*, translated by L. K. Born: Columbia University Press.

John Ferguson, *The Enthronement of Love*: Mr. John Ferguson.

The Little Flowers of St. Francis, translated by T. Okey: Messrs. J. M. Dent & Sons, Ltd., and E. P. Dutton & Co., Inc.

Mahatma Gandhi, Essays and Reflections on his Life and Work, by Dr. S. Radhakrishnan: Messrs. George Allen & Unwin, Ltd.

Phyllis Garlick, *Pioneers of the Kingdom*: Miss P. L. Garlick and the Church Missionary Society.

Charles Gore: *The Philosophy of the Good Life*: Messrs. John Murray, Ltd.

Sir Richard Gregory, *Discovery*: Lady Gregory and the trustees of Sir R. Gregory.

H. M. Gwatkin, *Early Church History*: Miss E. R. Gwatkin.

J. L. and B. Hammond, *Lord Shaftesbury*: Messrs. Longmans, Green & Co., Ltd.

Abbot Harmion's letter translated in *Mont St. Michel and Chartres*, by Henry Adams: Messrs. Constable & Co., Ltd., and the Houghton Mifflin Co.

J. C. Harris, *Couriers of Christ*: the Livingstone Press.

F. Heiler, *The Gospel of Sadhu Sundar Singh*: Messrs. George Allen & Unwin, Ltd.

Lucy Hodgkin, *A Book of Quaker Saints*: Miss Lucy Hodgkin (Mrs. L. V. Holdsworth).

G. M. Hopkins, *Pied Beauty* and *Easter*: the Oxford University Press.

Sir Edwyn Hoskyns, *Cambridge Sermons*: the S.P.C.K.

Laurence Housman, *A Christmas Song*: Mr. Laurence Housman; *The Little Plays of St. Francis*: Mr. Housman and Messrs. Jonathan Cape, Ltd., and Messrs. Sidgwick and Jackson, Ltd.

Laurence Housman and C. H. K. Marten, *The Long Journey*: Messrs. Jonathan Cape, Ltd., and Basil Blackwell & Mott, Ltd.

F. E. Hutchinson, *Cranmer and the English Reformation*: Messrs. Hodder & Stoughton, Ltd.

W. R. Inge, *Personal Religion and the Life of Devotion*: Messrs. Longmans, Green & Co., Ltd.

Kilvert's Diary: Messrs. Jonathan Cape, Ltd., and Mr. T. Percival Smith.

Hanns Lilje, *The Valley of the Shadow*: the S.C.M. Press, Ltd.

Sir Richard Livingstone, *Some Tasks for Education*: the Cambridge University Press.

Martin Luther, *The Magnificat*: The Muhlenberg Press.

Theodore Maynard, *Apostle of Charity*: Messrs. George Allen & Unwin, Ltd. (U.S. copyright 1939 by The Dial Press).

Thomas Merton, *Elected Silence*: Messrs. Hollis & Carter, Ltd.; published in U.S. as *Seven Story Mountain* by Harcourt, Brace and Co.

Alice Meynell, *Easter Night*: Sir Francis Meynell.

U. K. Moore, 'By faith. . .': Mrs. U. K. Moore.

Jawaharlal Nehru, *The Discovery of India*: Mr. Krishna Menon, and The John Day Company, Inc.

Norman Nicholson, *The Shepherd's Carol*: Mr. Norman Nicholson and Messrs. Faber & Faber, Ltd.

W. E. Orchard, *The King's Mount*: the Rev. W. E. Orchard.

Pascal, *Pensées*, translated by W. F. Trotter (Everyman's Library): Messrs. J. M. Dent & Sons, Ltd., and E. P. Dutton & Co., Inc.

John Patten, *These Remarkable Men*: Mr. John Patten.

Henri Perrin, *Priest-Workman in Germany*: Messrs. Sheed & Ward, Ltd.

A. T. Quiller-Couch, *The Roll-Call of Honour*: Miss A. T. Quiller-Couch and Messrs. Thomas Nelson & Sons, Ltd.

R. B. Rackham, *The Acts of the Apostles*: Messrs. Methuen & Co., Ltd.

H. A. Reinhold, *The Spear of Gold*: the Rev. H. A. Reinhold.

F. D. Roosevelt, *Public Papers and Addresses*: Random House, New York.

Sir Ronald Ross, verse quoted by Sir R. Gregory: Messrs. John Murray, Ltd.

S. Kenneth Ruck, in *Social Reformers of the Nineteenth Century*, edited by Hugh Martin: the S.C.M. Press, Ltd.

Dorothy L. Sayers, *The Man Born to be King*: Miss D. L. Sayers and Messrs. Victor Gollancz, Ltd. Copyright 1943 by Dorothy L. Sayers.

Albert Schweitzer, *On the Edge of the Primeval Forest*, and *The Quest of the Historical Jesus*: Messrs. A. & C. Black, Ltd., and The Macmillan Company; *My Life and Thought*: Messrs. George Allen & Unwin, Ltd. (U.S. copyright 1933, 1949, by Henry Holt & Co., Inc.).

Captain Scott's Diary: Messrs. John Murray, Ltd.

George Seaver, *The Faith of Edward Wilson*, and Introduction by A. Cherry Garrard to *Edward Wilson of the Antarctic* by George Seaver: Messrs. John Murray, Ltd.; *Albert Schweitzer, the Man and his Mind*: Messrs. A. & C. Black, Ltd., and Harper & Brothers.

viii   ACKNOWLEDGEMENTS

Seneca, translation of Ep. xli: Miss D. W. Hackman.

Lucy Seymer, *Florence Nightingale*: Messrs. Faber & Faber, Ltd.

Bernard Shaw, *St. Joan*: the Society of Authors and the Public Trustee.

B. H. Streeter and A. J. Appasamy, *The Sadhu*: Macmillan & Co., Ltd.

Rabindranath Tagore, *Gitanjali* and *Fruit Gathering*: Messrs. Macmillan & Co., Ltd., the Trustees of the Tagore Estate, and The Macmillan Company.

William Temple, *Repton School Sermons, Christ in His Church*, and *Readings in St. John's Gospel*: Messrs. Macmillan and Mrs. Temple; *The Universality of Christ*: the S.C.M. Press, Ltd.

St. Teresa's Works, Stanbrook Abbey translation: the Lady Abbess; F. Allison Peers's translation: Messrs. Sheed & Ward, Ltd.

Francis Thompson, *Easter Sunday*: Sir Francis Meynell and Messrs. Hollis & Carter, Ltd.

Arnold Toynbee, *Civilization on Trial*: the Oxford University Press.

Thomas Traherne, *Poems* and *Centuries of Meditation*: Messrs. P. J. and A. E. Dobell.

Freda Troup, *In Face of Fear*: Messrs. Faber & Faber, Ltd.

Turgenev, *Dream Tales and Prose Poems*, translated by Constance Garnett: Messrs. Heinemann, Ltd., and The Macmillan Company.

Evelyn Underhill, *The House of the Soul*: Messrs. Methuen & Co., Ltd. *Immanence*: J. M. Dent & Sons, Ltd., and E. P. Dutton & Co., Inc.

Helen Waddell: *The Desert Fathers* and *Medieval Latin Lyrics*: Messrs. Constable & Co., Ltd.

C. V. Wedgwood, *William the Silent*: Miss C. V. Wedgwood and Messrs. Jonathan Cape, Ltd., and Yale University Press.

J. S. Whale, *Christian Doctrine*: the Cambridge University Press.

A. N. Whitehead, *Science and the Modern World*: the Cambridge University Press and The Macmillan Co. (U.S. copyright 1925 by The Macmillan Co.).

Janet Whitney, *Elizabeth Fry*: the author and Messrs. George G. Harrap & Co., Ltd.

Charles Williams, *He Came Down From Heaven*: Messrs. Faber & Faber, Ltd.

Bishop J. L. Wilson, broadcast address: the Rt. Rev. J. L. Wilson.

R. F. Wilson, *Life of St. Vincent de Paul*: Messrs. Longmans, Green & Co., Ltd.

Nicholas Zernov, *St. Sergius*: the S.P.C.K.

In one or two cases, where attempts to get in touch with the author's present representatives have been made without success, permission to include short extracts has been assumed. The Florence Nightingale Letter is in the possession of Walthamstow Hall, Sevenoaks, and is reproduced with the kind concurrence of Sir Harry Verney.

CONTENTS

PART THREE
THE FRUIT OF THE KINGDOM

PART FOUR
SERVANTS OF THE KINGDOM

PART FIVE
THE KINGDOM PERFECTED

PART ONE

THE APPROACH TO THE
KINGDOM

I. FORERUNNERS

The Advice of Erasmus

'*Thou shalt find many things helping to honest living, neither is it to be refused whatsoever an author (yea though he be a gentile) teacheth well . . . it shall be profitable to taste of all manner of learning of the gentiles, if so it be done with caution and judgment discreetly. Furthermore with speed and after the manner of a man that intendeth but to pass over the country only and not to dwell or inhabit, in conclusion (which thing is chiefest of all) if everything be applied and referred to Christ.*'

ERASMUS (*c.* 1456–1536),
The Manual of the Christian Knight

1. The Emperor Asoka

Asoka lived as ruler of the greater part of India in 273 B.C. Only the south-east and part of the south were beyond his sway.

The old dream of uniting the whole of India under one supreme government fired Asoka. . . . His armies triumphed and there was a terrible slaughter. When news of this reached Asoka he was stricken with remorse and disgusted with war. Unique among the victorious monarchs and captains in history he decided to abandon warfare in the full tide of victory . . and his mind turned, under the influence of Buddha's gospel, to conquests and adventure in other fields. What Asoka felt and how he acted are known to us in his own words in the numerous edicts he issued, carved in rock and metal. 'No longer', says one of the edicts, 'would Asoka tolerate any more killing or taking into captivity. True conquest consists of the conquest of men's hearts by the law of duty or piety.' The edict further says 'Moreover, should anyone do him wrong, that too must be borne with by His Sacred Majesty.'

This astonishing ruler, beloved still in India and in many other parts of Asia, devoted himself to the spread of Buddha's teaching, to righteousness and goodwill, and to public works got for the good of the people. He was no passive spectator of events, lost in contemplation and self improvement. He laboured hard at public business and declared that he was always ready for it.—'At all times and all places, whether I am dining, in my bedroom or in my closet, in my carriage or in my palace gardens, the official reporters should keep me informed of the people's business. . . . At any hour and at any place work I must for the commonweal.'

Everywhere an appeal was made to the mind and the heart; there was no force or compulsion. Ardent Buddhist as he was, he showed respect and consideration for all other faiths. He proclaimed in an edict—'All sects deserve reverence for one reason or another. By thus acting a man exalts his own sect and at the same time does service to the sects of other people.'

Asoka died in 232 B.C. after ruling strenuously for forty-one years. Of him H. G. Wells says in his *Outline of History*: 'Amidst the tens of thousands of names of monarchs that crowd the columns of history, their majesties and graciousnesses and serenities and royal highnesses and the like, the name of Asoka shines, and shines almost alone, a star. From the Volga to Japan his name is still honoured. China, Tibet, and even India, though it has left his doctrine, preserve the tradition of his greatness.'

JAWAHARLAL NEHRU, The Discovery of India

2. The Greek View of Virtue

The Greek word ἀρετή (pronounced arété) which we translate as 'virtue' or 'excellence' meant primarily 'efficiency at a task'. It was the philosopher Aristotle, Plato's greatest pupil, who defined it as 'the right condition of the soul'.

Human beings have bodies, minds, and characters. Each of these is capable of what the Greeks call 'virtue'. The virtue or excellence of the body is health and fitness and strength, the firm and sensitive hand, the clear eye; the excellence of the mind is to know and to understand and to think, to have some idea of what the world is and of what man has done and has been and can be; the excellence of the character lies in the great virtues. This trinity of body, mind and character is man: man's aim, besides earning his living, is to make the most of all three, to have as good a mind, body and character as possible; and a liberal education, a free man's education, is to help him to this; not because a sound body, mind and character help to success, or even because they help to happiness, but because they are good things in themselves, and because what is good is worth while, simply because it is good.

SIR RICHARD LIVINGSTONE, The Future in Education

3. The Conscience of Socrates

Socrates, on trial for impiety, addresses his judges.

'When I was ordered by the Generals whom you, O men of Athens, chose to command me, at Potidaea and Amphipolis and Delium, I remained where they placed me, like any other man, facing death; strange, indeed, would be my conduct, if now, when . . . God orders me to fulfil the philosopher's mission of searching into myself and other men, I were to desert my post through fear of death, or any other fear. . . . For the fear of death is indeed the pretence of wisdom and not real wisdom, being a pretence of knowing the unknown; and no one knows whether death, which men in their fear apprehend to be the greatest evil, may not be the greatest good. Is not this ignorance of a disgraceful sort, the ignorance which is the conceit that a man knows what he does not know? And in this respect only I believe myself to differ from men in general, and may perhaps claim to be wiser than they are—that whereas I know but little of the world below, I do not suppose that I know: but I do know that injustice and disobedience to a better, whether God or man, is evil. . . . Men of Athens, I honour and love you; but I shall obey God rather than you. . . . Nothing will injure me, for a bad man is not permitted to injure a better than himself . . . they may perhaps kill me, or drive me into exile, or deprive me of civil rights; and may imagine, and others may imagine, that they are inflicting a great injury upon me: but there I do not agree. . . . Someone will say: Yes, Socrates, but cannot you hold your tongue, and then you may go into a foreign city, and no one will interfere with you? Now I have great difficulty in making you understand my answer to this. For if I tell you that to do as you say would be a disobedience to the God, and therefore that I cannot hold my tongue, you will not believe that I am serious; and if I say again that daily discourse about virtue . . . is the greatest good of man . . . you are still less likely to believe me. Yet I say what is true.'

[His judges condemn him to death.]

PLATO (427–347 B.C.), *Apology of Socrates*,
Jowett's translation (slightly altered)

4. Socrates Speaks of Death

Socrates was condemned to death for doing what he thought right: before leaving the court he made a farewell speech to his judges, ending with these words.

'We shall see that there is great reason to hope that death is good; for one of two things—either death is a state of . . . utter unconsciousness, or as men say, there is a change and migration of the soul from this world to another. Now if you suppose that there is no consciousness, but a sleep like the sleep of him who is undisturbed even by dreams. . . . I say that to die is gain; for eternity is then only a single night. But if death is a journey to another place, and there, as men say, all the dead abide, what good . . . can be greater than this? What would not a man give if he might converse with Orpheus and Hesiod and Homer? . . . What infinite delight would there be in conversing with them and asking them questions! In another world they do not put a man to death for asking questions: assuredly not.

'Wherefore, O judges, be of good cheer about death and know of a certainty, that no evil can happen to a good man, either in life or after death. He and his are not neglected by the gods; . . . For which reason, also, I am not angry with my condemners, or with my accusers; they have done me no harm, although they did not mean to do me any good; and for this I may gently blame them.

'. . . The hour of departure has arrived, and we go our ways —I to die and you to live. Which is better God only knows.'

PLATO (427–347 B.C.), *Apology of Socrates*, Jowett's translation

5. The Death of Socrates

Socrates in prison is speaking to his friends Simmias and Crito.

'Let a man be of good cheer about his soul, who, having cast away the pleasures and ornaments of the body as alien to him and working harm rather than good, has sought after the pleasures of knowledge; and has arrayed the soul, not in some foreign attire, but in her own proper jewels, temperance, and justice, and courage, and nobility, and truth—in these adorned she is ready to go on her journey to the world below, when her hour comes. You, Simmias and Cebes, and all other men will depart at some time or other. Me already, as a tragic poet would say, the voice of fate calls.'

When he had done speaking, Crito said: 'And have you any commands for us, Socrates—anything to say about your children, or any other matter in which we can serve you?'

'Nothing particular, Crito', he replied: 'only, as I have always told you, take care of yourselves; that is a service which you may be ever rendering to me and mine and to all of us,. whether you promise to do so or not.' . . .

'We will do our best,' said Crito: 'and in what way shall we bury you?'

'In any way that you like; but you must get hold of me, and take care that I do not run away from you.' Then he turned to us, and added with a smile: 'I cannot make Crito believe that I am the same Socrates who have been talking and conducting the argument; he fancies that I am the other Socrates whom he will soon see, a dead body—and he asks, How shall he bury me? And though I have spoken many words in the endeavour to show that when I have drunk the poison I shall leave you and go to the joys of the blessed, these words of mine, with which I was comforting you and myself, have had, as I perceive, no effect upon Crito. . . . I would not have him sorrow at my hard lot, or say at the burial, Thus we lay out Socrates, or, Thus we follow him to the grave, or bury him; for false words are not only evil in themselves, but they infect the soul with evil. Be of good cheer then, my dear Crito, and say that you are burying my body only, and do with that whatever is usual, and what you think best.' . . .

Now the hour of sunset was near, for a good deal of time had passed while he was within. . . . Soon the jailer, who was the servant of the Eleven, entered and stood by him, saying: 'To you, Socrates, whom I know to be the noblest and gentlest and best of all who ever came to this place, I will not impute the angry feelings of other men, who rage and swear at me, when, in obedience to the authorities, I bid them drink the poison—indeed, I am sure that you will not be angry with me; for others, as you are aware, and not I, are to blame. And so fare you well, and try to bear lightly what must needs be—you know my errand.' Then bursting into tears he turned away and went out.

Socrates looked at him, and said: 'I return your good wishes, and will do as you bid.' . . .

Then raising the cup to his lips, quite readily and cheerfully he drank off the poison. And hitherto most of us had been able to control our sorrow; but now when we saw him drinking, and saw too that he had finished the draught, we could no longer forbear, and in spite of myself my own tears were flowing fast; so that I covered my face and wept, not for him, but at the thought of my own calamity in having to part from such a friend. Nor was I the first. . . .

Socrates alone retained his calmness: 'What is this strange outcry?' he said. 'I sent away the women mainly in order that they might not misbehave in this way, for I have been told that a man should die in peace. Be quiet then, and have patience.' When we heard his words we were ashamed, and refrained our tears.

PLATO (427–347 B.C.), *Phaedo*, Jowett's translation

6. *The Justice of God*

Plato, who in his youth was a disciple of Socrates, wrote these words in his old age.

God, as the old tradition declares, holding in his hand the beginning, middle and end of all that is, travels according to his nature in a straight line towards the accomplishment of his end. Justice always accompanies him and is the punisher of those who fall short of the divine law. To justice he who would be happy holds fast, and follows in her company with all humility and order; but he who is lifted up with pride, or elated by wealth, or rank or beauty, who is young and foolish and has a soul hot with insolence and thinks that he has no need of any guide or ruler, he, I say, is left deserted by God; and being thus deserted, he takes to him others who are like himself, and dances about, throwing all things into confusion, and many think that he is a great man; but in a short time he pays the penalty which justice cannot but approve, and is utterly destroyed, and his family and city with him.

PLATO (427–347 B.C.), *Laws*, Jowett's translation

7. God in Nature and in Man

The author of this passage, the younger Seneca, was a distinguished Roman, brother of Gallio, the governor before whom St. Paul appeared at Corinth. His philosophy is representative of the Stoics.

God is near you, with you, within you. A divine spirit has its dwelling place in our hearts, always watchful of that which is evil in us, always guarding that which is good. As we deal with him so does he in his turn deal with us. And when we turn to look at the good man, we see that none is good apart from the workings of God. Surely a man cannot raise himself above the reach of fortune except by the help of the divine. God it is who gives sublime and lofty counsel. . . . If a wood shows itself to the view with ancient trees that have soared beyond the common height, a wood that shuts out the sight of the sky with its canopy of branches, one layer of them protecting the other, that wood by the giant structure of its trees, its seclusion, the marvellous depth of shadow unbroken in the open air, will bring you the assurance of the presence of the divine. . . . If you behold a human being free from terror in the face of dangers, unsmirched by covetous desires, blessed in the midst of misfortunes, tranquil when encompassed by storms, looking upon mortal men from some pinnacle above them, standing on a level with the gods, will not reverence for such a man come into your heart? Will you not say, 'That character is too great, too lofty for me to believe that it can possibly be akin to the frail form in which it dwells?' A force from God has come down into such a man. A spirit that soars above the world, that is controlled and indifferent to all vicissitudes, looking upon them as beneath its notice, a spirit that scorns all that we fear or desire, is animated by an influence from heaven. Such a spirit leaves its greater part to dwell still in the home from which it came down.

SENECA (c. 5 B.C.–A.D. 65), *Epistle* XLI, D. W. Harkman's translation

8. We are all children of God

Epictetus was a Greek slave of the first and second centuries A.D. who ultimately obtained his freedom and taught philosophy at Rome and Nicopolis. This passage is from his teaching.

If these statements of the philosophers are true that God and men are akin, there is but one course open to men, to do as Socrates did: never to reply to one who asks his country, 'I am an Athenian,' or 'I am a Corinthian,' but 'I am a citizen of the universe.' For why do you say that you are an Athenian, instead of merely a native of the little spot on which your bit of a body was cast forth at birth? Plainly you call yourself Athenian or Corinthian after that more sovereign region which includes not only the very spot where you were born, and all your household, but also generally that region from which the race of your forbears has come down to you. When a man has learnt to understand the government of the universe and has realised that there is nothing so great or sovereign or all-inclusive as this frame of things wherein men and God are united, and that from it come the seeds from which are sprung not only my own father or grandfather, but all things that are begotten and that grow upon earth, . . . why should he not call himself a citizen of the universe and a son of God?

EPICTETUS (c. A.D. 55–c. 135), *Discourses*, Matheson's translation

9. The Praise due to God

If we had sense we ought to do nothing else in public and in private, than praise and bless God and pay Him due thanks.

Ought we not, as we dig and plough and eat, to sing the hymn to God? 'Great is God that He gave us these instruments wherewith we shall till the earth. Great is God that He has given us hands, . . . and the power to grow without knowing it, and to draw our breath in sleep.' At every moment we ought to sing these praises and, above all, the greatest and divinest praise, that God gave us the faculty to comprehend these gifts and to use the way of reason. . . . If, indeed, I were a nightingale I should sing as a nightingale, if a swan as a swan: but as I am a rational creature I must praise God. This is my task and I do it: and I will not abandon this duty, so long as it is given me; and I invite you all to join in this same song.

EPICTETUS (c. A.D. 55–c. 135), *Discourses*, Matheson's translation

10. *The Opportunities of every Soul*

We sometimes ask, 'What of the good men who lived before the time of Christ or in pagan lands, and never had the opportunity of being Christians?' Here is the answer of a modern writer.

We must believe that the possibilities, provided by God of learning through suffering in this world, have always afforded a sufficient means of salvation to every soul that has made the best of the spiritual opportunity offered to it here, however small that opportunity may have been. . . .

A pagan soul, no less than a Christian soul, has ultimate salvation within its reach; but a soul which has been offered, and has opened itself to the illumination and grace that Christianity conveys, will, while still in this world, be more brightly irradiated with the light of the other world than a pagan soul that has won salvation by making the best in this world, of the narrower opportunity here open to it. The Christian soul can attain, while still on Earth, a greater measure of man's good than can be attained by any pagan soul in this earthly stage of its existence. . . .

It is this individual spiritual progress in this world for which we pray when we say, 'Thy will be done in Earth as it is in Heaven'. It is for the salvation that is open to all men of good will—pagan as well as Christian, primitive as well as civilized —who make the most of their spiritual opportunities on Earth, however narrow these opportunities may be, that we pray when we say, 'Thy Kingdom come'.

ARNOLD J. TOYNBEE, *Civilization on Trial*

II. THE QUEST OF THE SPIRIT

11. *'What shall I do to be saved?'*

John Bunyan, in this passage from *The Pilgrim's Progress*, describes the plight of every man in this world.

As I walked through the wilderness of this world, I lighted on a certain place where was a Den, and as I laid me down in that place to sleep, and, as I slept, I dreamed a dream. I dreamed, and behold, I saw a man clothed with rags, standing in a certain place, with his face from his own house, a book in his hand, and a great burden upon his back.

. . . Now I saw, upon a time, when he was walking in the fields, that he was, as was his wont, reading in his book, and greatly distressed in his mind; and, as he read, he burst out, . . . crying, What shall I do to be saved?

I saw also, that he looked this way and that way, as if he would run; yet he stood still, because, as I perceived, he could not tell which way to go. I looked then, and saw a man named Evangelist coming to him, who asked, Wherefore dost thou cry?

He answered, Sir, I perceive by the book in my hand, that I am condemned to die, and after that to come to judgement; and I find that I am not willing to do the first, nor able to do the second.

. . . Then said Evangelist, If this be thy condition, why

standest thou still? He answered, Because I know not whither to go.

. . . Then said Evangelist, pointing with his finger over a very wide field, Do you see yonder wicket-gate? The man said, No. Then said the other, Do you see yonder shining light? He said, I think I do. Then said Evangelist, Keep that light in your eye, and go up directly thereto: so shalt thou see the gate; at which when thou knockest, it shall be told thee what thou shalt do.

JOHN BUNYAN (1628–88), *The Pilgrim's Progress*

12. *A Prayer of Love*

St. Augustine wrote these words, thinking how God had drawn him to Himself when he cared nothing for God.

Late have I loved Thee, O Beauty so ancient and so new; late have I loved Thee! For behold Thou wert within me, and I outside; and I sought Thee outside and in my unloveliness fell upon those lovely things that Thou hast made. Thou wert with me and I was not with Thee. I was kept from Thee by those things, yet had they not been in Thee, they would not have been at all. Thou didst call and cry to me and break open my deafness: and Thou didst send forth Thy beams and shine upon me and chase away my blindness: Thou didst breathe fragrance upon me, and I drew in my breath and do now pant for Thee: I tasted Thee, and now hunger and thirst for Thee: Thou didst touch me, and I have burned for Thy peace.

ST. AUGUSTINE (354–430), *Confessions*

13. *The Pulley*

When God at first made Man,
Having a glass of blessings standing by,
'Let us,' said He, 'pour on him all we can;
Let the world's riches, which dispersed lie,
Contract into a span.'

So strength first made a way;
Then beauty flowed, then wisdom, honour, pleasure:
When almost all was out, God made a stay,
Perceiving that, alone of all His treasure,
Rest in the bottom lay.

'For if I should,' said He,
'Bestow this jewel also on My creature,
He would adore My gifts instead of Me,
And rest in Nature, not the God of Nature;
So both should losers be.

'Yet let him keep the rest,
But keep them with repining restlessness;
Let him be rich and weary, that at least,
If goodness lead him not, yet weariness
May toss him to my Breast.'

GEORGE HERBERT (1593–1633)

14. True Rest

'Great art Thou, O Lord, and greatly to be praised; great is
Thy power, and Thy wisdom infinite. . . . Yet would man
praise Thee; he, but a particle of Thy creation. . . . Thou
awakest us to delight in Thy praise; for Thou madest us for
Thyself, and our heart is restless, until it repose in Thee.'

ST. AUGUSTINE (354–430), *Confessions*

15. To Find out God

I sought Thee round about, O Thou my God,
To find Thy abode:
I said unto the Earth, 'Speak, art thou He?'
She answered me,

'I am not.' I enquired of creatures all,
In general,
Contained therein: they with one voice proclaim
That none amongst them challenged such a Name.

I asked the Seas, and all the Deeps below,
My God to know:
I asked the reptiles, and whatever is
In the abyss:
Even from the shrimp to the leviathan
My enquiry ran:
But in those deserts, which no line can sound,
The God I sought for was not to be found.

I asked the Air if that were He, but know
It told me, 'No':
I from the towering eagle to the wren
Demanded then,
If any feathered fowl 'mong them were such:
But they, all much
Offended with my question, in full quire
Answered, to find my God I must look higher.

And now, my God, by Thy illumining Grace,
Thy glorious Face
(So far forth as Thou wilt discovered be)
Methinks though invisible and infinite,
To human sight,
Thou in Thy Mercy, Justice, Truth, appearest,
In which to our frail senses Thou com'st nearest.

O, make us apt to seek and quick to find,
Thou God most kind:
Give us Love, Hope, and Faith in Thee to trust,
Thou God most just:

Remit all our offences, we entreat,
Most Good, most Great:
Grant that our willing though unworthy guest
May, through Thy grace, admit us 'mongst the blest.

THOMAS HEYWOOD (d. c. 1650)

16. *Peace*

The poet's search for peace leads him to the Prince of Peace, Christ, who 'sweetly lived' and was put to death by his foes for us.

Sweet Peace, where dost thou dwell? I humbly crave,
Let me once know.
I sought thee in a secret cave,
And ask'd if Peace were there.
A hollow wind did seem to answer, 'No;
Go seek elsewhere.'

I did; and going did a rainbow note:
Surely, thought I,
This is the lace of Peace's coat:
I will search out the matter.
But while I look'd, the clouds immediately
Did break and scatter.

Then went I to a garden, and did spy
A gallant flower,
The Crown Imperial. Sure, said I,
Peace at the root must dwell.
But when I digg'd, I saw a worm devour
What show'd so well.

At length I met a rev'rend good old man,
Whom when for Peace
I did demand, he thus began:
'There was a Prince of old
At Salem dwelt, who liv'd with good increase
Of flock and fold.

'He sweetly liv'd: yet sweetness did not save
His life from foes.
But after death out of His grave
There sprang twelve stalks of wheat;
Which many wond'ring at, got some of those
To plant and set.

'It prospered strangely, and did soon disperse
Through all the earth;
For they that taste it do rehearse
That virtue lies therein;
A secret virtue, bringing peace and mirth
By flight of sin.

'Take of this grain, which in my garden grows,
And grows for you;
Make bread of it; and that repose
And peace, which ev'ry where
With so much earnestness you do pursue,
Is only there.'

GEORGE HERBERT (1593–1633)

III. THE QUEST OF THE MIND

17. Asking Questions of God

It has been said that men should not presume to question God's ways.
But a modern Christian poet argues that we must and should ask
questions.

The Book of Job . . . has saved Christendom from being misled
by Saint Paul's rash refusal to allow the thing formed to ask
questions of him that formed it, the pot of the potter: . . . No
pot—so far—has asked questions of the potter in a voice the
potter can understand; when it does, it will be time enough to
compare pots to men. The criticism is not aimed at Saint Paul

who dropped the phrase in the midst of a great spiritual wrestle, not as a moral instruction. But it has been used too often by the pious to encourage them to say, in love or laziness, 'our little minds were never meant. . . .' Fortunately there is the book of Job to make it clear that our little minds were meant. A great curiosity ought to exist concerning divine things. Man was intended to argue with God. . . . The Lord demands that his people shall demand an explanation from him. Whether they understand it or like it when they get it is another matter, but demand it they must and shall. Humility has never consisted in not asking questions; it does not make men less themselves or less intelligent, but more intelligent and more themselves.

CHARLES WILLIAMS (1886–1945), *He Came Down from Heaven*

18. The Adventure of the Spirit

Here are some words of a distinguished modern philosopher.

There has always been a conflict between religion and science; and . . . religion and science have always been in a state of continual development. In the early days of Christianity, there was a general belief among Christians that the world was coming to an end in the lifetime of people then living. . . . The belief proved itself to be mistaken and Christian doctrine adjusted itself to the change. . . . In the seventeenth century the motion of the earth was condemned by a Catholic tribunal. A hundred years ago, the extension of time demanded by geological science distressed religious people. . . .

A clash is not a disaster, it is an opportunity. . . . In the early medieval times, Heaven was in the sky and Hell was underground; volcanoes were the jaws of Hell. . . . In this instance the clash between religion and science . . . has been greatly to the benefit of . . . religion by dispersing these medieval fancies. . . .

Any verbal form of statement which has been before the world for some time discloses ambiguities. . . . It is here that the impersonal criticism of science and philosophy comes to the aid of religious evolution. . . .

The worship of God is not a rule of safety . . . it is an adventure of the spirit, a flight after the unattainable.

A. N. WHITEHEAD (b. 1861), *Science and the Modern World*

19. *Grasping Truth*

Edward Wilson went with Scott on his last expedition to the Antarctic as doctor and zoologist. He endured the terrible winter journey with Bowers and Cherry-Garrard when they went in search of Emperor Penguin eggs: and he was one of the five who reached the South Pole in January 1912. These words are from his diary.

The more we try the clearer becomes our insight, and the more we use our thinking faculties the quicker they become in their power of grasping points of truth.

Truths are not things we can pick up without taking trouble to hunt for them. And when we find a truth we really possess it, because it is bound to our heart by the process by which we reached it . . . through trouble, difficulty or sorrow . . . a man binds it into his life. But what is easily come by is easily lost.

Every bit of truth that comes into a man's heart burns in him and forces its way out, either in his actions or in his words. Truth is like a lighted lamp in that it cannot be hidden away in the darkness because it carries its own light.

EDWARD WILSON (1872–1912)
(from *The Faith of Edward Wilson*, by George Seaver)

IV. A STORY OF THE JOURNEY

The eight extracts that begin here all come from *The Pilgrim's Progress*. A previous extract told how Christian began his journey. These show some of the obstacles and adventures he met on his way to the Celestial City.

20. *The Slough of Despond*

Now, I saw in my dream, . . . that they drew near to a very miry slough, that was in the midst of the plain; and they, being heedless, did both fall suddenly into the bog. The name of the slough was Despond. Here, therefore, they wallowed for a time, being grievously bedaubed with the dirt; and Christian, because of the burden that was on his back, began to sink in the mire.

Then, said Pliable, Ah! neighbour Christian, where are you now?

Truly, said Christian, I do not know.

At this Pliable began to be offended, and angrily said to his fellow, Is this the happiness you have told me all this while of? If we have such ill speed at our first setting out, what may we expect betwixt this and our journey's end? May I get out again with my life, you shall possess the brave country alone for me. And, with that, he gave a desperate struggle or two, and got out of the mire on that side of the slough which was next to his own house: so away he went, and Christian saw him no more.

Wherefore Christian was left to tumble in the Slough of Despond alone: but still he endeavoured to struggle to that side of the slough that was . . . next to the wicket-gate; the which he did, but could not get out, because of the burden that was upon his back: but I beheld in my dream, that a man came to him, whose name was Help, and asked him, What he did there?

Sir, said Christian, I was bid go this way by a man called

Evangelist, who directed me also to yonder gate, that I might escape the wrath to come; and as I was going thither I fell in here.

But why did not you look for the steps?

Fear followed me so hard, that I fled the next way and fell in.

Then said he, Give me thy hand: so he gave him his hand, and he drew him out, and set him upon sound ground, and bid him go on his way.

JOHN BUNYAN (1628–88), *The Pilgrim's Progress*

21. *Good-Will tells Christian the way he must go*

And therefore, good Christian, come a little way with me, and I will teach thee the way thou must go. Look before thee; dost thou see this narrow way? THAT is the way thou must go; it was cast up by the patriarchs, prophets, Christ, and His Apostles; and it is as straight as a rule can make it. This is the way thou must go.

But, said Christian, are there no turnings or windings, by which a stranger may lose his way?

Yes, there are many ways butt down upon this, and they are crooked and wide. But thus thou mayest distinguish the right from the wrong, the right only being straight and narrow.

Then I saw in my dream, that Christian asked him further if he could not help him off with his burden that was upon his back; for as yet he had not got rid thereof, nor could he by any means get it off without help.

He told him, As to thy burden, be content to bear it, until thou comest to the place of deliverance; for there it will fall from thy back of itself.

Then Christian began to gird up his loins, and to address himself to his journey. So the other told him, that by that he was gone some distance from the gate, he would come at the house of the Interpreter, at whose door he should knock, and he would show him excellent things. Then Christian took his leave of his friend, and he again bid him God-speed.

JOHN BUNYAN (1628–88), *The Pilgrim's Progress*

22. *The Cross*

Now I saw in my dream, that the highway up which Christian was to go, was fenced on either side with a wall, and that wall was called Salvation. Up this way, therefore, did burdened Christian run, but not without difficulty because of the load on his back.

He ran thus till he came at a place somewhat ascending, and upon that place stood a cross, and a little below, in the bottom, a sepulchre. So I saw in my dream, that just as Christian came up with the cross, his burden loosed from off his shoulders, and fell from off his back, and began to tumble, and so continued to do till it came to the mouth of the sepulchre, where it fell in, and I saw it no more.

Then was Christian glad and lightsome, and said, with a merry heart, 'He hath given me rest by his sorrow, and life by his death.' . . . He looked therefore and looked again, even till the springs that were in his head sent the waters down his cheeks. Now . . . behold, three Shining Ones came to him and saluted him with 'Peace be to thee.' So the first said to him, 'Thy sins be forgiven thee,' the second stripped him of his rags, and clothed him 'with a change of raiment;' the third also set a mark on his forehead, and gave him a roll with a seal upon it, which he bade him look on as he ran, and that he should give it in at The Celestial Gate. So they went their way. . . . Then Christian gave three leaps for joy, and went on singing.

JOHN BUNYAN (1628–88), *The Pilgrim's Progress*

23. *The Hill Difficulty*

I beheld, then, that they all went on till they came to the foot
of the Hill Difficulty; at the bottom of which was a spring.
There were also in the same place two other ways besides that
which came straight from the gate; one turned to the left hand,
and the other to the right, at the bottom of the hill; but the
narrow way lay right up the hill, and the name of the going up
the side of the hill is called Difficulty. Christian now went to
the spring, and drank thereof, to refresh himself, and then
began to go up the hill. . . .

The other two also came to the foot of the hill; but when
they saw that the hill was steep and high, and that there were
two other ways to go, . . . they were resolved to go in those
ways. Now the name of one of those ways was Danger, and
the name of the other Destruction. So the one took the way
which is called Danger, which led him into a great wood; and
the other took directly up the way to Destruction, which led
him into a wild field, full of dark mountains, where he stumbled
and fell, and rose no more. . . .

I looked, then, after Christian, to see him go up the hill,
where I perceived he fell from running to going, and from
going to clambering upon his hands and his knees, because of
the steepness of the place. Now, about the midway to the top
of the hill was a pleasant arbour, made by the Lord of the hill
for the refreshing of weary travellers; thither, therefore, Christian got, where also he sat down to rest him. Then he pulled
his roll out of his bosom, and read therein to his comfort. . . .
Thus pleasing himself awhile, he at last fell into a slumber,
and thence into a fast sleep, which detained him in that place
until it was almost night; and in his sleep his roll fell out of his
hand. Now, as he was sleeping, there came one to him, and
awaked him, saying, 'Go to the ant, thou sluggard; consider
her ways, and be wise.' And with that Christian started up,

and sped him on his way, and went apace, till he came to the top of the hill.

Now when he was got up to the top of the hill, there came two men running to meet him; the name of one was Timorous, and of the other, Mistrust; to whom Christian said, Sirs, what's the matter? You run the wrong way. Timorous answered that they were going to the City of Zion, and had got up that difficult place; but, said he, the further we go, the more danger we meet with; wherefore we turned, and are going back again.

Yes, said Mistrust, for just before us lie a couple of lions in the way, whether sleeping or waking we know not, and we could not think, if we came within reach, but they would presently pull us in pieces.

Then said Christian, You make me afraid, but whither shall I fly to be safe? . . . If I can get to the Celestial City, I am sure to be in safety there. I must venture. . . . I will yet go forward. So Mistrust and Timorous ran down the hill, and Christian went on his way.

But, thinking again of what he had heard from the men, he felt in his bosom for his roll, that he might read therein and be comforted; but he felt, and found it not. Then was Christian in great distress, and knew not what to do, for he wanted that which used to relieve him, and that which should have been his pass into the Celestial City. . . . At last he bethought himself that he had slept in the arbour that is on the side of the hill; and falling down upon his knees, he asked God's forgiveness for that his foolish act, and then went back to look for his roll. But all the way . . . oftentimes he chid himself for being so foolish to fall asleep in that place, which was erected only for a little refreshment for his weariness. . . .

How far might I have been on my way by this time! I am made to tread those steps thrice over, which I needed not to have trod but once; yea now also I am like to be benighted, for the day is almost spent. Oh! that I had not slept.

Now by this time he was come to the arbour again, where for a while he sat down and wept; but at last . . . looking sorrowfully down under the settle, there he espied his roll; the which, with trembling and haste, he catched up and put it into his bosom. . . . And he gave thanks to God . . . and with joy and tears betook himself again to his journey. But oh, how nimbly now did he go up the rest of the hill! . . . And he lift up his eyes, and behold there was a very stately palace before him, the name of which was Beautiful. . . . And he made haste and went forward, that if possible he might get lodging there.

Now, before he had gone far, he entered into a very narrow passage, which was about a furlong off of the porter's lodge; and looking very narrowly before him as he went, he espied two lions in the way. Now, thought he, I see the dangers that Mistrust and Timorous were driven back by. (The lions were chained, but he saw not the chains.) Then he was afraid, and thought nothing but death was before him. But the porter at the lodge, whose name is Watchful, perceiving that Christian made a halt as if he would go back, cried unto him, saying, Is thy strength so small? Fear not the lions, for they are chained, and are placed there for trial of faith where it is, and for discovery of those that had none. Keep in the midst of the path, and no hurt shall come unto thee. . . .

Then I saw that he went on, trembling for fear of the lions, but taking good heed to the directions of the porter; he heard them roar, but they did him no harm. Then he clapped his hands, and went on till he came and stood before the gate [of the palace].

JOHN BUNYAN (1628–88), *The Pilgrim's Progress*

24. Christian's Encounter with Apollyon

But now, in this Valley of Humiliation, poor Christian was hard put to it; for he had gone but a little way, before he espied a foul fiend coming over the field to meet him; his name is Apollyon. Then did Christian begin to be afraid, and to cast in his mind whether to go back or to stand his ground. But he considered again that he had no armour for his back; and therefore thought that to turn the back to him might give him the greater advantage with ease to pierce him with his darts. Therefore he resolved to venture and stand his ground. . . .

So he went on, and Apollyon met him. Now the monster was hideous to behold; he was clothed with scales like a fish, he had wings like a dragon, feet like a bear, and out of his belly came fire and smoke, and his mouth was as the mouth of a lion. When he came up to Christian, he beheld him with a disdainful countenance, and thus began to question with him.

Whence come you? and whither are you bound?

I am come from the City of Destruction, which is the place of all evil, and am going to the City of Zion.

By this I perceive thou are one of my subjects, for all that country is mine, and I am the prince and god of it. How is it, then, that thou hast run away from thy king? Were it not that I hope thou mayest do me more service, I would strike thee now, at one blow, to the ground.

I was born, indeed, in your dominions, but your service was hard, and your wages such as a man could not live on, 'for the wages of sin *is* death.' Therefore when I was come to years, I did as other considerate persons do, look out, if, perhaps, I might mend myself. . . .

And the Prince whom I now serve and honour is merciful, and ready to forgive. . . .

Then Apollyon broke out into a grievous rage, saying, I am

an enemy to this Prince: I hate his person, his laws and people.
I am come out on purpose to withstand thee. . . .

Then Apollyon straddled quite over the whole breadth of
the way, and said, I am void of fear in this matter: prepare
thyself to die: for I swear by my infernal den, that thou shalt
go no further: here will I spill thy soul.

And with that he threw a flaming dart at his breast, but
Christian had a shield in his hand, with which he caught it,
and so prevented the danger of that.

Then did Christian draw, for he saw it was time to bestir
him: and Apollyon as fast made at him, throwing darts as
thick as hail; by the which, notwithstanding all that Christian
could do to avoid it, Apollyon wounded him in his head, his
hand and foot. This made Christian give a little back: Apollyon, therefore, followed his work amain, and Christian again
took courage, and resisted as manfully as he could. This sore
combat lasted for above half a day, even till Christian was
almost quite spent; for you must know that Christian, by
reason of his wounds, must needs grow weaker and weaker.

Then Apollyon, espying his opportunity, began to gather up
close to Christian, and wrestling with him, gave him a dreadful
fall: and with that Christian's sword flew out of his hand. Then
said Apollyon, I am sure of thee now. And with that he almost
pressed him to death, so that Christian began to despair of life:
but as God would have it, while Apollyon was fetching of his
last blow, thereby to make a full end of this good man, Christian
nimbly stretched out his hand for his sword and caught it . . .
and with that gave Apollyon a deadly thrust, which made him
give back, as one that had received his mortal wound. Christian
perceiving that, made at him again, saying, 'Nay, in all these
things, we are more than conquerors through him that loved us.'

And with that Apollyon spread forth his dragon's wings and
sped him away, that Christian for a season saw him no more.

JOHN BUNYAN (1628-88), *The Pilgrim's Progress*

25. Christian's Opinion of Talkative

Christian and his friend Faithful had met another traveller on their journey.

Now did Faithful begin to wonder [at their companion]; and stepping to Christian he said to him, What a brave companion have we got! Surely this man will make a very excellent pilgrim.

At this Christian modestly smiled, and said, This man, with whom you are so taken, will beguile, with that tongue of his, twenty of them that know him not.

Do you know him then?

Know him! Yes—better than he knows himself.

Pray, what is he?

His name is Talkative: he dwelleth in our town. I wonder that you should be a stranger to him . . . and notwithstanding his fine tongue, he is but a sorry fellow.

Well, he seems to be a very pretty man.

That is, replied Christian, to them who have not thorough acquaintance with him; for he is best abroad; near home, he is ugly enough. . . .

But I am ready to think you do but jest, because you smiled.

God forbid that I should jest in this matter, or that I should accuse any falsely! . . . This man is for any company, and for any talk: . . . he talketh of prayer, of repentance, of faith; but he knows but only to talk of them. . . .

Yes, said Faithful, I see that saying and doing are two things: and hereafter I shall better observe this distinction. . . .

This Talkative is not aware of; he thinks that hearing and saying will make a good Christian, and thus he deceiveth his own soul. Hearing is but the sowing of the seed; talking is not sufficient to prove that fruit is indeed in the heart and life: and let us assure ourselves, that at the day of doom men shall be judged according to their fruits. It will not be said then, Did you believe? but, Were you doers or talkers only? and accordingly shall they be judged. The end of the world is compared to our harvest; and you know men at harvest regard nothing but fruit.... And I will add another thing: Paul calleth some men, yea, and those great talkers, too, 'sounding brass and tinkling cymbals', that is, as he expounds them in another place . . . things without life, without the true faith and grace of the gospel. . . .

Faithful. Yes, if a man have all knowledge he may yet be nothing, and so consequently be no child of God. When Christ said, 'Do ye know all these things?' and the disciples had answered, 'Yes,' he addeth, 'Blessed are ye if ye do them.' He doth not lay the blessing in the knowing of them, but in the doing. . . . Indeed, to know is a thing that pleaseth talkers and boasters; but to do is that which pleaseth God.

JOHN BUNYAN (1628–88), *The Pilgrim's Progress*

26. Evangelist speaks of their Victory over Trials

After Christian and Faithful had passed through many difficulties they met Evangelist again.

Right glad am I, said Evangelist, not that you have met with trials, but that you have been victors; and for that you have, notwithstanding many weaknesses, continued in the way.

I say, right glad am I of this thing, and that for mine own sake and yours. I have sowed, and you have reaped: and the day is coming when both he that sowed and they that reaped shall rejoice together; that is, if you hold out: 'for in due season ye shall reap, if ye faint not.' The crown is before you, and it is an incorruptible one; 'so run, that you may obtain it.' Some there be that set out for this crown, and, after they have gone far for it, another comes in, and takes it from them; hold fast, therefore, that you have; let no man take your crown. . . . Let the kingdom be always before you, and believe steadfastly concerning things that are invisible. Let nothing that is on this

side the other world get within you; and above all, look well
to your own hearts; . . . set your faces like a flint; you have
all power in heaven and earth on your side.

JOHN BUNYAN (1628–88), *The Pilgrim's Progress*

27. *Doubting Castle*

Christian is on his pilgrimage, accompanied now by Hopeful.

At last, lighting under a little shelter, they sat down until the
daybreak; but, being weary, they fell asleep. Now there was,
not far from the place where they lay, a castle called Doubting
Castle, the owner whereof was Giant Despair; and it was in his
grounds they now were sleeping: wherefore he, getting up in
the morning early, and walking up and down in his fields,
caught Christian and Hopeful asleep in his grounds. Then
with a grim and surly voice, he bid them awake; and asked
them whence they were, and what they did in his grounds. . . .
Then said the Giant, You have this night trespassed on me, by
trampling in and lying on my grounds, and therefore you must
go along with me. . . . The Giant, therefore, drove them before
him, and put them into his castle, into a very dark dungeon,
nasty and stinking to the spirits of these two men. Here then
they lay from Wednesday morning till Saturday night, without
one bit of bread, or drop of drink, or light, or any to ask how
they did. . . .

Now, Giant Despair had a wife, and her name was Diffi-
dence. So when he was gone to bed he told his wife what he
had done. . . . Then he asked her also what he had best to do
further to his prisoners. . . . She counselled him that when he
arose in the morning he should beat them without any mercy.
So, when he arose, he getteth him a grievous crab-tree cudgel,
and goes down into the dungeon to them, and there first falls
to rating them as if they were dogs. . . . Then he falls upon
them, and beats them fearfully, in such sort, that they were

not able to help themselves, or to turn them upon the floor. This done, he withdraws and leaves them, there to condole their misery, and to mourn under their distress. So all that day they spent the time in nothing but sighs and lamentations.

The next night, she, talking to her husband about them further, and understanding they were yet alive, did advise him to counsel them to make away themselves. So when the morning was come, he goes to them in a surly manner as before, and perceiving them to be very sore with the stripes that he had given them the day before, he told them, that since they were never like to come out of that place, their only way would be forthwith to make an end of themselves. . . . Then did the prisoners consult between themselves, whether it was best to take his counsel or not. . . .

Well, towards evening, the Giant goes down into the dungeon again, to see if the prisoners had taken his counsel; but when he came there he found them alive; and truly, alive was all; for now, for want of bread and water, and by reason of the wounds they received when he beat them, they could do little but breathe. But, I say, he found them alive; at which he fell into a grievous rage, and told them that, seeing they had disobeyed his counsel, it should be worse with them than if they had never been born.

At this they trembled greatly, and I think that Christian fell into a swoon; but coming a little to himself again, they renewed their discourse about the Giant's counsel.

Now Christian again seemed for doing it, but Hopeful made his reply again, as followeth:

My brother, said he, rememberest thou not how valiant thou hast been heretofore? Apollyon could not crush thee, nor could all that thou didst hear, or see, or feel, in the Valley of the Shadow of Death. What hardship, terror, and amazement hast thou already gone through! And art thou now nothing but fear! Thou seest that I am in the dungeon with thee, a far weaker man by nature than thou art; also this Giant hath wounded me as well as thee, and hath also cut off the bread and water from my mouth; and with thee I mourn without the light. But let us exercise a little more patience. . . . Wherefore let us bear up with patience as well as we can.

Now, night being come again, and the Giant and his wife being in bed, she asked him concerning the prisoners. . . . To which he replied, They are sturdy rogues, they choose rather to bear all hardship, than to make away themselves. Then said she, Take them into the castle yard tomorrow, and show them the bones and skulls of those thou hast already despatched, and make them believe, ere a week comes to an end, thou also wilt tear them in pieces, as thou hast done their fellows before them.

So, when morning was come, the Giant goes to them again, and takes them to the castle yard and (shows them) as his wife has bidden him. . . . Go, get you down to your den again; and with that he beat them all the way thither.

They lay, therefore, all day on Saturday in a lamentable case, as before. . . .

Well, on Saturday, about midnight, they began to pray, and continued in prayer till almost break of day.

Now, a little before it was day, good Christian, as one half amazed, brake out in a passionate speech: What a fool, quoth he, am I, thus to lie in a stinking dungeon, when I may as well walk at liberty! I have a key in my bosom, called Promise, that will, I am persuaded, open any lock in Doubting Castle.

Then said Hopeful: That is good news, good brother; pluck it out of thy bosom, and try.

Then Christian pulled it out of his bosom, and began to try at the dungeon door, whose bolt gave back, and the door flew open with ease, and Christian and Hopeful both came out. Then he went to the outward door that leads to the castle-yard, and with his key, opened that door also. After, he went

to the iron gate, for that must be opened too, but the lock
went damnable hard, yet the key did open it. Then they thrust
open the gate to make their escape with speed . . . and they
went on and came to the King's highway, and so were safe.

JOHN BUNYAN (1628–88), *The Pilgrim's Progress*

V. DIRECTIONS FOR THE WAY

28. The Pilgrimage

Sir Walter Raleigh wrote this poem when he was imprisoned in the
Tower of London. (The scallop-shell was the badge of pilgrims in the
Middle Ages.)

Give me my scallop-shell of quiet,
My staff of faith to walk upon,
My scrip of joy, immortal diet,
My bottle of salvation,
My gown of glory, hope's true gage;
And thus I'll take my pilgrimage.

Blood must be my body's balmer;
No other balm will there be given;
Whilst my soul, like quiet palmer,
Travelleth towards the land of heaven;
  Over the silver mountains,
  Where spring the nectar fountains:
    There will I kiss
    The bowl of bliss,
And drink mine everlasting fill
Upon every milken hill.
My soul will be a-dry before;
But, after, it will thirst no more.

SIR WALTER RALEIGH (1552(?)–1618)

29. A Story of St. Christopher

St. Christopher lived in the fourth century after Christ. This traditional story about him is here given as it was written centuries later.

It came in his mind that he would seek the greatest prince that was in the world, and him would he serve and obey. And so far he went that he came to a right great king, of whom the renown generally was that he was the greatest of the world. And when the king saw him, he received him into his service, and made him dwell in his court. Upon a time a minstrel sang before him a song in which he named oft the Devil, and the King, who was a Christian man, when he heard him name the Devil, made anon the sign of the cross on his visage. And when Christopher saw that, he had a great marvel what sign it was, and wherefore the King made it, and he demanded of him. And because the King would not say, he said, 'If thou tell me not I shall no longer dwell with thee;' and then the King told him, saying: 'Alway when I hear the Devil named I fear that he should have power over me, and I garnish me with this sign, that he grieve me not nor annoy me!' Then Christopher said unto him: 'Doubtest thou the Devil that he hurt thee? Then is the Devil more mighty and greater than thou art. I am then deceived of my hope and purpose, for I had supposed I had found the most mighty and the greatest lord in the world, but I commend thee to God, for I will go seek him, for to be my lord and I his servant.'

And then he departed from this King and hasted him for to seek the Devil. And as he went by a great desert he saw a great company of knights, of which a knight cruel and horrible came to him and demanded whither he went, and Christopher answered him and said: 'I go to seek the Devil, for to be my master.' And he said: 'I am he that thou seekest.' And then Christopher was glad, and bound him to be his servant perpetual, and took him for his master and lord. And as they went together by a common way they saw a cross erect and standing. And as soon as the Devil saw the cross he was afeared and fled, and left the right way and brought Christopher about by a sharp desert. And after when they were past the cross, he brought him to the highway that they had left. And when Christopher saw that, he marvelled and demanded whereof he doubted and had left the high and fair way and had gone so far about by so rough a desert. And the Devil would not tell him in no wise. Then Christopher said to him: 'If thou wilt not tell me, I shall anon depart from thee, and serve thee no more.' Wherefore the Devil was constrained to tell him and said: 'There was a man called Christ which was hanged on the Cross, and when I see his sign I am sore afraid and flee from it wheresoever I see it.' To whom Christopher said: 'Then He is greater and more mightier than thou, when thou art afraid of this sign, and I see well that I have laboured in vain when I have not found the greatest law of the world. And I will serve thee no longer; go thy way then, for I will go with Christ.'

And when he had long sought and demanded where he should find Christ at last he came into a great desert, to an hermit that dwelt there, and the hermit preached to him of Jesus Christ and informed him in the Faith diligently. . . . Then the hermit said to him: 'Knowest thou such and such a river, where many be perished and lost?' To whom Christopher said: 'I know it well.'

Then said the hermit: 'Because thou art noble and high of stature and strong in thy members thou shalt be resident by the river, and thou shalt bear over all them that shall pass there, which shall be a thing right pleasing to Our Lord Jesus Christ whom thou desirest to serve, and I hope He shall show Himself to thee.' Then said Christopher: 'Certainly this service may I well do, and I promise to Him for to do it.' Then went

Christopher to this river and made there a dwelling-place for himself, and bare a pole in his hand instead of a staff by which he sustained himself in the water, and bare over all manner of people without ceasing. And there he abode, thus doing, many days.

And in a time, as he slept in his lodge, he heard the voice of a child which called him, and said: 'Christopher, come out and bear me over.' Then he awoke and went out and found no man. And when he was again in his house he heard the same voice and he ran out and found nobody. The third time he was called and came thither and found a child beside the edge of the river, which prayed him goodly to bear him over the water. And then Christopher lift up the child on his shoulders, and took his staff and entered the water for to pass. And the water of the river arose and swelled more and more; and the child was as heavy as lead, and always as he went farther the water increased more and more, and the child more and more waxed heavy, insomuch that Christopher had great anguish and was afeard to be drowned. And when he was escaped with great pain and passed the water, and set the child aground, he said to the child: 'Child, thou has put me in great peril; thou weighest almost as I had all the world upon me: I might bear no greater burden.' And the child answered: 'Christopher, marvel me nothing: for thou hast borne Him that created and made all the world, upon thy shoulders. I am Jesus Christ, the King whom thou servest in this work.'

From *The Golden Legend* (1270)

30. *A Prayer of an Indian Thinker*

Let me not pray to be sheltered from dangers, but to be fearless in facing them.

Let me not beg for the stilling of my pain, but for the heart to conquer it.

Let me not look for allies in life's battlefield, but to my own strength.

Let me not crave in anxious fear to be saved, but hope for the patience to win my freedom.

Grant me that I may not be a coward, feeling your mercy in my success alone; but let me find the grasp of your hand in my failure.

RABINDRANATH TAGORE (1861–1941), from *Fruit Gathering*

31. *What is the Use of the World?*

Call the world if you please 'The Vale of Soul-making.' Then you will find out the use of the world. . . .

I will call the world a School instituted for the purpose of teaching little children to read. I will call the human heart the Horn Book read in that school. And I will call the Child able to read, the Soul made from that School and its Horn Book. Do you not see how necessary a World of Pains and Troubles is to school an Intelligence and make it a Soul?

JOHN KEATS (1795–1821), *Letters*

32. *The Source of Spiritual Strength*

In this extract Margaret Bondfield, who was to become the first woman cabinet minister in Britain, describes what she learned from a series of lectures she attended as a trade union organizer.

These lectures opened up a new world of adventure, a spiritual world—an introduction to the mystery and dynamic force of prayer. Unlike other turns in the road of life, this experience was of slow growth—full of retreat, of backsliding, to use an old evangelical word. I do not think it possible to exaggerate the importance of the discoveries I made about life, and the relation of the self to the unseen world of the Spirit, and yet I find it hard to speak about; these are matters that cannot be taken on trust, they must be individually experienced and have no validity otherwise. In my case, a course of reading brought to me a sense of the *quality* of service given to the world by people like the Lady Julian of Norwich, Catherine of Siena, the Quaker Saints, Josephine Butler, and that great host of dedicated lives. My everyday trade union work took on a deeper significance. The doing of ordinary everyday things became lit up with that inner light of the Spirit which gave one strength and effectiveness; strength to meet defeat with a smile; to face success with a sense of responsibility; to be willing to do one's best without thought of reward; to bear misrepresentation without giving way to futile bitterness. Saint Theresa declared that: 'There are only two duties required of us—the love of God and the love of our neighbour, and the surest sign of discovering whether we observe these duties is the love of our neighbour'; and a great scholar has asserted that this love of God is not an emotion, although that may be experienced, it is a *principle of action*—it reinforces effort, it demands that we *do* something, not merely talk or feel sympathetic; we've got to use the new strength or it will break us.

That is the vital difference between those who drift with the stream, as I did at first, and those who, like the great souls down the ages, inspire, revive, and strengthen the corporate life of their generation.

MARGARET BONDFIELD (1873–1953), contribution to *What Life Has Taught Me* (edited by Sir J. Marchant, 1948)

33. *An Attitude to Life*

The continuation of the previous extract.

Another lesson that I learned was that the intensity of prayer is not measured by time, but by the reality and depth of one's awareness of unity with God. I learned to look on prayer not as a means of influencing the Creator in my favour, but as an awareness of the presence of God—everywhere.

I also learned a few helpful ideas about sin. Broadly speaking, I learned to recognise sin as the refusal to live up to the enlightenment we possess. To know the right order of values and deliberately to choose the lower ones. To know that, however much these values may differ with different people at different stages of spiritual growth, for one's self there must be no compromise with that which one *knows* to be the lower value.

I learned, too, that to condemn others is a grave mistake, since hatred, and even the wrong kind of criticism, is an evil which recoils upon its author and poisons every human relationship.

That does not mean we should be blind to the weaknesses or wickednesses of others, any more than to our own, but that we should learn to look on them as the limitations of birth and circumstance, limitations which it is our duty to help them to rise above. In this I have found that example and service are more helpful than advice or preaching.

It has enabled me to get some little glimpse of the meaning behind that great truth—that all the living are as one, in the Great Life of the Universe.

And it carries with it a deep sense of rest. It gives a meaning to life, and a happiness which nothing else can give and no one but ourselves can take away. It is a road to be travelled with a shout of joy—a most exciting road.

MARGARET BONDFIELD (1873–1953), contribution to *What Life Has Taught Me* (edited by Sir J. Marchant, 1948)

34. *The Call to Heroism*

An extract from a sermon preached in Repton School Chapel by William Temple, then Headmaster, and afterwards Archbishop of Canterbury.

Heroism is the same in every age. I wonder if any of you know the story of the Republic which was set up in Rome in 1848 to stand for liberty and justice; it was attacked by the old corrupt governments which surrounded it and which it had displaced, and Rome was besieged. It resisted for more weeks than the wiseacres supposed it could stand days, but at last it fell. On the day when the terms of capitulation were signed a vast concourse gathered in the open space in front of St. Peter's and there rode into the middle the man whose faith and courage had sustained them throughout—Garibaldi. When at last the cheering had died down, he said: 'I am going out from home, I offer neither quarters, nor provisions, nor wages. I offer hunger, thirst, forced marches, battles and death. Let him who loves his country with his heart and not his lips only, follow me.' They streamed after him into the hills, and because of his heroism and theirs, the kingdom of Italy is a fact in the world today.

'I offer neither quarters, nor provisions, nor wages. I offer hunger, thirst, forced marches, battles, death.' It is the very spirit of Christ's invitation: 'If any man will come after Me, let him deny himself, and take up his cross and follow Me.' It is an appeal to heroes. . . . Our Lord is literally demanding of those who would follow Him that they should put a rope round their necks; they are to be ready for literally anything. . . . There is no appeal to selfishness; there is no offer of reward except the reward of sharing the life and sufferings of Christ, which are the life and sufferings of God.

WILLIAM TEMPLE (1881–1944), *Repton School Sermons*

35. *Endless Effort*

From a letter to *The Times* written just after the outbreak of the Second World War.

Too many people think and speak as if peace were the natural state of the world, disturbed from time to time by wicked men like the Shepherd Kings, Sennacherib, Alexander, the Danes, the Normans, the Huns, Napoleon, and Hitler. There is no peace in Nature; peace is the greatest product of the human intellect. In Nature, not only is 'the mayfly torn by the swallow, the sparrow speared by the shrike,' but the cattle and the rabbits contend for the grass which is their food, and the roots of the grass and the roots of the trees wage ceaseless warfare. Even for inorganic matter there is no peace until the absolute death of absolute cold stills the eternal strife of every molecule, by myriads of collisions in every second of time, to maintain its share of the world's space.

Pax Romana, Pax Britannica, were products of long and wise thought and action by many great men. The world will have peace some time; for man is very great and becomes greater. Let us abstain from the folly of pretending again that we shall have peace by the removal of the Kaiser, the German Army, or Hitler, or the Nazis. There is no peace when the rabbits have driven cattle from the pasture, there is deadly war as to which rabbits shall starve and which thrive: when the grass has vanquished the fruit trees shall it be fescue or timothy that lives? When the fruit trees shade grassless earth, which tree's roots shall drain the roots of its neighbour?

If our minds are great enough now and our ideals are wise enough, the best men among us may set a new order in the world which will give it peace—trebling the value of every man's work and his time for happiness and the speed of discovery and the value of life. This year, next year, in a hundred years, in a thousand years this will be attained. Peace will not be won by conquest or obliteration: it must be invented and constructed and maintained by endless effort, such as is given now to the perfection of war.

DR. G. P. BIDDER, *The Times*, 23 Nov. 1939

36. Loyalty to Christ

Erasmus wrote this advice in his work *The Education of a Christian Prince* which he dedicated in 1516 to the sixteen-year-old Charles of Burgundy, the future Emperor Charles V.

'Whenever you think of yourself as a prince, remember you are a *Christian* prince! You should be as different from even the noble pagan princes as a Christian is from a pagan.

Do not think that the profession of a Christian is a matter to be lightly passed over, entailing no responsibilities unless, of course, you think the sacrament which you accepted along with everything else at baptism is nothing. . . . You share the Christian sacrament alike with all others—why not its teaching too? You have allied yourself with Christ—and yet will you slide back into the ways of Julius and Alexander the Great? You seek the same rewards as the others, yet you will have no concern with His mandates.

But on the other hand, do not think that Christ is found in ceremonies, in doctrines kept after a fashion, and in constitutions of the church. Who is truly a Christian? Not he who is baptized or anointed or who attends church. It is rather the man who has embraced Christ in the innermost feelings of his heart, and who emulates Him by his pious deeds. . . . You compel your subjects to know and obey your laws. With far more energy you should exact of yourself knowledge and obedience to the laws of Christ, your king! You judge it an infamous crime, for which there can be no punishment terrible enough, for one who has sworn allegiance to his king to revolt from him. On what grounds, then, do you grant yourself pardon and consider as a matter of sport and jest the countless times you have broken the laws of Christ, to whom you swore allegiance in your baptism, to whose cause you pledged yourself, by whose sacraments you are bound and pledged? . . .

You, too, must take up your cross, or else Christ will have

none of you. 'What,' you ask, 'is my cross?' I will tell you:
Follow the right, do violence to no one, plunder no one, sell
no public office, be corrupted by no bribes. To be sure, your
treasury will have far less in it than otherwise, but take no
thought for that loss, if only you have acquired the interest
from justice. . . . Let the concern for the state completely
cover your personal ambitions. If you cannot defend your
realm without violating justice, without wanton loss of human
life, without great loss to religion, give up and yield to the
importunities of the age! If you cannot look out for the
possessions of your subjects without danger to your own life,
set the safety of the people before your very life! But while
you are conducting yourself in this fashion, which befits a true
Christian prince, there will be plenty to call you a dolt, and
no prince at all. Hold fast to your cause. It is far better to be
a just man than an unjust prince.'

ERASMUS (1466–1536), *The Education of a Christian Prince*,
L. K. Born's translation

VI. THE APPROACH THROUGH WORSHIP

37. *What Worship is*

Two passages from Archbishop William Temple.

To worship is to quicken the conscience by the holiness of
God, to feed the mind with the truth of God, to purge the
imagination by the beauty of God, to open the heart to the
love of God, to devote the will to the purpose of God. All
this is gathered up in that emotion which most cleanses us
from selfishness because it is the most selfless of all emotions—
adoration.

WILLIAM TEMPLE (1881–1944), *The Hope of a New World* (1940)

'What worship means is the submission of the whole being to the object of worship. It is the opening of the heart to receive the love of God; it is the subjection of conscience to be directed by Him; it is declaration of the need to be fulfilled by Him; and as the result of all these together, it is the surrender of will to be used by Him. . . . Not as mere appreciative intelligence do we pray, but as children who want to be with their Father, as friends who must mark off certain times to enjoy the company of their Friend.'

WILLIAM TEMPLE (1881–1944), *The Church and its Teaching Today* (1936)

38. A Parable of Prayer

So have I seen a lark rising from its bed of grass, and soaring upwards, singing as he rises, and hopes to get to heaven and climb above the clouds; but the poor bird was beaten back with the loud sighings of an eastern wind, and his motion made irregular and inconstant, descending more at every breath of the tempest than it could recover by the libration and frequent weighing of his wings; till the little creature was forced to sit down and pant, and stay till the storm was over; and then it made a prosperous flight, and did rise and sing, as if it had learned music and motion from an angel, as he passed sometimes through the air, about his ministries here below: so is the prayer of a good man.

JEREMY TAYLOR (1613–67), *The Return of Prayers* (Part II)

39. On Prayer

In the book from which this is taken, *The Interior Castle*, St. Teresa likens the soul to a castle with many rooms. To pray well we must retire into the innermost room in silence.

Souls without prayer are like bodies, palsied and lame, having hands and feet they cannot use. Just so, there are souls so infirm and accustomed to think of nothing but earthly matters, that there seems no cure for them. It appears impossible for them to retire into their own hearts; they are so accustomed to be with the reptiles and other creatures which live outside the castle, as to come at last to imitate their habits. . . .

Let us speak no more of those crippled souls . . . we will now think of these others who at last enter the precincts of the castle; they are still very worldly, yet have some desire to do right, and at times though rarely, commend themselves to God's care. They think about their souls every now and then; although very busy, they pray a few times a month, with their minds generally filled with a thousand other matters, for where their treasure is, there is their heart also. . . . At length they enter the first rooms in the basement of the castle, accompanied by numbers of reptiles which disturb their peace, and prevent them seeing the beauty of the building; still it is a great gain to have found their way in at all.

ST. TERESA (1515–82), The Interior Castle,
Stanbrook Abbey translation

40. How Badly we Pray

But when we consider with a religious seriousness the manifold weaknesses of the strongest devotions in time of Prayer, it is a sad consideration. I throw myself downe in my Chamber, and I call in, and invite God, and his Angels thither, and when they are there, I neglect God and his Angels, for the noise of a Flie, for the ratling of a Coach, for the whining of a doore; I talke on, in the same posture of praying; eyes lifted up; knees bowed downe; as though I prayed to God; and, if God, or his Angels should aske me, when I thought last of God in that prayer, I cannot tell. Sometimes I finde that I had forgot what I was about, but when I began to forget it, I cannot tell. A memory of yester days pleasures, a feare of tomorrows dangers, a straw under my knee, a noise in mine eare, a light in mine eye, an any thing, a nothing, a fancy . . . troubles me in my prayer. . . . I turne to hearty and earnest prayer to God, and I fix my thoughts strongly (as I thinke) upon him, and before I have perfected one petition . . . the spirit of slumber closes mine eyes, and I pray drowsily; or . . . the spirit of deviation, and vaine repetition, and I pray giddily, and circularly, and returne againe and againe to that I have said before, and perceive not that I do so. . . . I consider not mine own purpose in prayer; and by this advantage, this doore of inconsideration, enters the seducing spirit, the spirit of error, and I pray not only negligently, but erroneously, dangerously for such things as disconduce to the glory of God, and my true happiness, if they were granted.

JOHN DONNE (*c*. 1573–1631), *Sermons*

41. Living always in God's Presence

This reading is from a letter of a humble lay-brother, Brother Lawrence, who worked in the kitchen of a monastery in the seventeenth century. He found that books did not help him to pray, but as he went about his work he tried to do everything as in God's presence.

'Having found in many books different methods of going to God, and divers practices of the spiritual life, I thought this would serve rather to puzzle me, than facilitate what I sought after, which was nothing but how to become wholly God's. . . . I renounced for the love of Him everything that was not He; and I began to live as though there was none but He and I in the world. . . . I worshipped Him the oftenest that I could, keeping my mind in His holy Presence, and recalling it as often as I found it wandered from Him. I found no small pain in this exercise, and yet I continued it notwithstanding all the difficulties that occurred . . . or disquieting myself. . . . I made this my business, as much all the day long as at the appointed

times of prayer . . . and though I have done it very imperfectly,
yet have I found great advantages by it. . . . When we are
faithful to keep ourselves in His holy Presence, and set Him
always before us; this not only hinders our offending Him . . .
at least wilfully, but it also begets holy freedom, and if I may
so speak, a familiarity with God where with we ask . . . the
graces we stand in need of.

BROTHER LAWRENCE (c. 1605–91), *The Practice of the Presence of God*,
English translation, London, 1892

42. God's Presence with Us

'Our Father who art in Heaven.' Do you suppose it is of little
consequence whether or not you know what this heaven is,
and where you must seek your most holy Father? . . . You
know that God is everywhere, which is most true. Now, the
place in which the King dwells is called his court; so wherever
God dwells, there is heaven, and you may feel sure that all
which is glorious is near His Majesty.

Remember what St. Augustine tells us—I think it comes in
his Meditations: how he sought God in many places and at last
found the Almighty within himself. It is of no slight importance for a soul given to wandering thoughts to realize this
truth, and to see that it has no need to go to heaven in order
to speak to the eternal Father or to enjoy His company. . . .
We are not forced to take wings to find Him, but have only to
seek solitude and to look within ourselves. You need not be
overwhelmed with confusion before so kind a Guest, but with
utter humility, talk to Him as to your Father: ask for what you
want as from a father: tell Him your sorrows and beg Him for
relief.

ST. TERESA (1515–82), *The Way of Perfection*,
E. Allison Peers's translation

43. Prayer

Be not afraid to pray—to pray is right.
Pray, if thou canst, with hope; but ever pray,
Though hope be weak, or sick with long delay;
Pray in the darkness, if there be no light.
Far is the time, remote from human sight,
When war and discord on the earth shall cease;
Yet every prayer for universal peace
Avails the blessed time to expedite.
Whate'er is good to wish, ask that of Heaven,
Though it be what thou canst not hope to see;
Pray to be perfect, though material leaven
Forbid the spirit so on earth to be:
   But if for any wish thou darest not pray,
   Then pray to God to cast that wish away.

HARTLEY COLERIDGE (1796–1849)

44. Worship in Work

This passage from Jeremy Taylor is an answer to those who say they have no time for religion.

He that is choice of his time will also be choice of his company and choice of his actions. . . . God hath given to man a short time here upon earth, and yet upon this short time eternity depends. . . . We must remember that the life of every man may be co-ordered, and indeed must, that it may be a perpetual serving of God. . . . For God provides the good things of the world to serve the needs of nature by the labours of the plough-man, the skill and pains of the artisan, and the dangers and traffic of the merchant; these men are in their calling the ministers of the divine providence and the stewards of the creation and servants of a great family of God, the world. . . . In their proportions also a king and a priest and a prophet, a judge and an advocate are doing the work of God. So that no man can complain that his calling takes him off from religion: his calling itself . . . is a serving of God.

JEREMY TAYLOR (1613–67), *Holy Living*

45. Brother Lawrence in the Kitchen

On the subject of this extract see No. 41.

Brother Lawrence had found such an advantage in walking in the presence of God, it was natural for him to recommend it earnestly to others; but his example was a stronger inducement than any arguments he could propose. His very countenance was edifying; such a sweet and calm devotion appearing in it, as could not but affect the beholders. And it was observed, that in the greatest hurry of business in the kitchen, he still preserved his recollection and heavenly mindedness. He was never hasty nor loitering, but did each thing in its season, with an even uninterrupted composure and tranquillity of spirit. 'The time of business,' said he, 'does not with me differ from the time of prayer; and in the noise and clatter of my kitchen, while several persons are at the same time calling for different things, I possess God in as great tranquillity as if I were upon my knees at the Blessed Sacrament.'

From *The Practice of the Presence of God: Letters and Conversations of Brother Lawrence*, English translation, London, 1892

46. Of the Tumbler of Our Lady

This is a story of the Middle Ages, with a meaning for today. (See the next passage also.)

[Once long ago there lived a minstrel or tumbler.] So much had he journeyed to and fro in so many places, . . . that he became a monk of a holy Order, for that he was weary of the world. He wholly relinquished his horses, and clothes, and money, and all that he had, and then he withdrew him from the world, and never more did he wish to return to it. Therefore he entered this holy profession, as has been said, at Clair-vaux.

And when that this tumbler, who was so graceful, and fair, and comely, and well formed, became a monk, he knew not how to perform any office that fell to be done there. Of a truth, he had lived only to tumble, to turn somersaults, to spring, and to dance. To leap and to jump, this he knew, but naught else, and truly no other learning had he, neither the 'Paternoster,' nor the 'Canticles,' nor the 'Credo,' nor the 'Ave Maria,' nor aught that could make for his salvation. . . .

[And he lamented much at this and] went prying about the Church until that he entered a crypt, and he crouched down nigh unto an altar, and hid himself there as best he could. And above the altar was the image of Our Lady, the Holy Mary. And in nowise did it surprise him that he felt in safety there. . . .

And when he . . . heard the bell ring for the Mass, . . . 'Ah!' said he, 'I am like unto a traitor! Even now each one is saying his response, and here am I a tethered ox, and I do naught here but browse, and waste food in vain. Shall I therefore neither speak nor act? By the Mother of God, this will I do, and never shall I be blamed for it. I will do that which I have learnt, and thus, after mine own manner, will I serve the Mother of God in her Church. The others do service with song, and I will do service with tumbling.'

And he took off his habit, and then stripped himself, and laid his garments beside the altar. . . .

Then he began to turn somersaults, now high, now low, first forwards, then backwards, and then he fell on his knees before the image, and bowed his head. 'Ah, very gentle Queen!' said he, 'of your pity, and of your generosity, despise not my service.' . . . And he bowed to the image, and worshipped it, for he paid homage to it as much as he was able. . . .

And when he heard the monks celebrating, he began to exert himself, and so long as the Mass dured, he ceased not to dance, and to jump, and to leap, until that he was on the point to faint, and he could not stand up, and thus he fell to the ground, and dropped from sheer fatigue. . . .

And longwhiles he led this life, and, at each hour precisely, he repaired to the image, to render service and homage. . . .

Well known was it that he went each day into the crypt, but no one, save God, knew what he did there, nor would he, for all the riches of the whole world, that any, save the supreme God alone, should know of his doing. . . . But God, who knew his purpose and his very great compunction, and the love which moved him to it, would not that his deeds should be hidden, but willed and suffered that (they) . . . should be known and made manifest, to the end that every one should know and understand and perceive that God refuses no one who lovingly labours for Him, in whatsoever manner it may be, provided he loves God, and does right.

Think you now that God would have prized his service if that he had not loved Him? By no means, however much he tumbled. But He prized it because of his love. . . .

Longwhiles did the good man live thus, but for how long time he so lived contented, I cannot tell unto you, but in the course of time sore trouble came to him, for one of the monks, who in his heart greatly blamed him that he came not to matins, kept watch on him. . . . And so closely did the monk pursue him, and follow him, and keep watch on him, that he distinctly saw him perform his service in a simple manner, even as I have told it unto you. . . .

And he went to the abbot, and rehearsed unto him, from beginning to end, all that he had learnt, even as you have heard it.

And the abbot arose, and said to the monk, 'On your vow of obedience, I command that you keep silence, and noise this not abroad, and that you so well observe this command, that you speak not of this matter save to me alone, and we will both go thither, and we shall see if this can be. . . .

And then they went thither quite quietly, and without delay they hid themselves in a covert nook nigh unto the altar, so that he saw them not. And the abbot, watching there, observed all the service of the novice, and the divers somersaults the which he turned, and how that he capered, and danced, and bowed before the image, and jumped, and leaped, until that he was nigh fainting. And so greatly was he overcome of fatigue, that he fell heavily to the ground. . . .

And anon the abbot looked, and he saw descend from the vaulting so glorious a lady, that never had he seen one so fair or so richly crowned, and never had another so beautiful been created. . . . And the sweet and noble Queen took a white cloth, and with it she very gently fanned her minstrel before the altar. And the noble and gracious Lady fanned his neck and body and face to cool him, and greatly did she concern herself to aid him, and gave herself up to the care of him; but of this the good man took no heed, for he neither perceived, nor did he know, that he was in such fair company. . . .

And full four times did the abbot and the monk witness, without hindrance, how that each hour he went there, and how that the Mother of God came there to aid and succour her liegeman. . . .

And thus passed the time, until that, a little while after, it came to pass that the abbot sent for him who was so good. And when he heard that he was sent for, and that it was the abbot who made enquiry for him, so greatly was he troubled, that he knew not what he should say. 'Alas,' said he, 'I am found out.' . . .

And weeping, so that his face was all wet, he came before the abbot, and he knelt before him in tears. 'Sire,' said he, 'for God's sake, have mercy! Would you drive me hence? Tell me all your behests, and all your bidding will I do.' . . .

And the holy abbot turned to him, and, all weeping, raised

him up. And he kissed both his eyes. 'Brother,' said he, 'be silent now, for truly do I promise unto you that you shall be at peace with us. God grant that we may have your fellowship so long as we are deserving of it. Good friends shall we be. Fair, gentle brother, pray for me, and I will pray in return for you. And so I beseech and command of you, my sweet friend, that you forthwith render this service openly, just as you have done it, and still better even, if that you know how.'

'Sire,' said he, 'are you in good earnest?'

'Yes, truly,' said the abbot, 'and I charge you, on pain of penance, that you no longer doubt it.'

Then was the good man so very joyous, so the story relates, that he scarce knew what he did. But despite himself, he was constrained to rest, for he had become all pale. And when that he was come to himself again, he was so overcome of joy, that he was seized with a sickness, of the which in a short space he died. But very cheerfully did he perform his service without ceasing, morning and evening, by night and by day, so that not an hour did he miss, until that he fell ill. . . .

Thus died the minstrel. Cheerfully did he tumble, and cheerfully did he serve, for the which he merited great honour, and none was there to compare unto him.

. . . Now let us pray God, without ceasing, that He may grant unto us so worthily to serve Him, that we may be deserving of His love. . . .

From the collection made by GAUTIER DE COINCI (13th cent.)

47. *The Right Attitude to Work*

The opening of this passage refers to the previous reading.

I wonder how many of you have read that remarkable short story by a French writer called *Le Jongleur de Notre-Dame*. In it the retired acrobat had gone to finish his life as a lay brother in a monastery, and one day the monks passing the chapel saw him doing an acrobatic turn in front of an image of the Madonna. It was all that he had to offer her. He was offering his skill and his effort. The observers passed on deeply impressed.

The acrobat had expressed in the simplicity of his action a profound truth, that we hold our accomplishments, our capacity, whatever it may be, from the hands of God, and we must, therefore, use it to His glory and for His purpose. It might seem that acrobatics have little to do with religion or service to God. But that view would be all wrong. Working at a machine or in an office, singing in a theatre or the housework done at home are all services, which, like the acrobatics, can be offered in a spirit which will satisfy our duty to God and will make others happier. We all of us have something worth while that we can offer, however humble it may be. Remember the story of the Widow's Mite. . . .

Very often today we are told that people are not doing their best in their work, that they are trying to get away with as much as they can in the form of reward from the country, whether in profits, salaries or wages, for as little contribution of effort as possible.

We are all of us, of course, only too liable to take that view of our responsibility, that is to regard it as a responsibility to ourselves and not to others—to do as little as we feel we need to satisfy our own desires. Indeed some people feel they need do nothing at all in return for the livelihood with which they are provided, except to try and enjoy themselves, but they are the few exceptions.

As long as we take a purely materialistic view of life that attitude may seem to be a natural one. If with ease anyone can make a large income in the Black Market, why trouble to work hard for a smaller but honest wage?

And from the materialistic point of view I don't know of any very effective answer, as long as one keeps within the letter of the law. . . .

Examining our own position—whatever it may be—from the Christian point of view we must come to the conclusion of the Jongleur of Notre-Dame that, quite apart from our own personal interests, we hold our accomplishments in trust from God to offer them in His service, and that service on earth is, as Christ taught us so thoroughly, to bring happiness and well-being to our fellow-men—to make our best contribution.

SIR STAFFORD CRIPPS (1889–1952), Sermon on Industrial
Sunday, 1947, published in *God in our Work*

48. *True Patriotism*

From a Sermon preached in Repton Chapel, 25 June 1911, on the Coronation of King George V.

If we are to be worthy citizens of the world, we must be members of some society which will mould us for the service of men. If we are to be good men, it must be by becoming good Englishmen; there is no other way open to us. Into our national patriotism we carry our devotion to family, school, university, trade union, or whatever it may be; and the more complete our loyalty in the narrow sphere, the more effective will our patriotism be. But just as we are the children of our parents and can never imagine ourselves except as their children, so we are in our innermost nature Englishmen. We are born members of a nation whose character has been given a very definite form by its peculiar history; we are each of us made what we are by the heroism of Alfred, the statecraft of William the Conqueror, by the resistance to tyranny led by the church in the person of Becket and Langton and the Seven Bishops, by the joyous grace of the Cavaliers and the stern dutifulness of the Puritans; great events and great men have played their part in shaping every one of us; but above all other formative influences must be placed great literature which springs from national character and history, and then reacts again upon them

—Shakespeare and Milton and Bunyan, the Book of Common Prayer, and, above all, the English Bible.

. . . But it is . . . important that our thoughts should not stop there. As we carry our affection for family or school into devotion to the country, so we must carry our patriotism forward into devotion to God and service to mankind. . . . Our wider citizenship in the Kingdom of God must act as a perpetual check on our national patriotism; or, rather, must act as the inspiration of our patriotism.

For if we are genuinely members of the Kingdom of God which Christ came on earth to found, we can never believe that to assist our nation in self-aggrandisement is any kind of service to it. . . . That Kingdom includes all men of all nations, and all are to bring their own contribution to the wealth of its life. As our civilisation is the work of Palestine, Greece and Rome, each bringing its peculiar treasures, spiritual devotion, intellectual passion and social order, so the perfected Kingdom of God will be built up by the inclusion of all that the different nations can offer.

WILLIAM TEMPLE (1881–1944), *Repton School Sermons*

49. *The Building of Chartres Cathedral*

Some of the most beautiful buildings in the world are our ancient cathedrals and churches. Many of these were built as an act of prayer and praise to God and were the work, not of one or two rich men employing an architect and a firm of builders, but of a whole community. Most of the artists and architects and craftsmen who created these buildings to the Glory of God are quite unknown. A man offered up his art and his labour as an act of worship. His name was only one of many, his work might be better or worse than that of others but it was offered with the same devotion, and so there was no need to single him out and record his name. This letter describing the building of Chartres Cathedral was written in 1145 by Abbot Harmion of St. Pierre-sur-Dives in Normandy to Tutbury Abbey in England.

Who has ever seen! Who has ever heard tell, in times past, that powerful princes of the world, that men brought up in honour and in wealth, that nobles, men and women, have bent their proud and haughty necks to the harness of carts, and that like beasts of burden, they have dragged to the abode of Christ these wagons, loaded with wines, grains, oil, store and wood, and all that is necessary for the wants of life, or for the construction of the Church? But while they draw their burdens, there is one thing admirable to observe, it is that often when a thousand persons and more are attached to the chariots, —so great is the difficulty,—yet they march in such silence that not a murmur is heard, and truly if one did not see the thing with one's eyes, one might believe that among such a multitude there was hardly a person present. When they halt on the road, nothing is heard but the confession of sins, and pure and suppliant prayer to God to obtain pardon. At the voice of the priests who exhort their hearts to peace, they forget all hatred, discord is thrown far aside, debts are remitted, the unity of hearts is established. But if anyone is so far advanced in evil as to be unwilling to pardon an offender, . . . his offering is instantly thrown from the wagon as impure, and he himself ignominiously and shamefully excluded from the society of the holy. There one sees the priests who preside over each chariot exhort every one to penitence, to confession of faults, to the resolution of better life! There one sees old people, young people, little children, calling on the Lord with a suppliant voice, and uttering to Him, from the depth of the heart . . . words of glory and praise!

After the people, warned by the sounds of trumpets and the sight of banners, have resumed their road, the march is made with such ease that no obstacle can retard it. . . . When they have reached the Church they arrange the wagons about it like a spiritual camp and during the night they celebrate the watch by hymns and canticles.

From 'The Building of Chartres Cathedral': a letter by ABBOT HAR-MION, published in *Mont St. Michel and Chartres*, by Henry Adams

50. *The Building of a Parish Church*

The previous reading described how a whole community shared in the work of building Chartres Cathedral. It was not only cathedrals that were built like this. Here is the description of the building of an English parish church—that of Bodmin in Cornwall.

Everyone seems to have given according to his means and up to his means. Many who gave money gave labour also, and many who could not give money laboured as best they might, and others gave what they could. We have gifts of lambs, of a cow, and of a goose, and one woman in addition to her subscription sold her brass cauldron . . . and all found its way into the common treasury. No age nor sex seems to have kept aloof.

(Vol. vii of the Camden Miscellany: *The Story of
Bodmin Parish Church*)

And again the chronicler of Ramsey says:

These workmen continued their labours as much from the fervour of devotion as from love of gain; some bore stones, others made mortar, and others again hoisted both on high by means of a mechanical wheel, so that, the Lord giving increase, the walls rose from day to day.

The decoration of the interior of these beautiful churches is described by a monk called Roger of Helmershausen who wrote a book on Divine Arts about 1120.

If David and Solomon were so solicitous to adorn God's house, how much more may the artist of our own day, when he serves the Church, feel himself inspired by the Sevenfold Spirit of God? Thus animated, he will strive to 'show forth to the beholders a vision of God's paradise, bright as springtide with flowers of every hue.' The walls and the vaults will be as gay as a meadow or an embroidered mantle; the glass will outshine them all. For deeper devotion there will be Christ's Passion, and the sufferings of the Saints, and their final reward of glory. 'Work therefore now, good man, happy in this life before God's face and man's, and happier still in the life to come;' for your daily work is a daily burnt-sacrifice to God.

Compiled from *Art and the Reformation*, by G. G. COULTON

51. *Thanksgiving*

If anyone would tell you the shortest, surest way to all happiness and all perfection, he must tell you to make a rule to yourself, to thank and praise God for everything that happens to you. For it is certain that whatever seeming calamity happens to you, if you thank and praise God for it, you turn it into a blessing. Could you therefore work miracles, you could not do more for yourself, than by this thankful spirit, for it heals with a word speaking, and turns all that it touches into happiness.

And although this be the highest temper that you can aim at, though it be the noblest sacrifice that the greatest saint can offer unto God, yet it is not tied to any time, or place or great occasion, but is always in your power, and may be the exercise of every day. For the common events of every day are sufficient to discover and exercise this temper, and may plainly show you how far you are governed in all your actions by this thankful spirit.

WILLIAM LAW (1686–1761)

52. *Praise*

In one salutation to thee, my God, let all my senses spread out and touch this world at thy feet.

Like a rain-cloud of July hung low with its burden of unshed showers, let all my mind bend down at thy door in one salutation to thee.

Let all my songs gather together their diverse strains into a single current and flow to a sea of silence in one salutation to thee.

Like a flock of homesick cranes flying night and day back to their mountain nests, let all my life take its voyage to its eternal home in one salutation to thee.

RABINDRANATH TAGORE (1861–1941), from *Gitanjali*

53. *St. Francis and Nature*

St. Francis of Assisi lived from 1181 to 1226. He was brought up as a well-to-do young man, till he gave up all his possessions to serve God with a few companions.

Wherever he found a flowering meadow, there he preached; and he called upon it to praise the Lord, even as if it had been a rational being. In the same manner did he treat the sown fields and the vineyards, the stones and the forests, all the fair meads, the running streams, the green gardens, the earth, the fire, the air and the wind. And he counselled them all with upright purity of heart to love God; and in a strangely hidden way he penetrated into the heart of each creature with his sharp-sightedness: as though he were penetrating into the glorious freedom of the Son of God.

From THOMAS OF CELANO's *Life of St. Francis*

54. *The Song of the Creatures*

O most high, almighty, good Lord God: to thee belong praise, glory, honour, and all blessing.

Praisèd be my Lord God, with all his creatures: and specially our brother the sun, who brings us the day and who brings us the light.

Fair is he, and shining with a very great splendour: O Lord, he signifies to us thee.

Praisèd be my Lord for our sister the moon: and for the stars, the which he has set clear and lovely in heaven.

Praisèd be my Lord for our brother the wind: and for air and cloud, calms, and all weather by the which thou upholdest in life all creatures.

Praisèd be my Lord for our sister water: who is very serviceable unto us, and humble and precious and clean.

Praisèd be my Lord for our brother fire, through whom thou givest us light in the darkness: and he is bright and pleasant and very mighty and strong.

Praisèd be my Lord for our mother the earth, the which doth sustain us and keep us: and bringeth forth divers fruits, and flowers of many colours, and grass.

Praisèd be my Lord for all those who pardon one another for his love's sake: and who endure weakness and tribulation.

Blessèd are they who peaceably shall endure: for thou, O most Highest, shalt give them a crown.

Praisèd be my Lord for our sister the death of the body: blessed are they who are found walking by thy most holy will.

Praise ye and bless ye the Lord and give thanks unto him: and serve him with great humility. Alleluya, alleluya!

ST. FRANCIS OF ASSISI (1181–1226), Matthew Arnold's translation

55. St. Francis Preaches to the Birds

And journeying on . . . St. Francis lifted up his eyes and beheld some trees by the wayside whereon were an infinite number of birds; so that he marvelled and said to his companions, 'Tarry here for me by the way and I will go and preach to my little sisters the birds.' And he entered into a field and began to preach to the birds that were on the ground; and anon those that were on the trees flew down to hear him, and all stood still the while St. Francis made an end of his sermon; and even then they departed not until he had given them his blessing. . . . And the substance of the sermon St. Francis preached was this, 'My little sisters the birds, much are ye beholden to God your Creator, and always and in every place ye ought to praise Him for that He hath given you—double and—triple vesture; He hath given you freedom to go into every place and also did preserve the seed of you in the ark of Noah, in order that your kind might not perish from the earth. Again, ye are beholden to him for the element of air which he hath appointed for you; moreover ye sow not, neither do ye reap, and God feedeth you and giveth you the rivers and the fountains for your drink; He giveth you the mountains and valleys for your refuge, and the tall trees wherein to build your nests, and forasmuch as ye can neither spin nor sew God clotheth you, you and your children: wherefore your Creator loveth you much, since He hath dealt so bounteously with you; and therefore beware little sisters mine, of the sin of ingratitude, but ever strive to praise God.' While St. Francis was uttering these words, all those birds began to open their beaks, and stretch their necks, and spread their wings and reverently to bow their heads to the ground, showing by their gestures and songs that the holy father's words gave them greatest joy: and St. Francis was glad and rejoiced with them, and marvelled much at so great a multitude of birds and at their manifold loveliness, and at their attention and familiarity, for which things he devoutly praised the Creator in them.

From *The Little Flowers of St. Francis*,
T. Okey's translation (Everyman)

56. St. Anthony Preaches to the Fishes

The Anthony here spoken of was a follower of St. Francis, and thus one of the first Franciscan friars.

It befell on a time when St. Anthony was at Rimini, where was a great multitude of heretics whom he desired to lead to the light of the true faith and to the paths of virtue, that he preached for many days and disputed with them concerning the faith of Christ and of the Holy Scriptures: and yet they not only consented not unto his words, but even hardened their hearts and stubbornly refused to hear him. Wherefore St. Anthony, by divine inspiration, went one day to the bank of the river, hard by the sea-shore, and standing there on the bank of the river, between it and the sea, began to speak to the fishes after the manner of a preacher sent by God, 'Hear the word of God, ye fishes of the sea and of the river, since the miscreant heretics scorn to hear it.' And when he had thus spoken, anon there came towards the bank such a multitude of fishes, great and small, and middling, that never before in those seas, nor in that river, had so great a multitude been seen; and all held their heads out of the water in great peace and gentleness and perfect order and remained intent on the lips of St. Anthony: for in front of him and nearest to the bank were the lesser fishes; and beyond them were those of middling size; and then behind, where the water was deepest, were the greater fishes. The fishes being then mustered in such order and array, St. Anthony began to preach to them solemnly, and spake thus, 'Ye fishes, my brothers, much are ye held, according to your power, to thank God, our Creator, who hath given you so noble an element for your habitation; for at your pleasure have ye waters, sweet and salt, and He hath given you many places of refuge to shelter you from the tempests; He hath likewise given you a pure and clear element and food whereby ye can live. God, your Creator, bountiful and kind, when He created you, commanded you to increase and multiply, and gave you His blessing. Moreover, He hath given you fins that ye may fare whithersoever it may please you. To you was it granted, by commandment of God, to preserve Jonah, the prophet, and after the third day to cast him forth on dry land, safe and whole. Ye did offer the tribute money to Christ, our Lord, poor little one, that had not wherewithal to pay. Ye, by a rare mystery, were the food of the eternal King, Christ

Jesus, before the resurrection and after. For all these things much are ye held to praise and bless God, that hath given you blessings so manifold and so great; yea, more even than to any other of His creatures.' At these and the like words and admonitions from St. Anthony, the fishes began to open their mouths and bow their heads, and by these and other tokens of reverence, according to their fashion and power, they gave praise to God.

From *The Little Flowers of St. Francis*, T. Okey's translation

57. *Pied Beauty*

Glory be to God for dappled things—
   For skies of couple-colour as a brinded cow;
    For rose-moles all in stipple upon trout that swim;
Fresh-firecoal chestnut-falls; finches' wings;
   Landscape plotted and pieced—fold, fallow, and plough;
    And all trades, their gear and tackle and trim.

All things counter, original, spare, strange;
   Whatever is fickle, freckled (who knows how?)
    With swift, slow; sweet, sour; adazzle, dim;
He fathers-forth whose beauty is past change:
    Praise him.

GERARD MANLEY HOPKINS (1844–89)

58. *God's Creatures*

We praise Thee, O God, for Thy glory displayed in all the creatures of the earth,
In the snow, in the rain, in the wind, in the storm; in all of Thy creatures, both the hunters and the hunted. . . .
They affirm Thee in living; all things affirm Thee in living; the bird in the air, both the hawk and the finch; the beast on the earth, both the wolf and the lamb; the worm in the soil and the worm in the belly.

Therefore man, whom Thou hast made to be conscious of
    Thee, must consciously praise Thee, in thought and in
    word and in deed.
Even with the hand to the broom, the back bent in laying the
    fire, the knee bent in cleaning the hearth, . . .
The back bent under toil, the knee bent under sin, the hands
    to the face under fear, the head bent under grief,
Even in us the voices of seasons, the snuffle of winter, the song
    of spring, the drone of summer, the voices of beasts and of
    birds, praise Thee.

T. S. ELIOT, from *Murder in the Cathedral*

59. *O Light Invisible*

O Light Invisible, we praise Thee!
Too bright for mortal vision,
O Greater Light, we praise Thee for the less;
The eastern light our spires touch at morning.
The light that slants upon our western doors at evening,
The twilight over stagnant pools at batflight,
Glowworm glowlight on a grass blade,
O Light Invisible, we worship Thee.

We thank Thee for the lights that we have kindled,
The light of altar and of sanctuary;
Small lights of those who meditate at midnight,
And lights directed through the coloured panes of windows
And light reflected from the polished stone,
The gilded, carven wood; the coloured fresco.
Our gaze is submarine, our eyes look upward
And see the light that fractures through unquiet water.
We see the light but see not whence it comes.
O Light Invisible, we glorify Thee!

.   .   .

And we must extinguish the candle, put out the light and
    relight it; forever must quench, forever relight the flame.
Therefore we thank Thee for our little light that is dappled
    with shadow.
We thank Thee, who hast moved us to building, to finding, to
    forming at the ends of our fingers and beams of our eyes.
And when we have built an altar to the Invisible Light, we may
    set thereon the little lights for which our bodily vision is
    made.
And we thank Thee that darkness reminds us of light.

O Light Invisible, we give Thee thanks for Thy great glory!

T. S. ELIOT, from *The Rock*

PART TWO

FESTIVALS OF THE KINGDOM

I. CHRISTMAS

60. *The Angels for the Nativity of Our Lord*

'Run, shepherds, run, where Bethlem blest appears,
We bring the best of news, be not dismayed;
A Saviour there is born, more old than years,
Amidst the rolling Heaven this Earth who stayed:
In a poor cottage inned, a Virgin Maid
A weakling did Him bear, Who all upbears;
There He in clothes is wrapt, in manger laid
To Whom too narrow swaddlings are our spheres.
Run, shepherds, run, and solemnize His Birth.
This is that night—no, day, grown great with bliss,
In which the power of Satan broken is;
In Heaven be glory, peace unto the Earth.'
    Thus singing, through the air the angels swam,
    And all the stars re-echoèd the same.

WILLIAM DRUMMOND (1584–1649)

61. *'I sing of a maiden'*

No one knows who wrote this fifteenth-century carol. [In the first
verse, 'makeles' means 'matchless'; 'ches'[1] means 'chose'.]

> I sing of a maiden
> That is makeles;
> King of all kings
> To her son she ches.
>
> He came al so still
> There his mother was,
> As dew in April
> That falleth on the grass.

---

[1] Pronounce to rhyme with 'less'.

He came al so still
To his mother's bour,
As dew in April
That falleth on the flour.

He came al so still
There his mother lay,
As dew in April
That falleth on the spray.

Mother and maiden
Was never none but she;
Well may such a lady
Goddes mother be.

From the Sloane MS., published in *The Oxford
Book of Carols*, and elsewhere

62. *A Christmas Carol*

The Christ-Child lay on Mary's lap,
His hair was like a light.
(O weary, weary were the world,
But here is all aright.)

The Christ-Child lay on Mary's breast,
His hair was like a star.
(O stern and cunning are the Kings,
But here the true hearts are.)

The Christ-Child lay on Mary's heart,
His hair was like a fire.
(O weary, weary is the world,
  But here the world's desire.)

The Christ-Child stood at Mary's knee,
His hair was like a crown,
And all the flowers looked up at Him,
And all the stars looked down.

GILBERT KEITH CHESTERTON (1874–1936),
from *The Wild Knight*

63. *A Christmas Song*

When from His throne the Godhead bowed
To human Form below,
The Heavens dropt down, and every cloud
Hung loath to let Him go.
O, bright the light, and white the night,
When, full of favour stored,
God's Maid lay down in Bethlehem town,
To wait the coming Lord!

Before His feet went down the snow
Amid the tranquil night,
Till all the world lay white below
To greet the Lord of Light.
O, bright the light, and white the night,
When, full of favour stored,
God's Maid lay down in Bethlehem town,
To wait the coming Lord!

The rugged hills and all the rocks
Were covered as with fleece;
The towns were seen like folded flocks
To wait the Prince of Peace.
O, bright the light, and white the night,
When, full of favour stored,
God's Maid lay down in Bethlehem town,
To wait the coming Lord!

Oh, like a flock in field and fold,
The wintry world lay then,
On that fair night in days of old
When Christ came down to men.
Oh, bright the light, and white the night,
When, full of favour stored,
God's Maid lay down in Bethlehem town,
To wait the coming Lord!

LAURENCE HOUSMAN

64. Shepherds' Carol

When the frost was white on the wool of our flocks
And stars like hailstones fell on the rocks,
When we held our fingers tight to the dirk
And sharpened our eyes on the slaty dark
That blocked the ghyll and blackened the scree,
It was never a light we thought to see.

When the light blazed on the spikes of the fell
We remembered the burning barns in the dale;
When our collies pricked up their ears, and we
Harked to the warning wind from the sea
That creaked in the reeds by the frozen mere,
It never was music we thought to hear.

When the music clamoured across the tarns
And voices rang from the singing cairns
Of a holy chieftain, a warrior priest,
Blown from the wondering isles of the west
On a full tide and a pulling wind,
It was never a child we thought to find.

But the music we heard and the light we saw
And the child we found in a cot of straw.

When we took the lambs that were dropped in the snow
And ran to the stones by the sacred tree,
It was never ourselves we thought to give—
But we gave ourselves that the lambs might live.

NORMAN NICHOLSON

65. *The King's Mount*

When Jesus was born in Bethlehem there were other animals in that stable besides the humble ass which brought His mother to the inn. There was the contemptuous camel, with a lip, the steed of some desert ranger. There was a proud war horse stabled there by a passing warrior. There was a strong bullock who drew the wagon of a great merchant. In the quiet of that Christmas night the four beasts munched their provender in silence.

We have all heard how that at midnight on Christmas Eve all the beasts in the world gain for a few fleeting moments the power of human speech; now this miracle began on this very night in the stable at Bethlehem. The four beasts watched the carpenter Joseph, his wife Mary and the new-born child who lay in the manger.

'Humph,' said the contemptuous camel, with a sniff, 'quite an ordinary child.'

'A little peasant child,' said the proud horse with a snort, 'a common little kid.'

The great ox gave a grunt and said, 'A weak miserable little thing,' and they all went on munching their hay and forgot about Joseph and Mary and the Babe in the manger.

Then outside the stable there was a sound of footsteps and men's voices, which could be faintly heard through the half-open stable door. The humble ass who had felt much too insignificant to join in the conversation of his betters (indeed he would have been severely snubbed had he dared to do anything so rash), turned his long ears to hear what the men were saying. Then for the first time that night he spoke. 'They are saying,' said the ass, 'that a King is born this day.' There was a stir among the noble beasts at that news. 'Ah, He will need me,' said the camel, 'to cross the trackless desert, for surely this King will be a great traveller, visiting all the cities of the world in His wisdom and magnificence.'

'He will need me,' said the horse, 'to ride in triumph through the streets of the cities that He conquers, for He will be a mighty warrior.'

'No, it is I whom He will need,' said the ox, 'for it is a bearer of great burdens to carry His merchandise, His gold and His silver that He will want the most.'

So they quarrelled that night as to which of them the newborn King would need, and of the Baby in the manger they thought nothing at all, only the humble ass who had said nothing, for he thought he was too humble to be used at all, looked with mild brown eyes at the mother and her child as Mary crooned over the manger-cradle the baby's first lullaby. . . .

But after all, it was on the humble ass that the King rode into His city in the end.

After the story told by W. E. ORCHARD

66. Journey of the Magi

In this poem by T. S. Eliot one of the three Wise Men is speaking of their journey from the East to Bethlehem.

A cold coming we had of it,
Just the worst time of the year
For a journey, and such a long journey:
The ways deep and the weather sharp,
The very dead of winter.

And the camels galled, sore-footed, refractory,
Lying down in the melting snow.
There were times we regretted
The summer palaces on slopes, the terraces,
And the silken girls bringing sherbet.
Then the camel men cursing and grumbling
And running away, and wanting their liquor and women,
And the night-fires going out, and the lack of shelters,
And the cities hostile and the towns unfriendly
And the villages dirty and charging high prices:
A hard time we had of it.
At the end we preferred to travel all night,
Sleeping in snatches,
With the voices singing in our ears, saying
That this was all folly.

Then at dawn we came down to a temperate valley,
Wet, below the snow line, smelling of vegetation;
With a running stream and a water-mill beating the darkness,
And three trees on the low sky,
And an old white horse galloped away in the meadow.
Then we came to a tavern with vine-leaves over the lintel,
Six hands at an open door dicing for pieces of silver,
And feet kicking the empty wine-skins,
But there was no information, and so we continued
And arrived at evening, not a moment too soon
Finding the place; it was (you may say) satisfactory.

All this was a long time ago, I remember,
And I would do it again, but set down
This set down
This: were we led all that way for
Birth or Death? There was a Birth, certainly,
We had evidence and no doubt. I had seen birth and death,

But had thought they were different; this Birth was
Hard and bitter agony for us, like Death, our death.
We returned to our places, these Kingdoms,
But no longer at ease here, in the old dispensation,
With an alien people clutching their gods,
I should be glad of another death.

                                                    T. S. ELIOT

67. Christmas 1944

Hanns Lilje, a German pastor, tells of his experiences in prison on
Christmas Eve, 1944. The prison Commandant, a humane man,
arranged for Dr. Lilje to visit the cell of Count X, who had asked to
see a pastor. They were joined there by a prisoner who had been
condemned to death, but whose chains had been removed and his
violin returned to him for the night.

At the Commandant's suggestion the violinist played a Christmas chorale, exquisitely; then, in this cell, and before this
congregation, I read the Gospel for Christmas Day: 'Now it
came to pass in those days there went out a decree . . . .' The
violinist played another Christmas chorale; in the meantime I
had been able to arrange my thoughts a little about the passage
in Isaiah which had filled my mind when I was summoned
downstairs. I said to my fellow-prisoners: 'This evening we are
a congregation, part of the Church of Christ, and this great word
of divine promise is as true for us to-day as it was . . . a year ago,
. . . and for all who this year receive it in faith. Our chief concern
now,' I said, 'is to receive this promise in firm faith, and to
believe that God, through Jesus Christ, has allowed the eternal
light to "arise and shine" upon this world which is plunged in
the darkness of death, and that He will also make this light to
shine for us. At this moment, in our cells, we have practically
nothing that makes the Christmas festival so familiar and so
lovely, but there is one thing left to us: God's great promise.
Let us cling to this promise and to Him, in the midst of the

darkness. Here and now, in the midst of the uncertainty of our prison life, in the shadow of death, we will praise Him by a firm and unshaken faith in His Word, which is addressed to us.' Then, in the midst of the cell, the Count knelt down upon the hard stone floor, and while I prayed aloud the beautiful old prayer of confession from Thomas à Kempis (which he himself had chosen) and then pronounced absolution, the tears were running silently down his cheeks. It was a very quiet celebration of the Sacrament full of deep confidence in God; almost palpably the wings of the Divine Mercy hovered over us, as we knelt at the altar in a prison cell on Christmas Eve. We were prisoners, in the power of the Gestapo—in Berlin. But the peace of God enfolded us: it was real and present, 'like a Hand laid gently upon us.'

Since the Commandant had obviously done all this without permission, and on his own personal responsibility, he could not allow any further conversation. The violinist played a closing chorale; I parted from my fellow-prisoner with a warm handshake, saying: 'God bless you, brother.' When we reached the corridor the Commandant shook my hand twice, with an iron grip; he was deeply moved: turning to me, he said: 'Thank you! You cannot imagine what you have done for me this evening, in my sad and difficult daily work.' I was immediately taken back to my cell, but I praised God, and indeed, I praised Him from my whole heart that in this building, under the shadow of death, and in the face of so much trouble and distress, a Christian congregation had assembled to celebrate Christmas. For it is possible to have every external sign of festivity and comfort and joyful celebrations, and yet not to have a true Christmas congregation, while in the shadow of death and in much trouble of heart a real Christian congregation can gather at Christmas. It is possible for the candles and the lights to blind our eyes, so that we can no longer see the essential element in Christmas; but the people who 'walk in darkness' can perhaps see it better than all who see only the lights of earth.

Shortly after Christmas, the Count was sent to a concentration camp. The violinist was killed by the Gestapo during the last days before the collapse; I have completely lost sight of the Commandant who, soon after this, was removed from his post because he had proved too humane. But the memory of my Christmas service in 1944, illuminated by the consoling and eternal Light of God, still remains with me.

HANNS LILJE, from *The Valley of the Shadow*,
translated by Olive Wyon

II. ASH WEDNESDAY

68. *How We regard our Sins*

Before I commit a sin it seems to me so shallow, that I may wade through it dry-shod from any guiltiness. But when I have committed it, it often seems so deep that I cannot escape without drowning. Thus I am always in the extremities; either my sins are so small that they need not my repentance, or so great that they cannot obtain thy pardon. Lend me, O Lord, a reed out of thy Sanctuary, truly to measure the dimension of my offences. But oh! as thou revealest to me more of my misery, reveal also more of thy mercy.

THOMAS FULLER (1608–61), *Good Thoughts in Bad Time s*

69. *The Unweeded Garden*

This is an extract from a letter written in prison by James Parnell, a Quaker preacher, who died in prison in 1656.

O, how beautiful is the spring in a barren field, where barrenness and deadness fly away. As spring comes on, the winter casts her coat and the summer is nigh. O, wait to see and read these things within. You that have been as barren and dead and dry without sap; unto you the Sun of Righteousness is risen with healing in his wings. . . . O, mind the secret sprigs and tender plants. Now you are called to dress the garden. Let not the weeds and wild plants remain. Peevishness is a weed; anger is a weed; self-love and self-will are weeds; pride is a wild plant; covetousness is a wild plant; lightness and vanity are wild plants. . . . And these things have had a room in your gardens, and have been tall and strong: and truth, innocence, and equity have been left out and could not be found, until the Sun of Righteousness arose and searched out that which was lost. Therefore, stand not idle, but come into the vineyard and work. Your work shall be to watch and keep out the fowls, unclean beasts, wild bears and subtle foxes. And he that is the Husbandman will pluck up the wild plants and weeds, and make defence about the vines. He will tell you what to do. He who is Father of the vineyard will be nigh you. And what is not clear to you, wait for the fulfilling.

JAMES PARNELL (d. 1656); quoted in *A Little Book of Quaker Saints*, by L. V. Hodgkin

70. 'Lord, have mercy'

When John Sebastian Bach sought to give musical expression to the very kernel of Christian truth, he turned to the Mass for his words. The B minor Mass opens with the poignant cry of the whole chorus and orchestra, Kyrie Eleison, Lord have mercy, and in the fugue which follows all the voices and instruments independently take up the theme; there are no other words, simply Kyrie Eleison.

No one who has ever heard it can doubt that in that universal cry for mercy we are led to the threshold of our religion. Nor is it merely a preliminary; the sense of utter human unworthiness is the permanent ground-bass through which the melody of the gospel of the mercy of God sounds in our ears, so that the suitable epitaph for a Christian is composed of two words only, 'Jesu, mercy.' This is far more impressive, far more Christian, than a catalogue of virtues, or of benevolent actions, or of intellectual achievements.

The overwhelming recognition of human sin controls the Old Testament and the New Testament alike, and no understanding of Our Lord's words and actions is possible if we persist in denying it.

SIR EDWYN HOSKYNS (1884–1937), from *Cambridge Sermons*

71. *The Guest*

A poem by an unknown author

Yet if His Majesty, our sovereign lord,
Should of his own accord
Friendly himself invite,
And say, 'I'll be your guest to-morrow night,'
How would we stir ourselves, call and command
All hands to work! 'Let no man idle stand!

'Set me fine Spanish tables in the hall;
See they be fitted all;
Let there be room to eat
And order taken that there want no meat.
See every sconce and candlestick made bright,
That without tapers they may give a light.

'Look to the presence: are the carpets spread,
The dazie o'er the head,
The cushions on the chairs,
And all the candles lighted on the stairs?
Perfume the chambers, and in any case
Let each man give attendance in his place!'

Thus, if a king were coming, would we do;
And 'twere good reason too;
For 'tis a duteous thing
To show all honour to an earthly King,
And after all our travail and our cost,
So he be pleased, to think no labour lost.

But at the coming of the King of Heaven
All's set at six and seven;
We wallow in our sin,
Christ cannot find a chamber in the inn,
We entertain Him always like a stranger,
And, as at first, still lodge Him in the manger.

From a Christ Church, Oxford, MS., published in
Oxford Book of XVIIth Century Verse, &c.

III. HOLY WEEK

72. *Palm Sunday*

On this day Christ rode into Jerusalem and the people strewed
branches in front of him.

Come, drop your branches, strew the way
   Plants of the day!
Whom sufferings make most green and gay.
The King of grief, the man of sorrow,
Weeping still like the wet morrow,
Your shades and freshness comes to borrow.

Put on, put on your best array;
Let the joy'd road make holy-day
And flowers, that into fields do stray
Or secret groves, keep the high-way.

Hark! how the children shrill and high
  Hosanna cry;
Their joys provoke the distant skie,
Where thrones and seraphins reply;
And their own Angels shine and sing
  In a bright ring:
  Such young, sweet mirth
  Makes heaven and earth
  Joyn in a joyful Symphony.

The harmless young and happy Ass
Is in these joys an high partaker,
Ordain'd and made to bear his Maker.

Dear feast of Palms, of Flowers and Dew!
Whose fruitful dawn sheds hopes and lights;
Thy bright solemnities did shew,
The third glad day through two sad nights.

I'll get me up before the Sun,
I'll cut me boughs off many a tree
And all alone full early run
To gather flowers to welcome thee.

HENRY VAUGHAN (1622–95)

73. 'The Last Supper'

Leonardo da Vinci finished his painting of *The Last Supper* on the refectory wall of a religious community in 1497.

Some three years had passed since he had begun to work in Santa Maria delle Grazie. One day the scaffold was taken away and people crowded into the refectory. A solemn hush fell upon the room. . . . The mystic drama, elsewhere to be contemplated in peaceful settings, here broke through the solacing dust of fifteen centuries and for the second time embroiled every spectator in its pathos and terror and guilt. To every man present it spoke and said:

Look! It happens in a room like this one you yourself are in. The table and the utensils are indeed the very same you know. Those are the creases of a freshly spread table-cloth, for it is the feast of the Passover. . . . Something terrible has happened. The Master has dropped His eyes mournfully, and stretching out His arms in forgiveness has said:

'Verily, verily, one of you shall betray me.'

The words are spoken simply, but they have thrown the disciples into confusion. On either side of Jesus is a swaying, gesticulating group. Every man is touched and involved. Peter has sprung to his feet; he whispers vehemently to John, who sits at the right hand of Jesus:

'Who? You must know. Tell us who, and let us fight.'

In his excitement Peter grabs a knife, lurches against Judas who, thrown forward, knocks over the salt. Judas is a study in fright. In his right fist he clutches a money-bag. Involuntarily he puts out his left hand, as though to ward off a blow.

'Surely,' he seems to stammer, 'you cannot mean. . . . You would not suspect me, by any chance. . . .' His face is drawn, his body tense. He is at bay.

Behind Peter is Andrew who holds up his hands in horror: 'Heaven shield us!'

Bartholomew and the younger James bend forward excitedly: 'Who is it, Master? Say who.'

On the left of Jesus, the elder James throws out his arms, and his head sinks in despair. Over his shoulder Thomas raises a forefinger like a question-mark.

'Let us consider,' he speculates. 'One, you say. . . .'

Philip bends forward: 'Is it I, Lord?' he pleads passionately. 'Thou knowest it is not I. Look Thou but into my heart.'

At the far end of the table the patriarch Simon stretches

forth his hands in protest: 'What can this mean? I do not understand it at all.'

Matthew and Thaddeus turn to him with the utmost excitement. Matthew appeals to him to speak to the Master. 'Speak,' urges Thaddeus. 'We will know who is the arch-fiend among us.'

And among the spectators many a man searched his conscience, asking, like Philip: 'Is it I, Lord?' Others, like Peter, searched the conscience of their neighbours.

'Leonardo is right,' murmured the humble and devout hearts. 'Judas, too, is close to the Lord, like all his flock. Not apart.'

JOSEPH COTTLER, *Man with Wings*

74. *The Garden of Gethsemane*

A meditation on the Agony of Jesus in the Garden, before his crucifixion.

Jesus suffers in His passion the torments which men inflict upon Him; but in His agony He suffers the torments which He inflicts on Himself; *turbare semetipsum*. This is a suffering from no human, but an almighty hand, for He must be almighty to bear it.

Jesus seeks some comfort at least in His three dearest friends, and they are asleep. He prays them to bear with Him for a little, and they leave Him with entire indifference, having so little compassion that it could not prevent their sleeping, even for a moment. And thus Jesus was left alone to the wrath of God.

Jesus is alone on the earth, without any one not only to feel and share His suffering, but even to know of it; He and Heaven were alone in that knowledge.

Jesus is in a garden, not of delight as the first Adam, where he lost himself and the whole human race, but in one of agony, where He saved Himself and the whole human race.

He suffers this affliction and this desertion in the horror of the night.

I believe that Jesus never complained but on this single occasion; but then He complained as if He could no longer bear His extreme suffering. 'My soul is sorrowful, even unto death.'

Jesus seeks companionship and comfort from men. This is the sole occasion in all His life, as it seems to me. But He receives it not, for His disciples are asleep.

Jesus will be in agony even to the end of the world. We must not sleep during that time.

Jesus, in the midst of this universal desertion, including that of His own friends chosen to watch with Him, finding them asleep, is vexed because of the danger to which they expose, not Him, but themselves; He cautions them for their own safety and their own good, with a sincere tenderness for them during their ingratitude, and warns them that the spirit is willing and the flesh weak.

Jesus, finding them still asleep, without being restrained by any consideration for themselves or for Him, has the kindness not to waken them, and leaves them in repose.

Jesus prays, uncertain of the will of His Father, and fears death; but when He knows it, He goes forward to offer Himself to death.

BLAISE PASCAL (1623–62), *Pensées*, W. F. Trotter's translation

75. *Thoughts in Prison*

An extract from the diary of Henri Perrin, a young Jesuit priest, who trained as a mechanic and volunteered to work alongside the French conscript workers in the German factories. After six months he was imprisoned for his religious activities.

. . . For a week I had been giving my whole mind to the Passion of Christ. At Jerusalem, as I knelt on the flagstones of Lithostrotos, where Jesus spent the first hours of Good Friday, I had been profoundly moved. How much more so now, at the thought of the hours He spent in prison. . . . During my long hours of silence, I saw Him in His cell, in the midst of the other prisoners. For He 'did time,' too, and so many others after Him, from Peter to Joan of Arc, from Paul to St. Louis. This would henceforward be a bond creating a special and unforgettable love. However, I passed long hours in His company—sometimes in my cell, sometimes in His prison, that cellar of Caiphas' house. I often wondered what He can have said to the other prisoners—for indeed He must have talked to them. He who was as able to console the wretched as to silence the Pharisees.

HENRI PERRIN, Priest-Workman in Germany,
translated by Rosemary Sheed

76. Good Friday: Rex Tragicus, or Christ going to His Cross

The poet, as he watches the scene in imagination, addresses Christ.

Put off Thy robe of purple, then go on
To the sad place of execution:
Thine hour is come; and the tormentor stands
Ready, to pierce Thy tender feet, and hands.
Long before this, the base, the dull, the rude,
Th' inconstant and unpurgèd multitude
Yawn for Thy coming; some ere this time cry,
How He defers, how loath He is to die!
Amongst this scum, the soldier with his spear,
And that sour fellow, with his vinegar,
His sponge, and stick, do ask why Thou dost stay?
So do the scurf and bran too: Go thy way,
Thy way, Thou guiltless Man, and satisfy
By Thine approach, each their beholding eye.
Not as a thief, shalt Thou ascend the mount,
But like a person of some high account:

The Cross shall be Thy stage; and Thou shalt there
The spacious field have for thy theatre.
Thou art that Roscius, and that marked-out man,
That must this day act the tragedian,
To wonder and affrightment: Thou art He,
Whom all the flux of nations comes to see;
Not those poor thieves that act their parts with Thee:
Those act without regard, when once a King,
And God, as Thou art, comes to suffering.
No, no, this scene from Thee takes life and sense,
And soul and spirit, plot and excellence.
Why then, begin, great King! ascend Thy throne,
And thence proceed to act Thy Passion
To such an height, to such a period raised,
As Hell, and Earth, and Heaven may stand amazed.
God, and good angels guide Thee; and so bless
Thee in Thy several parts of bitterness;
That those, who see Thee nailed unto the Tree,
May (though they scorn Thee) praise and pity Thee.
And we (Thy lovers) while we see Thee keep
The laws of action, will both sigh and weep;
And bring our spices, and embalm Thee dead;
That done, we'll see Thee sweetly burièd.

ROBERT HERRICK (1591–1674)

77. *Good Friday*

Alone to sacrifice Thou goest, Lord,
Giving Thyself to death whom Thou wilt slay.
For us Thy wretched folk is any word,[1]
Whose sins have brought Thee to this agony?

---

[1] *Quid nos miserrimi possumus dicere?* Suggested alternative rendering:

> Can ought be said for us, Thy wretched folk,
> Whose sins have brought Thee to this agony?

(*Compilers*)

For they are ours, O Lord, our deeds, our deeds.
Why must Thou suffer torture for our sin?
Let our hearts suffer for Thy passion, Lord,
That very suffering may Thy mercy win.

This is that night of tears, the three days space,
Sorrow abiding of the eventide,
Until the day break with the risen Christ,
And hearts that sorrowed shall be satisfied.

So may our hearts share in Thine anguish, Lord,
That they may sharers of Thy glory be:
Heavy with weeping may the three days pass,
To win the laughter of Thine Easter Day.

PETER ABELARD (1079–1142), Helen Waddell's translation

IV. EASTER

78. *Easter Night*

All night had shout of men and cry
    Of woeful women filled his way;
Until that noon of sombre sky
    On Friday, clamour and display
Smote him; no solitude had He,
    No silence since Gethsemane.

Public was Death; but Power and Might,
    But life again, and Victory,
Were hushed within the dead of night,
    The shutter'd dark, the secrecy,
And all alone, alone, alone
    He rose again behind the stone.

ALICE MEYNELL (1847–1922)

79. *Christ in the Tomb*

They took the body down from the Cross and one of the few rich men among the first Christians obtained permission to bury it in a rock tomb in his garden; . . . It was well that the tomb should be sealed with all the secrecy of an ancient eastern sepulchre and guarded by the authority of the Caesars. . . . (For) it was the end of a very great thing called human history; the history that was merely human. The mythologies and the philosophies were buried there, the gods and the heroes and the sagas. In the great Roman phrase, they had lived. But as they could only live, so they could only die; and they were dead.

On the third day the friends of Christ coming at daybreak to the place found the grave empty and the stone rolled away. In varying ways they realized the new wonder; but even they hardly realized that the world had died in the night. What they were looking at was the first day of a new creation, with a new heaven and a new earth; and in a semblance of the gardener God walked again in the garden, in the cool not of the evening but the dawn.

G. K. CHESTERTON (1874–1936), *The Everlasting Man*

80. *Easter*

A poet recalls how Christ rose from the dead in the early morning.

I got me flowers to straw Thy way,
I got me boughs off many a tree;
But Thou wast up by break of day,
And brought'st Thy sweets along with Thee.

Yet though my flowers be lost, they say
A heart can never come too late;
Teach it to sing Thy praise this day,
And then this day my life shall date.

GEORGE HERBERT (1593–1633)

81. *Easter*

Break the box and shed the nard;
Stop not now to count the cost;
Hither bring pearl, opal, sard;
Reck not what the poor have lost;
Upon Christ throw all away:
Know ye, this is Easter Day.

Build His church and deck His shrine,
Empty though it be on earth;
Ye have kept your choicest wine—
Let it flow for heavenly mirth;
Pluck the harp and breathe the horn:
Know ye not 'tis Easter morn.

Gather gladness from the skies;
Take a lesson from the ground;
Flowers do ope their heavenward eyes
And a spring-time joy have found;
Earth throws winter's robes away,
Decks herself for Easter Day.

Beauty now for ashes wear,
Perfumes for the garb of woe,
Chaplets for dishevelled hair,
Dances for sad footsteps slow;
Open wide your hearts that they
Let in joy this Easter Day.

Seek God's house in happy throng;
Crowded let his table be;
Mingle praises, prayer and song,
Singing to the Trinity.
Henceforth let your souls alway
Make each morn an Easter Day.

GERARD MANLEY HOPKINS (1844–89)

82. Easter

Most glorious Lord of Lyfe! that, on this day,
Didst make Thy triumph over death and sin;
And, having harrowed hell, didst bring away
Captivity, thence captive, us to win:
This joyous day, deare Lord, with joy begin;
And grant that we, for whom thou diddest dye,
Being with Thy deare blood clene washt from sin,
May live for ever in felicity!
And that Thy love we weighing worthily,
May likewise love Thee for the same againe;
And for Thy sake, that all lyke deare didst buy,
With love may one another entertayne!
   So let us love, deare Love, lyke as we ought,
   —Love is the lesson which the Lord us taught.

EDMUND SPENSER (1552?–99)

83. Easter Sunday

A translation from some lines of a medieval poet, an Irish scholar at
Liége.

Last night did Christ the Sun rise from the dark,
The mystic harvest of the fields of God,
And now the little wandering tribes of bees
Are brawling in the scarlet flowers abroad.
The winds are soft with birdsong; all night long
Darkling the nightingale her descant told,
And now inside Church doors the happy folk
The Alleluia chant a hundredfold.
O Father of thy folk, be thine by right
The Easter joy, the threshold of the light.

SEDULIUS SCOTTUS (848–74), Helen Waddell's translation
(*Medieval Latin Lyrics*)

84. *Easter Sunday, 16th April 1876*

This is from the diary of a young man, Francis Kilvert (1840–79), who spent his life as a curate in a country parish. The diary was only published after his death.

... I rose early and went out into the fresh brilliant morning between 6 and 7 o'clock. The sun had already risen some time but the grass was still white with the hoar frost. I walked across the Common between the Lady's Gates in the bright sunny quiet empty morning listening to the rising of the lark as he went up in all ecstasy of song into the blue unclouded sky and gave in his Easter morning hymn at Heaven's Gate. Then came the echo and answer of earth as the Easter bells rang out their joy peals from the Church Towers all round: Kington St. Michael leading the Choir, Chippenham Old Church following, and later on I heard the sound of the great bell booming down from Bremhill in the east over the ridge of Bencroft. It was very sweet and lovely, the bright silent sunny morning, and the lark rising and singing alone in the blue sky, and then suddenly the morning air all alive with the music of sweet bells ringing for the joy of the Resurrection. 'The Lord is risen,' smiled the sun. 'The Lord is risen,' sang the lark. And the Church bells in their joyous pealing answered from tower to tower 'He is risen indeed.'

Kilvert's Diary, edited by WILLIAM PLOMER

V. ASCENSION

85. *The Ascension*

Lift up your heads, great gates, and sing,
Now Glory comes, and Glory's King;
Now by your high all-golden way
The fairer Heaven comes home to-day.

Hark! now the gates are ope, and hear
The tune of each triumphant sphere;
Where every Angel as he sings
Keeps time with his applauding wings,
And makes Heaven's loftiest roof rebound
The echoes of the noble sound.

JOSEPH BEAUMONT (1616–99)

86. *The Effect of Christ's Ascension*

In the days of His earthly ministry, only those could speak to
Him who came where He was. If He was in Galilee, men could
not find Him in Jerusalem; if He was in Jerusalem, men could
not find Him in Galilee. But His Ascension means that He is
perfectly united with God; we are with Him wherever we are
present to God; and that is everywhere and always. Because
He is 'in Heaven' He is everywhere on earth; because He is
ascended, He is here now. Our devotion is not to hold us by
the empty tomb; it must lift up our hearts to heaven so that
we too 'in heart and mind thither ascend and with Him continually dwell'; it must also send us forth into the world to do
His will; and these are not two things, but one.

WILLIAM TEMPLE (1881–1944), *Readings in St. John's Gospel*

VI. WHITSUNTIDE

87. *The Holy Spirit*

A translation of a traditional Gaelic hymn, taken down in the Highlands of Scotland.

O Holy Spirit of great power,
Come down upon us and subdue us:
From Thy glorious mansion in the heavens
The light effulgent shed on us.

Father beloved of every naked one,
From Whom all gifts and goodness come,
Our hearts illumine with Thy mercy,
In Thy mercy shield us from all harm.

.   .   .

The knee that is stiff; O Healer, make pliant,
The heart that is hard make warm beneath Thy wing;
The soul that is wandering from Thy path,
Grasp Thou his helm and he shall not die.

Each thing that is foul cleanse Thou each,
Each thing that is hard soften Thou with Thy grace,
Each wound that is working as pain
O best of healers, make Thou whole!

From *Carmina Gadelica*: Hymns and Incantations orally collected
in the Highlands by Alexander Carmichael (1940)

88. *The First Disciples and the Holy Spirit*

The writer has been asking what the first disciples believed about the
Holy Spirit; this is his answer.

It was something more than a glorified Christ in the heavens in
which [the Apostles] believed. At the beginning John the Baptist had taught his disciples to expect from Christ the baptism
not of water only as in his baptism, but of the Spirit. Before
His death Jesus had sought to fill His disciples' minds with the
expectation of this gift. . . . And that Spirit had come in sensible power upon them some ten days after Jesus had disappeared for the last time from their eyes. . . . And this Spirit
was the spirit of God, but also, and therefore, the Spirit of
Jesus. Jesus was not then merely a past example, or a remote
Lord, but an inward presence and power. A mere example in
past history becomes in experience a feebler and feebler power.
. . . But the example of Jesus was something much more than

a memory. For He who had taught them in the past how to live was alive in the heavenly places and was working within them by His Spirit.

CHARLES GORE (1853–1932), *The Philosophy of the Good Life*

89. 'What does Pentecost represent?'

In this passage a modern scholar explains what happened when, as the New Testament tells us, the Holy Spirit came upon the Apostles at Pentecost.

What does Pentecost represent? What change is effected by the out-pouring of the Spirit?

The change lies in the relation of the Holy Spirit to the human spirit. This relation was made quite new. Previously the Holy Spirit had acted on men from without, like an external force; as the prophet Ezekiel describes it, 'the hand of the Lord was upon me.' But now the Holy Spirit acts from within. He is in man. . . . It was the union of the divine and human natures in the person of Jesus Christ which first made it possible for the divine Spirit to dwell in a human personality. . . .

On earth then tne day of Pentecost marks the beginning of this new relation. . . . And the characteristic of this life is Power. A transformation takes place, the apostles are new men, all fear of the Jews is gone. Peter, but now afraid of a servant girl, stands up boldly before all the people. The apostles' tongues are loosed and three thousand are converted. The work of the Church begins.

R. B. RACKHAM, *The Acts of the Apostles* (Westminster Commentaries, 1906)

VII. ALL SAINTS

About him all the sanctities of heaven
Stood thick as stars, and from his sight received
Beatitude past utterance.

JOHN MILTON (1608–74), *Paradise Lost*

90. All Saints' Day

It is the feast-day of all those who loved Jesus Christ, who gave Him their souls and their blood for pure love, who were without pride, without confidence in themselves, and who, because of that, shine with the greatest imaginable splendour.

LÉON BLOY (1846–1917), *Letters*

91. 'God's saints are shining lights . . .'

God's saints are shining lights; who stays
    Here long must pass
O'er dark hills, swift streams and steep ways
    As smooth as glass:
    But these all night,
    Like candles, shed
    Their beams and light
    Us into bed.
They are—indeed—our pillar fires
    Seen as we go;
They are that City's shining spires
    We travel to.

HENRY VAUGHAN (1622–95)

92. 'There are no two saints alike . . .'

It is a wonderful experience to discover a new saint. For God is greatly magnified and marvellous in each one of His saints, differently in each individual one. There are no two saints alike; but all of them are like God, like Him in a different and special way. In fact, if Adam had never fallen, the whole human race would have been a series of magnificently different and splendid images of God, each one of all the millions of men showing forth His glories and perfections in an astonishing new way, and each one shining with his own particular sanctity, a sanctity destined for him from all eternity as the most complete and unimaginable supernatural perfection of his human personality.

THOMAS MERTON, *Elected Silence*

93. How Saints are made

These words are spoken by the Archbishop, Thomas Becket, in T. S. Eliot's play. The Archbishop is preaching on Christmas morning and speaking of St. Stephen, the first martyr, whose day follows immediately after Christmas. A few days later, on 29 December, Thomas himself became a martyr when he was killed in his own cathedral at Canterbury.

We do not think of a martyr simply as a good Christian who has been killed, because he is a Christian: for that would be solely to mourn. We do not think of him simply as a good Christian who has been elevated to the company of the Saints: for that would be simply to rejoice: and neither our mourning nor our rejoicing is as the world's is. A Christian martyrdom is no accident. Saints are not made by accident. Still less is a Christian martyrdom the effect of a man's will to become a saint, as a man by willing and contriving may become a ruler of men. Ambition fortifies the will of man to become ruler over other men: it operates with deception, cajolery and violence, it is the action of impurity upon impurity. Not so in Heaven. A martyr, a saint, is always made by the design of God, for his love of men, to warn them and to lead them, to bring them back to his ways. A martyrdom is never the design of man, for the true martyr is he who has become the instrument of God, who has lost his will in the will of God; not lost it, but found it, for he has found freedom in submission to God. The martyr no longer desires anything for himself, not even the glory of martyrdom. . . . So in Heaven the Saints are most high, having made themselves most low.

T. S. ELIOT, *Murder in the Cathedral*

PART THREE

THE FRUIT OF THE KINGDOM

'But the fruit of the Spirit is love, joy, peace, longsuffering, gentleness, goodness, faith, meekness, temperance: against such there is no law.'

Galatians v. 22, 23

I. LOVE

94. The Test of Christian Love

Our Lord asks but two things of us: Love for Him and for our neighbour: this is what we must strive to obtain. . . . We cannot know whether we love God, although there may be strong reasons for thinking so, but there can be no doubt about whether we love our neighbour or no. Be sure that in proportion as you advance in fraternal charity you are increasing in your love of God. In this most important matter we should be most watchful in little things, and take no notice of the great works we plan during prayer. . . . It is amusing to see souls who, while they are at prayer, fancy they are willing to be despised and publicly insulted for the love of God, yet afterwards do all they can to hide their small defects; if anyone unjustly accuses them of a fault, God deliver us from their outcries! Let those who cannot bear such things take no notice of the splendid plan they made when alone. . . .

Prayer does not consist of such fancies. . . . No, our Lord expects *works* from us. . . . Beg our Lord to grant you perfect love for your neighbour. . . . If someone else is well spoken of, be more pleased than if it were yourself; this is easy enough, for if you were really humble, it would vex you to be praised. . . . Force your will, as far as possible, to comply in all things with (others') wishes although sometimes you may lose your own rights by doing so. Forget your self-interests for theirs, however much nature may rebel.

ST. TERESA (1515–82), *The Interior Castle*

95. Loving Others through the Imagination

The great secret of morals is love; or a going out of our own nature, and an identification of ourselves with the beautiful which exists in thought, action, or person, not our own. A man, to be greatly good, must imagine intensely and comprehensively; he must put himself in the place of another and of many others; the pains and pleasures of his species must become his own. The great instrument of moral good is the imagination.

P. B. SHELLEY (1792–1822), *A Defence of Poetry*

96. Loving God

He has loved us without being loved. . . . We are bound to Him, and not He to us, because before He was loved, He loved us . . . and created us. . . . There it is, then: we cannot . . . love Him with this first love. Yet I say that God demands of us, that as He has loved us without any second thoughts, so He should be loved by us. In what way can we do this, then . . .? I tell you, through a means which He has established, by which we can love Him freely . . .; that is, we can be useful, not to Him, which is impossible, but to our neighbour. . . . To show the love that we have for Him, we ought to serve and love every rational creature and extend our charity to good and bad . . . as much to one who does us ill service and criticises us as to one who serves us. For . . . His charity extends over just men and sinners.

ST. CATHERINE OF SIENA (1347–80), *Letter to Brother Matteo* (from *St. Catherine of Siena as seen in her Letters*, by V. D. Scudder)

97. '. . . The greatest of these is charity'

He who has charity is not jealous, nor envious, neither does he speak evil of his neighbour. He does not rejoice at the fall of others; he does not criminate the fallen, but he sorrows with him, and does what he can to comfort him. He does not pass by his brother in adversity; but he aids him, and even dies with

him. He who has charity does the will of God, and learns of
Him; for our own good Master Himself said: 'By this shall all
men know that ye are My disciples, if ye have love one to
another.' He that has charity thinks no one a stranger; but he
looks upon all men as his own kindred. He that has charity
endures all things, is long-suffering, and kind to all. . . . Truly
may we say that 'God is love, and that he that dwelleth in love
dwelleth in God.'

ST. EPHRAIM SYRUS (*c.* 306–73) (from *A Day Book from the Saints
and Fathers*, ed. J. H. Burn)

98. Universal Love

These words are spoken by the priest, Father Zossima, in Dostoevsky's
great novel.

. . . Love will teach us all things: but we must learn how to
win love; it is got with difficulty: it is a possession dearly
bought with much labour and in long time; for one must love
not sometimes only, for a passing moment, but always. There
is no man who doth not sometimes love: even the wicked can
do that.

And let not men's sin dishearten thee: love a man even in
his sin, for that love is a likeness of the divine love, and is the
summit of love on earth. Love all God's creation, both the
whole and every grain of sand. Love every leaf, every ray of
light. Love the animals, love the plants, love each separate
thing. If thou love each thing thou wilt perceive the mystery
of God in all; and when thou perceive this, thou wilt thence-
forward grow every day to a fuller understanding of it: until
thou come at last to love the whole world with a love that will
then be all-embracing and universal.

FEODOR DOSTOEVSKY (1823–81), *The Brothers Karamazof*, Robert
Bridges's version in *The Spirit of Man*

99. The Message of the Gospels

Edward Wilson went with Scott on his last expedition to the Antarctic as doctor and zoologist: he was one of the five who reached the South Pole in January 1912.

He writes in his diary:

. . I had spent some weeks or months without saying any prayers because I had come to consider them a useless waste of time. But everything else seemed to be becoming also a useless waste of time, excepting always the seeing of beauty in nature and the attempt to fix something of it on paper. But it seemed a funny thing that this should be the object for which life was given to us, and I began to wonder how one could find out what one was really put here for; and only then it struck me that in the New Testament, and especially in the teaching of Christ, one might be able to write down in one's own words once and for all whatever definite directions one could make out from His teaching. . . . I have done this for a year now, and my insight into the meaning of the Gospels has increased enormously, and though there are many directions which are definite and many which are contradictory, it seems to me that across every page may be written as a summary of its teaching —Love one another in Truth and Purity, as children, impulsively and uncalculatingly, not with reasoning and quibbling over what is the best way under the circumstances, but as though I were alone with God in everyone I met, not influenced therefore by any human law or convention, but faithfully offering them a true love in act and example, and at all costs to myself. Offer them the best, let them take it or leave it, never the second best or half best or best under the circumstances, but the best always.

EDWARD WILSON (1872–1912) (from *The Faith of Edward Wilson*, by George Seaver)

100. *Love and the Jail-birds*

An extract from the diary of Henri Perrin, a young Jesuit priest, who trained as a mechanic and volunteered to work with the French conscripts in the German factories. After six months he was imprisoned for his religious activities.

Writing of the other men in his cell he says: . . . several quite terrified me. . . . My 'Christian charity' was checked by the force of their hatred. Recently we had discussed helping the victims should there be another air raid. Several of them were violently against it. . . . More than ever I got the feeling of how de-Christianized their hearts had become. Forgiving insults, loving one's enemies, and all the fundamentals of Christianity, were unknown to them . . . they were so independent with their hatred, their egoism, even their arrogance. . . . How could one make them *see* Charity?

And then a week later: Yesterday I had had the delight of sharing with them the first parcel Jacques had got through to me. They said no more after I had replied quietly to their impatience: 'Why should we worry? God knows the day and the hour; He is our Father, and no harm can come to us.' I could now protest against the hatred that was killing them, and they didn't mind listening. . . . A quite different feeling was rising and growing within me—a certainty of Christ's love and longing for us. . . . A great many of those about me would be imprisoned under any law; in France, as here, they would be regular jail-birds. But I loved them better and better —and still I knew how little was my love for them compared to Christ's. It is easy enough for a man to be honest and a 'good Christian' and keeper of the 'moral law,' when he has his own little home, his purse well-filled—when he is well shod and well fed. It is far less easy for a man who has to live from day to day, roaming from city to city, from factory to factory. It is far less easy for someone just out of jail, with nothing to wear but old down-at-heel shoes and a shirt in rags. All of a sudden I understood Our Lord's words: 'I was in prison . . . and you visited me not.' All these men, lazy, outside the law, starving, these failures of all kinds—they were dear to Christ—they were Christ, waiting in prison for someone to lean over Him—and if we were true Christians, we would do them every kindness.

HENRI PERRIN, *Priest-Workman in Germany*,
translated by Rosemary Sheed

101. *Love, not Vengeance*

. . . If the wrong-doing of men fill thee with indignation and irresistible pain, so that thou desire even to take vengeance on the wrong-doers, then above all things resist that feeling. Go at once and seek suffering for thyself, as though thou thyself wert guilty of the wrong-doing. Accept that suffering, and endure it to the end, and so shall thine heart be comforted, and thou wilt understand how thou thyself art also guilty: for unto those evil-doers thou mightest have let shine thy light, even like the one sinless man; and thou didst not. If thy light had shone forth, it would have made clear the path for others, and the man who sinned would perchance have been saved by thy light. Or if it be that thou didst show thy light, and yet see'st not that any are saved thereby; nevertheless stand thou firm, and doubt not the virtue of the heavenly light. Believe that if they have not been saved now, they will be saved here-after: and if they should never be saved, then their sons will be saved; for thy light will not die even when thou art dead. The just man passeth away, but his light remaineth: and it is after the saviour's death that men are mostly saved. Mankind will reject and kill their prophets, but men love their martyrs and honour those whom they have done to death. Thou, moreover, art working for the whole, and for the future thou labourest. And look not for any outward reward, since, without that, thy reward on earth is already great: thine is the spiritual joy which only the righteous man findeth. . . .

FEODOR DOSTOEVSKY (1823–81), The Brothers Karamazof, Robert
Bridges's version in The Spirit of Man

102. 'Ahimsa' or Non-violence

In my opinion non-violence is not passivity in any shape or form. Non-violence as I understand it is the most active force in the world.

Non-violence is the weapon of the strongest and the bravest. The true man of God has the strength to use the sword, but will not use it, knowing every man is the Image of God. Literally speaking non-violence, means non-killing . . . [But] it really means that you may not offend anybody. . . . This is an ideal which we have to reach and it is an ideal to be reached even at this very moment, if we are capable of doing so. But it is not a proposition in geometry, it is not even like solving difficult problems in higher mathematics—it is infinitely more difficult. . . . You will have to pass many a sleepless night, and go through many a mental torture, before you can even be within measurable distance of this goal. . . . Under this rule there is no room for organized assassination, or for murders openly committed, or for any violence for the sake of your country . . . or even for guarding the honour of precious ones that may be under your charge. . . . This doctrine tells us that we may guard the honour of those under our charge by delivering our own lives into the hands of the men who would commit the sacrilege. And that requires far greater courage than delivering blows.

MAHATMA GANDHI (1869–1948) (from Mahatma Gandhi: Essays
and Reflections on his Life and Work)

103. Christianity and the Colour-bar

Michael Scott was arrested in South Africa after he had joined Indians who were passively resisting the restrictive legislation of the South African government against the Indian community. In his statement in Court, Scott said:

With regard to the personal references to myself from the Bench, and to the surprise that was expressed at my association with people of another class, namely my fellow prisoners, I must disclaim any such superiority of class or intelligence as that suggested, and state further that my religion knows no colour bar. It recognises no artificial barriers of race or class, indeed it must challenge any conception of racial inferiority for there cannot be 'Greek and Jew, circumcision and un-circumcision, barbarian, Scythian, bondman and freeman', but Christ is all in all.

MICHAEL SCOTT (quoted from *In Face of Fear*, by Freda Troup)

104. How can Truth and Non-violence prevail?

Michael Scott had gone from South Africa to the United Nations meetings at Lake Success to speak on behalf of the Herero tribe who were threatened with injustice.[1] After the meetings he found himself marooned at a friend's house during New York's heaviest snowstorm.
  He wrote:

I spent a good deal of time thinking about the enormous number of words that had been uttered during these debates on the problems of South Africa and of the Hereros who for me had become symbolical of all the landless and dispossessed people in the world. Words signifying all the passions and emotions, hopes and fears of humanity, words like snow crys-tals of all shapes and sizes, and I could wish they had as much

[1] See No. 148.

power as the delicate fluttering flakes whose accumulated mass had seemingly brought civilization to a standstill.

. . . Where can be found the moral force that the world requires? How can the hopes and fears and the longings of mankind for peace and the opportunity to live as children of God or as human beings, at least, not monsters, be turned into a power which can be brought to bear upon those who are responsible for the organization of peace?

Non-violence is much too negative a word to describe Satyagraha. Similarly, passive resistance is a description of only one aspect of a movement of the human spirit rather than a definition of the movement. . . . How, some are asking, can truth and non-violence prevail against all the power of a modern state? Perhaps the question would be better put the other way round. How can force, even if wielded by a powerful organization like the State, prevail against the truth? . . .

As Gandhi has consistently pointed out, there is no value in suffering as such, it is rather the readiness to suffer, to sacrifice the self rather than the principles which are of common concern, which is of value. . . .

All these concepts—love, creative purpose, self-sacrifice, non-violence are bound up in the word 'satyagraha'. As Gandhi conceived it, it is the Way of Life, rather than a mere political tactic, just as Christ's Gospel is a Way of life. . . . This is the profound religious truth which in God's good time will unite East and West.

MICHAEL SCOTT (from *In Face of Fear*, by Freda Troup)

105. The Little Black Boy

My mother bore me in the southern wild,
And I am black; but oh, my soul is white!
White as an angel is the English child,
But I am black, as if bereaved of light.

My mother taught me underneath a tree,
And, sitting down before the heat of day,
She took me on her lap and kissèd me,
And, pointing to the East, began to say:

'Look on the rising sun: there God does live,
And gives His light, and gives His heat away,
And flowers and trees and beasts and men receive
Comfort in morning, joy in the noonday.

'And we are put on earth a little space,
That we may learn to bear the beams of love,
And these black bodies and this sunburnt face
Are but a cloud, and like a shady grove.

'For, when our souls have learned the heat to bear
The cloud will vanish, we shall hear His voice,
Saying, "Come out from the grove, My love and care,
And round My golden tent like lambs rejoice."'

Thus did my mother say, and kissèd me,
And thus I say to little English boy.
When I from black, and he from white cloud free,
And round the tent of God like lambs we joy,

I'll shade him from the heat till he can bear
To lean in joy upon our Father's knee;
And then I'll stand and stroke his silver hair,
And be like him, and he will then love me.

WILLIAM BLAKE (1757-1827)

106. The White and the Coloured Races

Albert Schweitzer, one of the most gifted men of our age, gave up a brilliant career in Europe to become a medical missionary in West Africa.

Writing from the mission station at Lambaréné he says:

Physical misery is great everywhere out here. Are we justified in shutting our eyes and ignoring it because our European newspapers tell us nothing about it? We civilised people have been spoilt. If any one of us is ill the doctor comes at once. Is an operation necessary, the door of some hospital or other opens immediately. But let everyone reflect on the meaning of the fact that out here millions and millions live without help or hope of it. Every day thousands and thousands endure the most terrible sufferings, though medical science could avert them. Every day there prevails in many and many a far-off hut a despair which we could banish. Will each of (you) think what the last ten years of (your) family history would have been if they had been passed without medical or surgical help of any sort? It is time that we should wake from slumber and face our responsibilities!

. . . Ever since the world's far-off lands were discovered, what has been the conduct of the white peoples to the coloured ones? What is the meaning of the simple fact that this and that people has died out, that others are dying out, and that the condition of others is getting worse and worse as a result of their discovery by men who professed to be followers of Jesus? Who can describe the injustice and the cruelties that in the course of centuries they have suffered at the hands of Europeans? Who can measure the misery produced among them by the fiery drinks and the hideous diseases that we have taken to them? If a record could be compiled of all that has happened between the white and the coloured races, it would make a book containing numbers of pages, referring to recent

as well as to early times, which the reader would have to turn
over unread, because their contents would be too horrible.

We and our civilisation are burdened, really, with a great
debt. We are not free to confer benefits on these men, or not,
as we please; it is our duty. Anything we give them is not
benevolence but atonement. For every one who scattered injury
some one ought to go out and take help, and when we have
done all that is in our power, we shall not have atoned for the
thousandth part of our guilt.

ALBERT SCHWEITZER, *On the Edge of the Primeval Forest*

107. *White Men, Slaves, and Indians*

John Woolman, the eighteenth-century Quaker, like Albert
Schweitzer, from whom the previous reading was taken,
believed in the love of God to all creation. He would have
agreed with the Hindu writer who said that religion consisted
of tenderness toward all creatures. In John Woolman this conviction was so strong that he spent his life in trying to better
the lives of animals, of slaves and of all the poor unfortunate
creatures of God. He travelled about America on foot trying
to persuade people that slavery was wrong. At the outset, all
about him, in every department of life and human activity, in
the State and the Church he saw evidence of the strength of
slavery, yet he never hesitated. 'The candle of the Lord shone
about him' and his path lay clear and unmistakable.

He believed that most of the injustices and cruelties of the
world came from a selfish love of gain. He regarded the merely
rich man with unfeigned pity.

'The love of ease and gain [he wrote] are the motives in
general for keeping slaves.' He prayed that men might 'keep
to that spirit which teaches us to be content with things really
needful, and to avoid all superfluitie. By the labour of the
wretched slave many are supported in luxury. These slaves

are the people who have made no agreement to serve us, and who have not forfeited their liberty that we know of. These are the souls for whom Christ died, and for our conduct towards them we must answer before Him who is no respecter of persons.'

Woolman befriended the Indians as well as the slaves—though at that time fighting was going on and the white people 'were being slain and scalped at divers places'. But 'having for many years felt love in my heart towards the natives of this land who dwell far back in the wilderness, whose ancestors were formerly the owners and possessors of the land where we dwell, and who for a small consideration assigned their inheritance to us, I desired to visit some of them. Love was the first motion, and thence a concern arose to spend some time with the Indians, that I might feel and understand their life and the spirit they live in, if haply I might receive some instruction from them, or they might be in any degree helped forward by my following the leadings of truth among them.'

He believed the trade carried on with the Indians did them much harm. 'Where cunning people pass counterfeits and impose on others that which is good for nothing, it is considered as wickedness; but for the sake of gain to sell that which we know does people harm is an evil which demands the care of all true lovers of virtue to suppress. I was renewedly confirmed in a belief that if all our inhabitants lived according to sound wisdom and ceased from desire after wealth, and from all customs which are tinctured with luxury, the way would be open to live comfortably on honest employment without this wicked practice. As I walked about viewing those Indian histories which were painted on the sides of the trees in red and black and thinking on the innumerable afflictions which the proud, fierce spirit produceth in the world; on the miseries and distresses of the Indians when far from home and wounded by their enemies; of the restless unquiet state of mind of those who live in this spirit—the desire to cherish the spirit of love and peace among these people arose very fresh in me.

'A weighty and heavenly care came over my mind, and love filled my heart towards all mankind, and I longed that we might so attend to pure universal righteousness as to give no just cause of offence to all those who do not profess Christianity, whether they be the blacks from Africa or the natives of this continent.'

Compiled from JOHN WOOLMAN (1720–72), *Journal*

108. Love for all Creation

John Woolman realized that it is easy to ignore the wrongs we do not see. 'When trade is carried on productive of much misery, and they who suffer by it are many thousand miles off, the danger is the greater of not laying their suffering to heart. It is good for those who live in fulness to improve every opportunity of being acquainted with the hardships and fatigues of those who labour for their living and thus to think seriously with themselves: Am I influenced by true charity in fixing all my demands? . . . So far as true love influences our minds, so far we become interested in God's workmanship and feel a desire to make use of every opportunity to lessen distress and increase the happiness of creation. Here we have a prospect of one common interest from which our own is inseparable, so that to turn all we possess into the channel of universal love becomes the business of our lives.'

Towards the end of his life John Woolman sailed to England. He insisted on travelling steerage in order to get to know 'the poor wet toiling seamen' and in order too to hear from them of the voyages to Africa and how the slaves were brought on board 'in chains and fetters with hearts loaded with grief'.

Again he prays that 'being delivered from the entangling

expenses of a delicate and luxurious life we may learn contentment with little' and so cease from exploiting both sailors and slaves.

Even the misery of the sailors did not prevent him from feeling for the poor cocks and hens taken on board for a sea store. 'I observed the cocks crow while we were near the land, but afterwards I did not hear one of them crow till we came near the English coast. In observing their dull appearance and the pining sickness of some of them, I often remembered the Fountain of goodness, who gave being to all creatures, and whose love extends to caring for the sparrows. I believe where the love of God is verily perfected, and the true spirit of government watchfully attended to, a tenderness towards all creatures made subject to us will be experienced and a care felt in us that we do not lessen that sweetness of life in the animal creation which the great Creator intends for them under our government.'

In England too he was concerned for the horses driven to death in the Stage Coaches. 'So great is the hurry in the spirit of this world, that in aiming to do business quickly and to gain wealth, the creation at this day doth loudly groan.' At great inconvenience to himself he refused to travel in these coaches, journeying mostly on foot, nor would he send or receive letters by them.

The hardships he endured in his journeyings ended his life while on this English visit.

Compiled from JOHN WOOLMAN (1720–72), *Journal*

109. *A Dream of John Woolman's*

In a time of sickness once I was brought so near the gates of death that I forgot my name. Being then desirous to know who I was, I saw a mass of matter of a dull gloomy colour between the south and the east, and was told that this mass was human beings in as great misery as they could be and live, and that I was mixed with them, and that henceforth I might not consider myself as a distinct or separate being. In this state I remained several hours. I then heard a soft melodious voice, more pure and harmonious than any I had heard with my ears before; I believed it was the voice of an angel who spoke to the other angels; the words were 'John Woolman is dead.' I soon remembered that I was once John Woolman . . . and I greatly wondered what that heavenly voice could mean. I believed beyond doubting that it was the voice of an holy angel, but as yet it was a mystery to me.

I was then carried in spirit to the mines where poor oppressed people were digging rich treasures for those called Christians, and heard them blaspheme the name of Christ, at which I was grieved, for His name to me was precious. I was then told that those who oppressed them were said to be the followers of Christ, and they said among themselves, 'If Christ directed them to use us in this sort, then Christ is a cruel tyrant.'

All this time the song of the angel remained a mystery . . . until as I lay still for a time I at length felt a Divine power prepare my mouth that I could speak, and I then said, 'I am crucified with Christ, nevertheless I live; yet not I, but Christ liveth in me. And the life which I now live in the flesh I live by the faith of the Son of God, who loved me and gave himself for me.' Then the mystery was opened and I perceived there was joy in heaven over a sinner who had repented, and that the language 'John Woolman is dead' meant no more than the death of my own will.

JOHN WOOLMAN (1720–72), *Journal*

110. *A Story about St. Lawrence*

St. Lawrence was a Deacon of the Church of Rome who was put to death during a persecution of Christians in the third century.

When it was ascertained that St. Lawrence was the keeper of the treasures of the Church, he was arrested and ordered to give them up. He asked for a day's delay, at the end of which time he promised to produce all that was most precious. All night he hurried about Rome, in and out of its poorest streets and alleys, and, on the morrow, he appeared before the Court with a crowd of the poor, the maimed, the halt, the blind, and the sick. 'These,' said he, 'are what the Church holds most dear, and counts as her greatest treasures. The gold, which you so eagerly desire, is a vile metal, and serves to incite men to all manner of crimes. The light of Heaven, which these poor objects enjoy, is the true gold!'

Quoted from *A Lectionary of Christian Prose*, by A. C. BOUQUET

111. *The Saint and the King*

'Sire,' announced the servant to the King, 'the saint Narotham has never deigned to enter your royal temple.

'He is singing God's praise under the trees by the open road. The temple is empty of worshippers.

'They flock round him like bees round the white lotus, leaving the golden jar of honey unheeded.'

The King, vexed at heart, went to the spot where Narotham sat on the grass.

He asked him, 'Father, why leave my temple of the golden dome and sit on the dust outside to preach God's love?'

'Because God is not there in your temple,' said Narotham.

The King frowned and said, 'Do you know, twenty millions of gold went to the making of that marvel of art, and it was consecrated to God with costly rites?'

'Yes, I know it,' answered Narotham. 'It was in that year when thousands of your people whose houses had been burned stood vainly asking for help at your door.

'And God said, "The poor creature who can give no shelter to his brothers would build my house!"

'And He took His place with the shelterless under the trees by the road.

'And that golden bubble is empty of all but hot vapour and pride.'

The King cried in anger, 'Leave my land.'

Calmly said the saint, 'Yes, banish me where you have banished my God.'

RABINDRANATH TAGORE (1861–1941), from *Fruit Gathering*

112. St. Francis Preaches to the Sultan

St. Francis of Assisi lived from 1181 to 1226.

He [St. Francis] taught his followers that the Gospel was for all men. . . .

These were the days when the Christians were so busy hating and fighting the followers of Mohammed who had captured the Holy Land, that they had quite lost sight of the real missionary work of the Church. They had forgotten that Christ's way was to love and not to hate, and so they tried to force the Moslems to become Christians by defeating them in battle. Francis made the great adventure of trying another way. 'What is the use of trying to conquer the Sultan?' he said. 'We must win him by love instead.'

In the summer of 1219 Francis sailed with a little band of companions to preach the Gospel to the Moslems. He landed in Egypt and joined the army of the Crusaders which was carrying on the Fifth Crusade. With one of his companions he escaped from the lines of the Crusaders, and together they made their way towards the camp of the Saracens. They knew they went at the risk of their lives, for there was no safety in the track of desert which divided one army from the other. Yet they were as calm and unafraid as though the sand of the desert which they trod had been the open road in Assisi. And as they walked they sang the brave words of the twenty-third psalm: 'The Lord is my shepherd; I shall not want. . . . Yea, though I walk through the valley of the shadow of death, I will fear no evil: for thou art with me.'

Suddenly they were roughly seized and bound by wild and fierce Arabs who dragged them before one officer after another. To all Francis made the same calm reply: 'I am a Christian, take me to your lord.'

So at last Francis and his companion stood in the presence of the Sultan himself. 'Who are you, and whence do you come?' he asked.

'We have been sent not by man but by God,' Francis replied, 'to tell you and your people of the love of Christ.' Then Francis fearlessly preached his message to the eastern monarch.

The Sultan gazed in surprise and listened with respect to what Francis had to say. He was struck by the courage and enthusiasm of this Christian missionary who had risked his life to enter the enemy's camp. He asked him to remain with him, and Francis replied: 'If you and your people will become followers of Christ, for His love I will willingly remain with you.'

All honour was done to Francis in the camp of the Saracens, for they admired and respected his courage. But when he found that the Sultan was not prepared to follow Christ he decided that it was useless to remain there, and the Sultan allowed him to return to the Christian camp. His parting words to Francis were: 'Pray for me that God may show me that law and faith which are according to His own heart.'

P. L. GARLICK, *Pioneers of the Kingdom*

113. Raimon Lull

Raimon Lull (about 1235-1315) followed the example of St. Francis in seeking to win the Moslems for Christ by love not force. He went as a Christian missionary to the Saracens in the cities of North Africa.

The ship on which he had booked his passage was lying in the blue harbour ready to sail. On board were the missionary's books and possessions. Only Raimon Lull himself was not there. He was facing the hardest moment of his life. Though he knew the ship was waiting for him he could not leave his room in the town. For suddenly he had felt terribly afraid. He sat there alone, thinking of the unknown country to which he was going, of the fierce Saracens who had just triumphed over the Crusaders in Palestine and were bitterly angry because their brother Moors had been slain in Spain by Crusaders like Raimon's father. For the moment he forgot the real reason why he was sailing to meet these fierce and cruel men; he thought only of what they might do to him. Perhaps they would torture him or keep him imprisoned for life in a dark dungeon. No, he simply could not go.

So his belongings were brought ashore again. The boat sailed without him.

Feeling that he had failed his Master, Raimon Lull's shame and sorrow were so great that he became very ill with a high fever. But his courage was beginning to come back. When his friends brought him news that another ship was ready in the harbour and loaded to sail for the port of Tunis, he begged them to put his books on board and to carry him down to the ship. They did as he asked, but seeing how ill he was they carried him ashore again, in spite of all his pleading, just before the hour of sailing.

Soon came the news of a third ship that was making ready to sail, and Raimon Lull made up his mind that at all costs he would be put on board and would sail this time. As the ship sailed out of the harbour into the open sea, Lull felt the courage of Christ take hold of him in place of the old fears. 'From this moment,' he said, 'I was a new man. All fever left me almost before we were out of sight of land.' So the ship sailed southward to the great Moslem city of Tunis.

P. L. GARLICK, *Pioneers of the Kingdom*

114. *A Story of George Herbert*

George Herbert (1593–1633) was an English country parson and also a poet.

His chiefest recreation was music, in which heavenly art he was a most excellent master and composed many divine hymns and anthems, which he set and sung to his lute or viol; . . . his love of music was such, that he went usually twice every week, on certain appointed days, to the Cathedral Church in Salisbury. . . . But before his return thence . . . he would usually sing and play his part at an appointed private music meeting. . . . In one of his walks to Salisbury . . . he saw a poor man with a poorer horse, that was fallen under his load: they were both in distress and needed present help; which Mr. Herbert perceiving, put off his canonical coat, and helped the poor man to unload, and after to load his horse. The poor man blessed him for it; he blessed the poor man; and was so like the good Samaritan, that he gave him money to refresh both himself and his horse; and told him, that if he loved himself he should be merciful to his beast. Thus he left the poor man: and at his coming to the musical friends at Salisbury, they began to wonder that Mr. George Herbert which used to be so trim and clean, came into that company so soiled and discomposed; but he told them the occasion. And when one of the company told him he had disparaged himself by so dirty an employment, his answer was, that the thought of what he had done would prove music to him at midnight; and that omission of it would have upbraided and made discord in his conscience whensoever he should pass by that place. 'For if I be bound to pray for all that be in distress, I am sure that I am bound, so far as it is in my power, to practise what I pray for. . . . And now let us tune our instruments.'

IZAAK WALTON (1593–1683), *Life of George Herbert*

115. Father Damien

When Father Damien sailed as a missionary for the Hawaian Islands in 1864 he probably knew little and thought nothing of the ever-growing colony of lepers by then segregated in part of the Island of Molokai.

A day came when he happened to attend the dedication of a chapel recently erected on the Island of Mani. The Bishop, Monseigneur Maigret, was there, and in his address lamented that, owing to the scarcity of missioners, he was unable to send them a fixed pastor. Some young priests from the Picpus Congregation had just arrived for mission work, and before them Father Damien instantly spoke.

'Monseigneur,' said he, 'here are your new missioners. One of them could take my district; and if you will be kind enough to allow it, I will go to Molokai and labour for the poor lepers, whose wretched state of bodily and spiritual misfortune has often made my heart bleed within me.'

Thus simply was made, by an obscure priest on a far-away island, an offer of which the heroism, when the world came to know of it, made cowards shudder and brave men wish they had been braver. It was accepted and that same day, without any farewells, Father Damien embarked with the bishop on a boat that was taking some fifty lepers to Molokai. On arriving the bishop assembled the lepers and said: 'My children, you have been left alone and uncared for. You shall be so no longer. Behold I have brought you one who will be a father to you, and who loves you so much that for your sakes he does not hesitate to become one of you, to live and die with you.' So the bishop departed, and Damien was left to his mission.

From the first he never doubted that he would take the leprosy in time, as how—constantly living with the contagion, dressing the patients' sores, washing their bodies, even digging their graves—could he escape it? But he fell to work with a cheerful heart. He had lived with them about ten years before he began to suspect it. In his letters home he made no mention of his fate, but to his bishop he wrote:—'I cannot come to Honolulu, for leprosy has attacked me. There are signs of it on my left cheek and ear and my eyebrows are beginning to fall, I shall soon be quite disfigured. . . . The good God knows what is best for my sanctification, and I say gaily "Thy will be done," with a ready heart.'

Henceforward, in preaching to his flock, he no longer said 'My brethren' but 'We lepers.' By this time the tale of self-devotion had travelled among many nations of men; but their wonder and pity could not help him. 'He saved others; himself he could not save.' He went steadily forward to the end, instructing his fellow-outcasts, receiving their confessions, binding their sores, even feeding them, putting their food into their mouths when the leprosy had eaten away their hands—all the while facing the sight of that to which he must surely come.

In accordance with his own wish, his friends buried him beneath the pandanus tree whose boughs had been his roof when he first came to Molokai.

A. T. QUILLER-COUCH, *The Roll Call of Honour*

116. *Where to seek Love*

I thought Love lived in the hot sunshine,
But O he lives in the moony light!
I thought to find Love in the heat of day,
But sweet Love is the comforter of night.

Seek Love in the pity of others' woe,
In the gentle relief of another's care,
In the darkness of night and the winter's snow,
In the naked and outcast, seek Love there.

WILLIAM BLAKE (1757–1827), from *William Bond*

II. JOY

117. *Christian Joy*

Joy is the triumph of *life*, it is the sign that we are living our true life as spiritual beings. We are sent into the world to become something and to make something. The two are in practice so closely connected as to be almost inseparable. Our personality expands by creativeness and creates spontaneously as it expands. Joy is the signal that we are spiritually alive and active. Wherever joy is, creation has been; and the richer the creation the deeper the joy. . . . A great work of art or a great scientific discovery, gives greater joy to its maker than a work of merely technical or mechanical skill.

. . . Joy was a characteristic of the Christian community so long as it was growing, expanding, and creating healthfully. The time came when the Church ceased to grow, except externally in wealth, power and prestige; and these are mere outward adornments, or hampering burdens, very likely. They do not imply growth, or creativeness.

. . . God sent us into the world to create something, and to enrich our own personality in the process. In our wrestling with intractable material, we have to draw on what is *above* ourselves. We have to rely on God's help to make anything worth making. And in drawing upon this power above ourselves, we take this higher power *into* ourselves; we raise ourselves above ourselves. This is how creativeness and inner growth mutually condition each other.

I want you to think earnestly of the witness which joy on the one hand, and its antithesis, boredom, on the other, bear to the duty and happiness of creative work, that is to say, real work, on however small a scale. The happy people are those who are producing something; the bored people are those who are consuming much and producing nothing. . . . God punishes the useless by giving them pleasure without joy; and very wearisome they find it.

. . . Joy will be ours in so far as we are genuinely interested in great ideas outside ourselves. When we have once crossed the charmed circle and got outside ourselves, we shall soon realise that all true joy has an eternal and Divine source and goal. We are immortal spirits, set to do certain things in time; were it not so, our lives would lack any rational justification. The joy of achievement is the recognition of a task understood and done. It is done, and fit to take its place—however lowly a place—in the eternal order. . . . To do our duty in our own sphere, to try to create something worth creating, as our life's work, is the way to understand what joy is in this life, and by God's grace to earn the verdict: 'Well done, good and faithful servant; enter thou into the joy of thy Lord.'

W. R. INGE, *Personal Religion and the Life of Devotion*

118. St. Francis

The most astonishing thing in Francis' ascetic life is his freedom from all moroseness. In view of Jesus' injunction, that in fasting men should not appear sad, Francis was actually filled with a sunny serenity in the midst of his dark self-mortifications . . . and in this inexhaustible joy lies one of his greatest secrets. . . . His unspeakable gaiety flowered from the certainty of his redemption, and he considered it, with genial insight as one of his best weapons against the wiles of the Devil. He commanded the Brothers emphatically in his 'Rules': 'Ye shall take care that ye do not behave outwardly like melancholy hypocrites. But ye shall behave in the Lord, fresh and gay and accordingly agreeable'. . . . This shining joy of Francis is an uncontrovertible testimony to the fact that he had understood the Gospel in its deepest sense, as joy at the coming of the Kingdom—something which had been forgotten very early in the history of Christianity. . . . In the case of Francis, the joy of God erupted like a volcano.

WALTER NIGG, *Great Saints*, translated by William Stirling

119. Sir Thomas More

Sir Thomas More, Lord Chancellor of England from 1529 to 1532, was beheaded in 1535 because he would not recognize the Royal Supremacy over the Church which Henry VIII claimed. He was canonized in 1935.

Sir Thomas More, who enjoyed life to the full, and who in his Utopia wrote that God created man for happiness, faced suffering, imprisonment and death, not merely with endurance but with gaiety.

If his wife or children were troubled he would say to them, 'We may not look at our pleasure to go to heaven in feather beds; it is not the way, for our Lord went there by many tribulations and the servant may not look to be in a better case than his master.'

To his wife, who told him that if he would do what all the Bishops and learned men of the realm had done and obey the King he might leave his 'close filthy prison . . . shut up among mice and rats,' and go home to 'his right faire house,' his orchard and his garden, he replied, 'Is not this house as nigh heaven as my own?' To those who condemned him to death he said, 'More have I not to say, My Lordes, but that like as . . . St. Paul . . . consented to the death of St. Stephen, . . . yet be they now both twain holy Saints in Heaven, and shall continue there friends for ever, so I verily trust and shall therefore right heartily pray, that though your Lordshippes have now here in earth been Judges to my condemnation we may yet here after in Heaven merrily all meet together. . . . When mounting the scaffold he said gaily to the Lieutenant of the Tower, 'I pray you, master Lieutenant, see me safe up, and for my coming down let me shift for myself;' and to the Executioner he said with a cheerful countenance, 'Pluck up thy spirits man, and be not afraid of thy office.'

Yet Sir Thomas More describes himself as one filled with fear over all the mishaps of life. He turned for strength not to God's power but to Christ's weakness. He imagines Christ as saying to all who are afraid, 'Pluck up thy courage, faint heart; what though thou be fearful, sorry, and weary, . . . be of good comfort; for I myself have vanquished the whole world, and yet felt I far more fear, sorrow and weariness. . . . He that is strong hearted may find a thousand glorious valiant martyrs whose example he may right joyously follow. But thou now, O timorous and weak, silly sheep, think it sufficient for thee only to walk after me; which am thy Shepherd and Governor, and so mistrust thyself and put thy trust in me.'

Compiled from WILLIAM ROPER (1496–1578), Life of More, and
SIR THOMAS MORE (1478–1535), Treatise on the Passion

120. 'Be not . . . of a sad countenance'[1]

Give no place to despondency. This is a dangerous temptation of the adversary. Melancholy contracts and withers the heart, and renders it unfit to receive the impressions of grace. It magnifies and gives a false colouring to objects, and thus renders your burdens too heavy to bear. . . .

A sad exterior is more sure to repel than attract to piety. It is necessary to serve God, with a certain joyousness of spirit,

[1] Matt. vi. 16.

with a freedom and openness, which renders it manifest that His yoke is easy; that it is neither a burden nor inconvenience.

If you would please God, be useful to others, and happy yourself, you must renounce this melancholy disposition. It is better to divert your mind with innocent recreations than to nourish melancholy. . . .

Let the desire to please God and honour Him, by an exterior all sweet, all humble, all cordial and cheerful, arouse and animate your spirit.

> JEANNE MARIE GUYON (1648–1717), from *A Day Book from the Saints and Fathers*, ed. J. H. Burn

121. *Renewal*

A Song of Praise to God in Spring

Unfold! unfold! Take in His light,
Who makes thy cares more short than night.
The joys which with His day-star rise
He deals to all but drowsy eyes;
And, what the men of this world miss,
Some drops and dews of future bliss.

Hark! how His winds have changed their note,
And with warm whispers call thee out!
The frosts are past, the storms are gone,
And backward life at last comes on;
The lofty groves in express joys
Reply unto the turtle's voice;
And here in dust and dirt, O here,
The lilies of His love appear!

> HENRY VAUGHAN (1622–95)

122. 'To be pleased with all that God hath done'

Thomas Traherne was a poet and mystic. A mystic is one who sees the Kingdom of Heaven all about him, the divine in the ordinary, the eternal in the things of this life. Traherne, because he saw the world thus, lived always in the spirit of joy.

> No Business Serious seemed but one; No Work
> But one was found; and that did in me lurk.
>   D'ye ask me What? It was with Cleerer Eys
> To see all Creatures full of Deities;
> Especially Ones self: And to Admire
> The Satisfaction of all True Desire:
> Twas to be Pleasd with all that God hath done;
> Twas to Enjoy *even All* beneath the Sun:
> Twas with a Steddy and immediat Sence
> To feel and measure all the Excellence
> Of Things: Twas to inherit Endless Treasure,
> And to be fild with Everlasting Pleasure.

.   .   .

THOMAS TRAHERNE (1634?–1704), from *Dumnesse*

123. Living in Paradise

Your enjoyment of the world is never right, till every morning you awake in Heaven; see yourself in your Father's Palace, and look upon the skies, the earth and the air as Celestial Joys: having such a reverend esteem of all as if you were among the angels.

You never enjoy the world aright, till the sea itself floweth in your veins, till you are clothed with the heavens, and crowned with the stars: and perceive yourself to be the sole heir of the whole world, and more than so, because men are in it who are everyone sole heirs as well as you. Till you can sing and rejoice and delight in God, as misers do in gold, and Kings in sceptres, you never enjoy the world. . . .

The world is a mirror of infinite beauty, yet no man sees it. It is a temple of Majesty, yet no man regards it. It is the region of Light and Peace, did not men disquiet it. It is the Paradise of God.

THOMAS TRAHERNE (1634?–1704), *Centuries of Meditation*

124. *Happiness and Vision*

William Blake was an artist, but also a mystic and a poet who illustrated his own work with wonderful drawings.

I feel that a man may be happy in this world and I know that this world is a world of imagination and vision. I see everything I paint in this world but everybody does not see alike. To the eye of a miser a guinea is far more beautiful than the sun and a bag worn with the use of money has more beautiful proportions than a vine filled with grapes. The tree which moves some to tears of joy is in the eyes of others only a green thing which stands in the way. As a man is so he sees.

When the sun rises, do you not see a round disk of fire something like a gold piece? O no, no, I see an innumerable company of the Heavenly host crying 'Holy, Holy, Holy, is the Lord God Almighty.' I do not question my bodily eye any more than I would question a window concerning sight. I look through it and not with it.

WILLIAM BLAKE (1757–1827)

III. PEACE

125. *Peace*

My Soul, there is a country
Far beyond the stars,
Where stands a wingèd sentry
All skilful in the wars:
There above noise, and danger,
Sweet Peace sits crowned with smiles,
And One born in a manger
Commands the beauteous files.
He is thy gracious Friend,
And—O my Soul, awake!—
Did in pure love descend
To die here for thy sake.
If thou canst get but thither,
There grows the flower of Peace,
The Rose that cannot wither,
Thy fortress, and thy ease.
Leave then thy foolish ranges,
For none can thee secure
But One, Who never changes,
Thy God, thy life, thy cure.

HENRY VAUGHAN (1622–95)

126. *'Be still . . .'*

Be still and cool in thy own mind and spirit from thy own thoughts, and then thou wilt feel the principle of God, to turn thy mind to the Lord, from whom life comes; whereby thou mayest receive His strength, and power to allay all blusterings, storms and tempests. That is it which works up into patience, into innocency, into soberness, into stillness, into staidness, into quietness, up to God with His power. . . .

Therefore be still awhile from thy own thoughts, searching, seeking, desires, and imaginations, and be staid in the principle of God in thee, that it may raise thy mind up to God; . . . and thou wilt find strength from Him, and find Him to be a God at hand, a present help in the time of trouble and of need.

GEORGE FOX (1624–91), *Letter to Lady Claypole*, 1658 (published in *Journals*, 1902 and 1952 eds.)

127. *Living peaceably*

First, keep thyself in peace and then thou shalt be able to keep peace among others.

A peaceable man doth more good than he that is well learned.

A passionate man draweth even good into evil, and easily believeth the worst.

A peaceable man turneth all things to good.

He that is in peace is not suspicious. But he that is discontented and troubled, is tossed with divers suspicions: he is neither quiet himself, nor suffereth others to be quiet.

He often speaketh that which he ought not to speak; and omitteth what it were more expedient for him to do.

He considereth what others are bound to do, and neglecteth that which he is bound to do himself.

First, therefore, have a careful zeal over thyself, and then thou mayest justly show thyself zealous also of thy neighbour's good.

Second, thou knowest well how to excuse and colour thine own deeds, but thou art not willing to receive the excuses of others.

It were more just that thou shouldst accuse thyself, and excuse thy brother.

If thou wilt thyself be borne with, bear also with another.

Behold how far off thou art yet from true charity and

humility; for that knows not how to be angry with any, or to be moved with indignation, but only against one's self.

It is no great matter to associate with the good and gentle: for this is naturally pleasing to all, and every one willingly enjoyeth peace, and loveth those best that agree with him.

But to be able to live peaceably with hard and perverse persons, or with the disorderly, or with such as go contrary to us, is a grace, and a most commendable and manly thing.

THOMAS À KEMPIS (c. 1380–1471), *The Imitation of Christ*

128. Tranquillity of Heart

He hath great tranquillity of heart that setteth nothing by praisings or blamings.

He whose conscience is clean, he will soon be content and pleased.

Thou art not the holier though thou be praised nor the more vile though thou be blamed or dispraised.

What thou art, that thou art; that God knoweth thee to be and thou canst be said to be no greater.

If thou take heed what thou art within thou shalt not reck what men say of thee: man looketh on the visage and God on the heart; man considereth the deeds and God praiseth the thoughts.

THOMAS À KEMPIS (c. 1380–1471), *The Imitation of Christ*

129. The Secret of Happiness

Socrates was wont to say, They are most happy and nearest the gods that needed nothing. And coming once up unto the Exchange at Athens, where they that traded, asked him What will you buy? What do you lack?, after he had gravely walked up into the middle, spreading forth his hands and turning about: Good gods, said he, who would have thought there were so many things in the world which I do not want?—and so left the place under the reproach of Nature. He was wont to say That happiness consisted not in having many, but in needing the fewest things. . . . We need heaven and earth, our senses, souls and bodies to be enjoyed. Which, God of his mercy having freely prepared, they are most happy that so live in the enjoyment of these, as to need no accidental, trivial things, no splendours, pomps and vanities.

THOMAS TRAHERNE (1634?–1704), *Centuries of Meditation*

130. Contentedness

'Contentedness in all accidents brings great peace of spirit . . . (consider) I am fallen into the hands of publicans . . . and they have taken all from me: what now? Let me look about me. They have left me the sun and moon, fire and water, . . . and many friends to pity me, and some to relieve me, and I can still discourse; and unless I list they have not taken away my merry countenance, and my cheerful spirit, and a good conscience; they still have left me the providence of God, and all the promises of the gospel, and my religion, and my hopes of heaven, and my charity to them too: and still I sleep and digest, I eat and drink, I read and meditate, I can walk in my neighbour's pleasant fields, and see the varieties of natural beauties, and delight in all that in which God delights, that is, in virtue and wisdom, in the whole creation, and in God himself.'

JEREMY TAYLOR (1613–67), *Holy Living*

131. The Boyhood of Sundar Singh

This is the beginning of the story of an Indian who lived from 1889 to about 1929, and sought 'that peace which the world cannot give'.

A strange guest is standing before the door of an English house: a tall, upright figure in a long, saffron-coloured robe, with a large turban wound round his head. His olive complexion and his black beard proclaim his Indian birth; his dark eyes, with their gentle expression, reveal a heart at rest, and they shine with an infinite kindness. The stranger gives his name to the girl who opens the door: Sâdhu Sundar Singh. The girl gazes at him for a moment in astonishment, then she hastens to call her mistress: 'There is someone at the door who wishes to see you, ma'am; I can't pronounce his name, but he looks like Jesus Christ!'

. . . Sundar Singh comes of an ancient, aristocratic, and wealthy Sikh family. He was born on the 3rd of September 1889 in the village of Rampur . . . where his father . . . was . . . lord of the manor. His home was not only full of material comfort, but of true piety. Sundar's mother, a cultivated and religious woman, . . . instructed her son in the sacred writings of the Sikh religion as well as of Hinduism. She trained him in daily devotional habits. . . . 'You must not be superficial and worldly like your brothers,' she used to say to him. 'You must seek peace of soul and love of religion, and one day you will become a holy Sâdhu.' . . . (But) the peace for which Sundar Singh longed so passionately did not come from his ancestral faith, but from afar. In the mission school of his native place . . . he learnt to know the New Testament. . . . At first he refused to have anything to do with it. He was most indignant. 'Why should he read the Bible?' . . . Others, too, warned him against the Bible. 'Don't read the Bible,' they said, 'for there is a secret power in it which will turn you into a Christian.'

Sundar's hatred of Christianity grew so strong that he became the avowed leader of a group of pupils who declared themselves the 'enemies of Christianity.' . . . He even went so far as to throw stones and dung at Christians, and he ordered his father's servants to do the same. . . . But in spite of this fanatical hatred the mysterious book of the Christians would not leave him alone.

FRIEDRICH HEILER, *The Gospel of Sâdhu Sundar Singh*, abridged translation by Olive Wyon

132. The Conversion of Sundar Singh

The story of his conversion, which occurred on December 18, 1904, is best given in his own words. . . . 'Preachers and Christians in general had often come to me and I used to resist them and persecute them. . . . In the presence of my father I cut up the Bible and other Christian books and put kerosene oil upon them and burnt them. . . . I was faithful to my own religion, but I could not get any satisfaction or peace, though I performed all the ceremonies and rites of that religion. So I thought of leaving it all and committing suicide. Three days after I had burnt the Bible, I woke up about 3.0 o'clock in the morning, had my usual bath and prayed, 'O God, if there is a God, wilt thou show me the right way or I will kill myself.' My intention was, that if I got no satisfaction, I would place my head upon the railway line when the 5.0 o'clock train passed by, and kill myself. . . . I was praying and praying, but got no answer. . . . At 4.30 a.m. I saw something of which I had no idea at all previously. In the room where I was praying I saw a great light. I thought the place was on fire. I looked round, but could find nothing. . . . Then as I prayed and looked into the light, I saw the form of the Lord Jesus Christ. . . . If it had been some Hindu incarnation I would have prostrated myself before it. But it was the Lord Jesus Christ whom I had been insulting a few days before. . . . I heard a voice saying in Hindustani, 'How long will you persecute me? I have come to save you, you were praying to know the right way. Why do you not take it?' The thought then came to me, 'Jesus Christ is not dead but living and it must be He Himself.' So I fell at his feet and got this wonderful Peace which I could not get anywhere else. This was the joy I was wishing to get. This was heaven itself. When I got up the vision had all disappeared; but although the vision disappeared the Peace and Joy have remained with me ever since.'

Full of joy, he roused his father, exclaiming: 'I am a Christian.' 'You are off your head, my boy,' said the bewildered man; 'go away and sleep! The day before yesterday you burnt the Bible, and now all of a sudden you say you are a Christian! How can you explain such behaviour?' Sundar replied: 'Because I have seen Him. Until now I always said, "He is simply a man who lived 2,000 years ago." But today I have seen Him Himself, the living Christ, and I intend to serve Him, for I have felt his power. He has given me the peace which no-one else could give. Therefore I know that He is the living Christ. I will, and I must, serve Him.'

B. H. STREETER and A. J. APPASAMY, The Sadhu

133. The Servant and his Master

On Sadhu Sundar Singh see the two previous readings. The man in the story had the peace which comes from simple humility.

Said the Sadhu: 'Only men called of God should enter His service as preachers. To these, though of poor intellect, God will give a message.'

'There was once a sweeper who became a Christian. He gave his heart to Christ. He found that peace in Him, and was saved, and so could bear witness for Him. People would say, "There is something in him that we have not got." In his preaching he was listened to with great attention. A passer-by asked, "Why are they listening so respectfully to a sweeper?" The sweeper said, "When my Saviour was going to Jerusalem riding on an ass, the people brought clothes and spread them under his feet. They did not spread their clothes under the feet of Christ but under the feet of the ass. Why do that for an ass? Because the King of Kings was riding on that ass."'

SADHU SUNDAR SINGH (quoted from The Sadhu, by B. H. Streeter
and A. J. Appasamy)

134. Solitary Confinement

Hanns Lilje, a German pastor, describes his reactions to his arrest and imprisonment by the Gestapo on 19 August 1944.

Like most people in a similar position I was at first quite cheerful, and was sure I'd only be here for a few days! But when I looked out of the window, and saw the tops of some tall trees rising in their majesty above the high walls, their dark green foliage standing out against the cloudless blue of the August sky, suddenly—just as I felt very early that morning—I had an inexplicable feeling that possibly I would still be here when these trees were yellow and bare. It was a depressing thought. I felt as if someone had struck me.

Then fear and panic began to creep over me, like an evil beast creeping out of its den. I began to see myself and my position very clearly. The dirty cell, with its iron bars—while the blue vault of the cloudless summer sky outside scarcely seemed real any longer. I felt myself enclosed by an invisible wall, the wall of the dark and dangerous and menacing present, against which an individual is outwardly defenceless. I realized that I might 'disappear' within this prison, and that no one would ever know what had become of me.

The more I reflected on the details of my situation, the tighter was the grip of fear. Slowly it began to dawn on me that those dark spots on the floor were not due to dirt, but to blood, which no amount of scrubbing would remove. The dark patch by the bed must have been caused by some unfortunate person who had cut his arteries. . . .

At this moment I made a resolve. I determined to mobilize all my faculties of spiritual and mental resistance. . . .

At last, one of the most precious gifts was granted me— which has been of priceless value to me throughout my life— the gift of sleep. I laid myself down on the plank bed to sleep; I was needing it very badly, for I had had a very long, eventful day. So in spite of the hard bed, and the incessant noise, and even in spite of the horrible, brilliant lamp which glared down upon us all night long, I slept in peace and quietness; when I woke up next morning, I felt greatly refreshed and strengthened; and everything looked different.

It was Sunday, the 20th of August, 1944—my forty-fifth birthday: a day of radiant sunshine, just the kind of weather I had hoped to have at this time of the year. 'Broad August' was shining in a dazzling vault of light, and the earth was bathed in glowing heat. Suddenly, from a window in another wing, I heard someone whistling the first line of a familiar hymn. I was electrified, sprang to the window, and as soon as my unknown companion ceased whistling I answered with the chorale: 'Oh for a thousand tongues to sing. . . .'

Then, over the roofs floated the sound of distant bells. I tried to guess the time by the position of the sun; hour after hour I lived through this Sunday morning: picturing the waiting congregation, and in spirit I held the service with my people.

HANNS LILJE, *The Valley of the Shadow*, translated by Olive Wyon

135. Peace in Prison

Pastor Hanns Lilje's story, continued from the previous reading.

In our usual daily contacts with our guards, like putting our water-jugs outside the cell, or in taking our clean towels from them, I would simply say 'Thank-you', not with any special emphasis, but as one does if one is well brought up. It was quite astonishing to see how differently various men reacted to these simple little words. In any case it often opened up the way for me to make contact with those who desired it, and sometimes gave me an opportunity for serious conversation.

Once I completely upset the equilibrium of an old, dried-up official by using this word. This happened in Tegel, and it was during the first difficult days in Tegel when the order to be chained was still quite new. One evening this man had to fasten my fetters before I went to sleep; when he had finished I couldn't resist saying to him, in a very polite and courteous voice. 'Thank you very much'. He stood still and stared at me; then he went out of the cell; and in a moment or two he came back again, and said in an awkward, rough voice: 'No need to thank me for a thing like that!' I replied: 'Well, you have only done your duty!'—an expression dear to the heart of any good German official! If he had not lost the power of expressing emotion and tenderness, he would have done so now, but this was beyond him, so shaking his head he strode out of the room, murmuring to himself.

And so the time passed, in darkness and uncertainty. My solitude was complete; apart from the few necessary words exchanged between me and my guards I was completely silent. Each morning, at midday, and in the evening, meals were brought to me; this was all the contact between my cell and the outside world. I had no watch; I hadn't a scrap of paper for writing or reading; only the four bare walls of the cell; that was all. I realized that I must gather up all my mental and spiritual forces, in order not to go to pieces; I had no contact with the outside world at all.

And yet the consolation of God did not fail. One of His lesser consolations was the fact that one day when I was looking out of my window I saw a falcon flying round in the sky. The sky was absolutely cloudless, and the sun shone down into the grey bare quadrangle of the prison courtyard, which seemed devastatingly empty under the summer sky. Suddenly, the falcon rose into the light blue above us and wheeled around with his glorious wings—a wonderful picture of freedom. There was nothing in this empty prison courtyard to attract him, so far as I could see, so I had the impression that God had sent him; and the words of Calvin on the 104th Psalm flashed into my mind with a deep sense of consolation: 'Status mundi in Dei laetitia fundatus est.' [The world stands because it is founded on the joy of God.] When the supernatural world is a present reality and more powerful than that of our external world, then even the smallest ray of its glory illumines our path, and lights up our life with a ray of eternal significance.

HANNS LILJE, *The Valley of the Shadow*, translated by Olive Wyon

136. Meeting God in Prison

Pastor Hanns Lilje's story, continued from the two previous readings.

Since I was in some measure prepared for my arrest, and was therefore not thrown completely off my balance when it came, it merely had the effect of a shock which helped me to be mentally and spiritually alert (temptations to lose one's balance came later). Physically, regular, comparatively long sleep enabled me to make up for a good deal of sleep that I had lost; by the time that I had to submit to these interrogations I was fully rested. The scarcity of food in those first hot summer days of my imprisonment did me no harm at all. They simply acted as a good training or ascetic discipline. Further, I tried to keep my body in good condition by gymnastic exercises and a morning run round my cell, for I wanted to avoid appearing before my tribunal as a pale and unhealthy prisoner. In addition to physical discipline, I added mental and spiritual exercises. I tried to discipline my mind very strictly, in order to resist the temptation to let one's mind wander chaotically hither and thither. I made a strictly ordered rule-of-life for each day, which included regular meditation and prolonged periods of prayer, followed by periods of thought on theological and ecclesiastical questions. The result of these reflections still helps me in my work to-day. Since I had no paper to write down the result of my thinking I not only repeated it over and over again, in order to impress it upon my memory, but I also frequently translated my thoughts into English, or French, or even into Latin, and this, in itself, did my memory a great deal of good. Under these circumstances, I could only repeat passages from the Bible, and verses from the hymn-book, which I had retained in my memory. How grateful I am to all my teachers who had made me learn by heart hymns and poems, Greek lyrics, Latin odes, or Hebrew psalms! They provided me with a treasure which in those hard days was literally priceless. During those weeks of strict confinement and solitude I wanted to guard against a feeling that I had lost all touch with time, so I managed to make a few marks on the wall with a rusty nail where the guard would not notice it; this was really a little calendar, worked out on a system of my own. When I looked at it I could see at once how many days, weeks, and months I had been in prison. . . .

Among us there were some who triumphed over this final solitude with a kind of noble humanism. . . . But for myself, and for many others in this building, it was a fundamental truth that we were only able to overcome this final terrible solitude by our meeting with God.

HANNS LILJE, *The Valley of the Shadow*, translated by Olive Wyon

IV. LONG-SUFFERING

137. *Long-suffering*

The author of these words was a famous preacher and saint of the ancient Church, John Chrysostom (that is 'the Golden-Mouthed')

A certain wise man said—'A man that is long-suffering is abundant in understanding'; and comparing it with a strong city, he said it was stronger than that; for it is both an invincible weapon and a sort of impregnable tower, easily beating off all annoyances: and as a spark falling into the keep doth it no injury, but is itself easily quenched, so whatever unexpected thing falls upon a long-suffering soul speedily vanishes, but the soul it disturbs not; for of a truth there is nothing so impenetrable as long-suffering. You may talk of armies, money, horses, walls, arms, or anything else, you will name nothing like long-suffering; for he that is surrounded by these, being overcome by anger, is upset, like a worthless child, and fills all with confusion and tempest; but the long-suffering man, settled as it were in a harbour, enjoys a profound calm. Though he may be surrounded with loss, the rock is not moved: though thou bruise him with stripes, thou hast not wounded the adamant. The possessor of this passive virtue hath a kind of long and noble soul, whose great strength is love.

ST. JOHN CHRYSOSTOM (c. 347–407) (from *A Day Book from the Saints and Fathers*, ed. J. H. Burn)

138. The Balance of Afflictions and Blessings

St. Rosa of Lima, who lived in Peru (1586–1617), experienced much illness in her life. This passage is her description of what she learned in a vision about suffering.

Then, in the hands of the Lord, I saw a great scales, with balances and squadrons of angels, illustrious with festive ornament, who bowed before the Divine Majesty. They were joined by hosts of the souls of the blessed, who made ceremonious reverence before the Saviour, and then drew apart. The Angels, taking the balances, began to load afflictions, laying some upon others as if they wished to discover exactly the severity of each one, and when they were perplexed by this, Christ intervened and took upon Himself the office of arbiter. He made the scales true, and from the piles upon the balances distributed afflictions to the souls present there, setting aside for me a heavy portion of adversity. Afterwards, placing new weights upon the balances, blessings were heaped upon blessings, and as the angels leaned to read the weight Christ intervened again, His omnipotent arm alone being equal to the task. He marked it exactly, and with great attention divided among the souls as many blessings as He had given them afflictions. To your handmaid He distributed inestimable riches. This done the Saviour raised His voice and said with majesty: 'Know that the grace corresponds to tribulation. This is the one true Scales of Paradise.' And when I heard Him speak I longed to rush out into the plaza and tell all people the truth. My soul almost left my body in its eager ardour, feeling that it could better travel through every land on its mission alone. For no one would cry out against his heavy cross if he knew the balances on which it has been weighed.

SAINT ROSA OF LIMA (1586–1617)

139. Pope Gregory Encourages a Missionary

The Gregory mentioned here is Gregory the Great, who was Pope when Saxon England was a heathen country where no Christian missionaries had ever preached. Augustine, whom Gregory sent, became the first Archbishop of Canterbury.

Gregory . . . sent Augustine, and several other God-fearing monks with him, to preach the word of God to the English nation. They having, in obedience to the Pope's commands, undertaken that work, were on their journey seized with a sudden fear, and began to think of returning home, rather than proceed to a barbarous, fierce and unbelieving nation, to whose very language they were strangers; and this they unanimously agreed was the safest course. In short, they sent back to Augustine, who had been appointed to be consecrated bishop in case they were received by the English, that he might by humble entreaty, obtain of the holy Gregory, that they might not be compelled to undertake so dangerous, toilsome, and uncertain a journey. The Pope, in reply, sent them a hortatory epistle, persuading them to proceed in the work of the Divine word, and rely on the assistance of the Almighty. The purport of which letter was as follows:

'*Gregory, the servant of the servants of God, to the servants of our Lord.*

'Forasmuch as it had been better not to begin a good work, than to think of desisting from that which has been begun, it behoves you, my beloved sons, to fulfil the good work, which by the help of our Lord, you have undertaken. Let not therefore the toil of the journey, nor the tongues of evil-speaking men, deter you; but with all possible earnestness and zeal perform that which, by God's direction, you have undertaken, being assured that much labour is followed by an eternal reward.

'. . . Almighty God protect you with His grace, and grant that I may, in the heavenly country, see the fruits of your labour, inasmuch as, though I cannot labour with you, I shall partake in the joy of the reward, because I am willing to labour. God keep you in safety, my most beloved sons.

Dated 23rd July, [A.D. 596].'

BEDE (673–735), *The Ecclesiastical History of the English Nation*

140. *St. Sergius*

St. Sergius lived in the fourteenth century in a Russia that had been conquered by the Mohammedan Tartars from Central Asia. His example and teaching inspired Dimitri, Prince of Moscow, and his subjects to fight for Christian civilization. He learned the art of Christian living during three years which he spent quite alone in the depths of a Russian forest.

. . . St. Sergius went away into the wilderness for exactly the same reason as his famous predecessors. He desired to discipline his mind and body, purify his heart from selfishness and fear, so as to offer his entire being to the service of his Creator and Redeemer.

St. Sergius' biography mentions the wild beasts which first were a menace to him. This danger however was temporary, for they soon were reconciled to the monk who had no intention of interfering with their habits. Some of them even became attached to St. Sergius, especially a big bear who used to pay regular visits to the youth in order to share his meals. . . .

Although it required exceptional strength of character to face unarmed the possible attacks of the beasts of the forest and to endure the burden of loneliness and complete isolation, all this was nothing compared to the main trials which St. Sergius had to suffer, that of the gales and frosts of a Russian winter. In the winter there is some affinity between the ocean and immense plains of Russia. They are both revelations of the majesty and terrifying power of Nature. Those who have experienced storms both at sea and in the Russian plains know how similar is the effect which these uncontrollable forces produce upon the human mind. The snow blizzard descends upon man with the sound of the roaring sea, blinding him, paralysing his mind and body and crushing his will to survive. . . . He was at times buried for days and nights under his white cover, unable to see the light till the blizzard had passed over and he could dig out a passage to the fresh air. . . .

St. Sergius met his enemies as a true Russian knight, throwing away all the armour of protection, trusting in God's help and in the strength of his young body. The Russians are renowned for their exceptional long-suffering and endurance and St. Sergius raised these national features to the highest possible level, using them as a means to the complete mastery of his body and soul. No one knows what privations and agonies he experienced during the years of his retirement, but we know that the time of trial was crowned with a complete victory, for when his disciples began to gather round him they found him strong in body, clear in mind, resolute and gentle in his will. St. Sergius did not ruin his health, he did not upset his spiritual balance, he reached the goal which he set himself from the start, and having learnt to master his entire being he was able to bring it to a state fit for service of his Master.

NICOLAS ZERNOV, *St. Sergius*

141. *Hugh Latimer*

Hugh Latimer was a bishop and preacher of the sixteenth century—a leader of the Reformation in England who was condemned to death in the reign of Queen Mary.

[During his imprisonment Latimer] spent long hours in reading and re-reading his well-loved New Testament. He had all his life been constant in prayer, and now in these last days he spent more time than ever on his knees, sometimes kneeling for so long that he was not able to rise without help. It is not without interest that we learn of the chief subjects of his prayer. First he desired that he might have grace to be firm to the end, that God would give him strength to suffer any kind of cruel death rather than prove false to the truth that was in his heart. He was by no means too confident of himself, knowing that he was old and weak, and shrinking from fresh bodily suffering, and so it was for strength and courage that he most earnestly and constantly prayed. Next, he prayed for the establishment and restoration of the true Gospel in England; and this he 'did so inculcate and beat into the ears of the Lord God as though he had seen God before him, and spoke unto Him face to face.' His third prayer was for the Princess Elizabeth, whom he constantly brought before God by name, looking to her to be a 'comfort to the comfortless realm of England.'

At last, on 16th October 1555, they [Latimer and Ridley] were led out to be burnt, Cranmer, his heart sad within him, watching the little procession from his window in the prison tower. Ridley was neatly dressed in a furred black gown with a fur tippet round his neck; Latimer in his old cloak, covering a shroud. 'Be of good comfort Master Ridley, and play the man. We shall this day light such a candle, by God's Grace, in England, as I trust shall never be put out.'

R. M. and A. J. CARLYLE, *Hugh Latimer* ('Leaders of Religion' series)

142. Colonel Hutchinson in Prison

This extract is from the biography of Colonel Hutchinson which was written by his wife. He was a public figure of the seventeenth century, a Parliamentarian who was attacked by the extremists of his own side as well as by the Royalists. After the Restoration he was imprisoned first in the Tower of London and then in Sandown Castle where he died in 1664.

His wife bore all her own toils joyfully enough for the love of him, but could not but be very sad at the sight of his un-deserved sufferings; and he would very sweetly and kindly chide her for it, and tell her that if she were but cheerful, he should think this suffering the happiest thing that ever befell him; he would also bid her consider what reason she had to rejoice that the Lord supported him, and how much more intolerable it would have been if the Lord had suffered his spirits to have sunk, or his patience to have been lost under this. . . .

Another time, when she was telling him she feared they had but placed him on the sea-shore in order to transport him to Tangier, he told her, if they had, God was the same God at Tangier as at Owthorpe; prithee, said he, trust God with me, if he carry me away he will bring me back again. . . .

When many ill usages he had received from godly people have been urged to him, he would say, that if they were truly the people of God, all their failings were to be borne. . . . Once when his wife was lamenting his condition, having said many things to comfort her, he told her he could not have been without this affliction, for if he had flourished while all the people of God were corrected, he should have feared he had not been accounted among His children, as he had not shared

their lot. Then would he with thankfulness repeat the kind
and gentle dealings of the Lord at all times towards him, and
erect a firm and mighty hope upon it, and wonderfully encourage her to bear it patiently, not only by words, but by his own
admirable example.

LUCY HUTCHINSON (b. 1620), *Memoirs of the Life of Colonel*
Hutchinson

143. John Bunyan in the Dock

John Bunyan, the tinker-preacher, was imprisoned in 1660 for preaching. He wrote:

'After I had laid in prison above seven weeks, the quarter-
sessions were to be kept in Bedford—and when my jailer had
set me before these justices, there was a bill of indictment preferred against me.'

And finally he hears his sentence:

'"You must be had back again to prison and there lie for
three months following; and at three months' end, if you do
not submit to go to church to hear divine service, and leave
your preaching, you must be banished from the realm: and if,
after such a day as shall be appointed you to be gone, you shall
be found in this realm, or be found to come over again without
special licence from the king, you must stretch by the neck for
it, I tell you plainly;" and so he bid my jailer have me away.

'I told him as to this matter, I was at a point with him; for if
I were out of prison to-day, I would preach the Gospel again
to-morrow, by the help of God. . . .

'Thus I departed from them; and I can truly say, I bless the
Lord Jesus Christ for it, that my heart was sweetly refreshed
in the time of my examination, and also afterwards at my
returning to the prison, so that I found Christ's words more
than bare trifles, where he saith, "I will give you a mouth and
wisdom which all your adversaries will not be able to gain-say
or resist," and that his peace no man can take from us.'

John Bunyan remained imprisoned for twelve years, during which time he wrote many books, including *The Pilgrim's Progress*.

Compiled from JOHN BUNYAN (1628–88)

144. *'As stiff as a tree and as pure as a bell'*

George Fox, the founder of the Society of Friends, was imprisoned in Scarborough Castle in 1666 and wrote this description in his journal.

One day the governor of Scarborough castle, Sir Jordan Crosland, came to see me. I desired the governor to go into my room and see what a place I had. I had got a little fire made in it, and it was so filled with smoke that when they were in it they could hardly find their way out again. . . . I told him I was forced to lay out about fifty shillings to stop out the rain, and keep the room from smoking so much. When I had been at that charge and had made it somewhat tolerable, they removed me into a worse room, where I had neither chimney nor fire hearth.

This being to the sea-side and lying much open, the wind drove in the rain forcibly, so that the water came over my bed, and ran about the room, that I was fain to skim it up with a platter. And when my clothes were wet, I had no fire to dry them; so that my body was benumbed with cold, and my fingers swelled, that one was grown as big as two. . . . Afterwards I hired a soldier to fetch me water and bread and something to make a fire of, when I was in a room where a fire could be made. Commonly a threepenny loaf served me three weeks, and sometimes longer, and most of my drink was water, with wormwood steeped or bruised in it. . . . As to friends I was as a man buried alive, for though many came far to see me, yet few were suffered to come to me. The officers often threatened that I should be hanged over the wall.

. . . But I told them that if that was what they desired and it was permitted them, I was ready; for I never feared death nor sufferings in my life, but I was known to be an innocent, peaceable man, free from all stirrings and plottings, and one that sought the good of all men. Afterwards, the Governor growing kinder, I spoke to him when he was going to London, and desired him to speak to Esquire March, Sir Francis Cobb, and some others, and let them know how long I had lain in prison, and for what, and he did so.

After I was released I would have made the Governor a present for his civility and kindness he had of late showed me; but he would not receive anything; saying, Whatever good he could for me and my friends, he would do it, and never do them any hurt. He continued loving unto me unto his dying day. The officers also and the soldiers were mightily changed, and became very respectful to me; when they had occasion to speak of me they would say, 'He is as stiff as a tree and as pure as a bell; for we could never bow him.'

GEORGE FOX (1624–91), *Journal*

145. On His Blindness

When I consider how my light is spent
    Ere half my days in this dark world and wide,
    And that one talent which is death to hide
    Lodged with me useless, though my soul more bent
To serve therewith my Maker, and present
    My true account, lest He returning chide,
    'Doth God exact day-labour, light denied?'
    I fondly ask. But Patience, to prevent
That murmur, soon replies, 'God doth not need
    Either man's work or his own gifts. Who best
    Bear his mild yoke, they serve him best. His state
Is kingly: thousands at his bidding speed,
    And post o'er land and ocean without rest;
    They also serve who only stand and wait.'

JOHN MILTON (1608–74)

146. The Persecution of the Early Church

The early Christians were persecuted at various times before A.D. 300, but the greatest and most systematic persecution of the Church was the last, which is here described.

The signal was given on February 23rd 303 A.D. by the demolition of the great church at Nicomedia. Next day the First Edict of the Persecution was issued. The Churches were to be destroyed, the Scripture to be burned. [This Edict was issued by the Emperor Diocletian because] 'men were forsaking the old worship of the gods and going astray after novel and disgraceful superstitions, . . . such worthless persons must be punished for endeavouring in their blindness to destroy the good gifts which the mercy of the gods has granted to us.'

No sooner was the Edict posted up at Nicomedia than some Christians tore it down. . . . The offender was burned according to law for treason. The next thing was a fire in the palace and another a fortnight later—both of course set down to the Christians. . . . Diocletian was wild with rage and suspicion, used torture daily, put to death his favourite Christian chamberlains and burned whole families in one fire. [Another Edict issued by Maximian] ordered that all persons without exception in their respective cities should offer sacrifice and make libations to the gods. . . . A dreadful time followed, the burning of a whole community in Phrygia took place. Neither young nor old were spared. . . . But no efforts could keep up for long the full horror of the persecution.

. . . The young deacon Athanasius . . . had seen the horrors of the persecution, and the slaughter of his early teachers was an abiding memory: but his eyes are fixed on the eternal word, and he never for a moment lowers them to revenge. . . . [He writes] 'The powers of sin are overthrown. The old fear of death is gone. . . . Even the barbarians have laid aside their fightings and their murders, and learned in Christ a new life of peace and purity. . . . The works of Christ are more in number than the sea, his victories are countless as the waves, his presence is brighter than the sunlight.'

H. M. GWATKIN, *Early Church History*

147. *A Modern Persecution*

The persecution of the Church in Madagascar during the nineteenth century.

A great . . . assembly was called . . . at which every tribe was to be represented. . . . The day came, and fifteen thousand troops were drawn up on the plain. With great ceremony . . . the Royal Decree was read demanding that all who had received baptism, or had entered into the new society, should report to the public officers within a month, under penalty of death. . . .

Then came the great winnowing; many who had seemed to be Christians failed in the testing, and swung over to extremes of licentiousness to save their lives. On the other hand, the pure metal began to show itself in one of the cruellest persecutions the Christian Church has ever known. People were required to deliver up all books, to desist from all worship, to pray to idols. Men, women and children were hunted down, slain by the spear, poisoned, hurled over a precipice, flogged, burnt, exiled in heavy chains, reduced to hunger and poverty.

The little church, just emerging from paganism, was faced with fire and terror. . . . With what result? It increased tenfold. Scattered to the wilds, hiding in caves, and gathering on hillsides, they 'witnessed a good confession' and held fast to their faith. The fires of persecution flared up and died down from time to time, but without any cessation of cruelty. After fourteen years the queen said: 'I have killed some; I have made some slaves till death; I have put some in long and heavy fetters; and still you continue praying. How is it that you cannot give that up?' Hundreds were killed, thousands were flogged and fined . . . but still the Church grew. . . . Prisoners won over their gaolers, and soldiers on guard over the condemned were converted to Christ. . . .

After twenty-six years of persecution the queen died and one of the first acts of her son and successor . . . was to proclaim religious liberty to all his subjects. Then followed some of the most wonderful and pathetic scenes in the history of any people. Out of the recesses of the forests, from the caves in the mountains, from hidden prisons and secret hiding-places, came men and women who had been outcasts for years. Along the roads leading up to the capital, and the paths to their villages, they came as if risen from the dead. Some bore the scars of chains and fetters, some worn to skeletons by hunger and fever, they dragged themselves back to liberty and life to witness to the victory of Love over force.

Compiled from J. C. HARRIS, *Couriers of Christ* (revised and edited by Joyce Reason)

148. The Hereros

The Hereros are one of the tribes of South-West Africa whose lands have been taken from them by European settlers. Michael Scott was asked by them to carry their petition to the United Nations meeting at Lake Success. This petition asked for the return of their lands.

Before leaving for America Michael Scott joined the Hereros at a solemn gathering at Okahandja at the graves of their ancestors. He writes:

Standing there in that grotto of green palm trees one's soul was sick with shame at the thought of the treatment which this proud people have received at the hands of the white race. . . . By force of arms, by the irrepressible, irresistible stealth of a perverted Christianity, . . . they stole the lands of the Hereros, drove them into the desert, deprived them of their cattle, violated their women and children, starved them, shot them. How skilfully and cunningly they were betrayed. . . . Strange it seemed as one stood praying with them by the graves of their dead, how faithful they have been to the religion in which they were weaned from the worship of the Holy Fire handed on by successive chiefs, from no one knows whence or whom. . . .

Chief Hosea, standing erect in the strong sun with his hat in his hand, prayed: 'You are the Great God of all the Earth and the Heavens. We are so insignificant. In us there are many defects. But the power is yours to make and to do what we cannot do. You know all about us. For coming down to earth you were despised, and mocked, and brutally treated because of those same defects in the men of those days. And for those men you prayed because they did not understand what they were doing, and that you came only for what is right. Give us the courage to struggle in that way for what is right. O Lord, help us who roam about. Help us who have been placed in Africa and have no dwelling place of our own. Give us back a dwelling place. O God, all power is yours in Heaven and Earth. Amen.'

Compiled from FREDA TROUP, *In Face of Fear*

149. *The Christian's Secret Strength*

An extract from the diary of Henri Perrin, a young Jesuit priest, who trained as a mechanic and volunteered to work with the French conscripts in the German factories. After six months he was imprisoned for his religious activities.

. . . It was hard to feel on the edge of society, exiled from one's country, and one's head would sometimes unwillingly bow beneath the humiliation.

Yet still, over all these limitations and humiliations, I felt astonishingly and profoundly free; I felt a flame, a secret little life of liberty beating away inside me, a liberty I could never lose. They could keep me locked up; they could take me to a Concentration Camp to-morrow, they could torture me and make me cry out with pain, but they could never touch the sanctuary where my soul watched, where I was alone master.

They might deceive me, abuse me, weaken me; they might get words out of me when my mind staggered from their cruelty, words which they could take as an admission; they could kill me. But they could never force my will, for it could never belong to them; it was between myself and God, and no one else could ever touch it.

How could they expect to reduce a Christian to slavery so easily? Did they really think that walls and chains and warders could bind Christians' activities? Poor wretches! For months now I had been seeing the very opposite thing happening. I was becoming daily surer that I was doing more for my little communities between the four walls of my cell than in our apostolic week-ends. 'Be glad if you are persecuted for my sake.' . . .

If our enemies knew how, far from fettering the liberty of Christians, they so often multiplied their activity—I almost said their harmfulness—they would chase them all out of the prisons. . . . They might forbid us any access to the material world, but the other could then only seem richer and more beautiful: they might bring our bodies into slavery, but thus they would only liberate other men who were waiting for the liberation of Christ: they might mutilate Christians, but we knew that then Christ in His Mystical Body would grow.

HENRI PERRIN, Priest-Workman in Germany,
translated by Rosemary Sheed

150. 'My grace is sufficient for thee'[1]

On Sunday morning, 13 October 1946, a Bishop stood before a microphone at Broadcasting House, London, and addressed a vast audience.

He had travelled a very long way, and had brought with him a unique story, which had already become one of the epics of the World War. This speaker was the Right Rev. Leonard Wilson, Bishop of Singapore.

I speak to you this morning from personal experience of God's comfort and strength. I was interned by the Japanese; I was

[1] 2 Cor. xii. 9.

imprisoned by their military police for many months; I suffered many weary hours of beatings and tortures. Throughout that time I never turned to God in vain; always He helped and sustained. I wish to speak of these experiences, the key-note of which could be summed up in St. Paul's words, 'More than conquerors'.[1]

. . . I was interned in March, 1943, and sent to Changi Jail. Here the conditions were appallingly crowded, but life was not too difficult until October of that year, when the [Japanese] military police, . . . raided the prison, searched all our luggage and arrested some sixty of us. A few were released almost immediately; others remained for many months; fifteen died from their treatment.

It is not my purpose to relate the tortures they inflicted upon us, but rather to tell you of some of the spiritual experiences of that ordeal. I knew that this was to be a challenge to my courage, my faith, and my love.

I remember Archbishop Temple, in one of his books, writing that if you pray for any particular virtue, whether it be patience, or courage, or love, one of the answers that God gives to us is an opportunity for exercising that virtue. After my first beating I was almost afraid to pray for courage lest I should have another opportunity of exercising it; but my unspoken prayer was there, and without God's help I doubt whether I would have come through. Long hours of ignoble pain were a severe test. In the middle of torture they asked me if I still believed in God. When, by God's help, I said, 'I do,' they asked me why God did not save me. By the help of His Holy Spirit I said, 'God does save me. He does not save me by freeing me from pain or punishment, but He saves me by giving me the Spirit to bear it'; and when they asked me why I did not curse them I told them that it was because I was a follower of Jesus Christ, who taught us that we were all brethren.

[1] Rom. viii. 37. Cf. St. Paul's experiences, 2 Cor. xi. 23 ff.

I did not like to use the words 'Father forgive them.' It seemed too blasphemous to use our Lord's words; but I *felt* them, and I said, 'Father, I know these men are doing their duty. Help them to see that I am innocent.' When I muttered 'Forgive them,' I wondered how far I was being dramatic, and if I really meant it; because I looked at their faces as they stood round, taking it in turn to flog me, and their faces were hard and cruel, and some of them were evidently enjoying their cruelty. But, by the Grace of God, I saw those men not as they were, but as they had been. Once they were little children, with their brothers and sisters—happy in their parents' love, in those far-off days before they had been conditioned by their false nationalist ideals. And it is hard to hate little children.

So I saw them not as they were, but as they were capable of becoming, redeemed by the power of Christ, and I knew that I should say 'Forgive.'

It is true that there were many dreary moments, especially in the early morning, in a crowded, filthy cell with hardly any power to move because of one's wounds; but here again I was helped tremendously by God. There was a tiny window at the back of the cell, and through the bars I could hear the song of the Golden Oriole. I could see the glorious red of the flame of the forest tree; and something of God, something of God's indestructible beauty, was conveyed to my tortured mind. Behind the flame-trees I glimpsed the top of Wesley's church, and was so grateful that the Church had preserved many of Wesley's hymns. One that I said every morning, we sang today: 'Christ whose glory fills the skies.'

Gradually the burden of this world was lifted, and I was carried into the presence of God and received from Him the strength and peace which were enough to live by, day by day.

This joy of prayer was used by God to help others. Many non-Christians came to ask me to teach them to pray, because prayer evidently meant so much to those of us who were Christians. We were not supposed to talk to each other, but when the guard were not looking I told them some of the elementary things of prayer—thanking Him, being sorry for things done wrong and praying for others. And so we formed a wider fellowship than any I had known before, a fellowship of suffering humanity. Prisoners knew that, when they were taken out of the cell for questioning or torture, there were others of us behind praying for them—praying that if it be God's will they should not suffer, but that if they suffered they would be given the Spirit to bear it and not involve others.

But there were other battles to be fought. I do not know how many of you know what real hunger is, but the temptation to greed is almost overwhelming. Here again we were helped. There was a young Roman Catholic in the cell. He was a privileged prisoner; he was allowed food from the outside. He could have eaten all of it, and more than all of it, but never a day passed without his sharing it with some people of the cell. It was a small amount we got, but what an enormous difference it made! It raised the whole tone of our life, and it was made possible for others to follow his noble example—to learn to share with one another.

After eight months I was released, and for the first time got into the sunlight. I have never known such joy. It seemed like a foretaste of the Resurrection. For months afterwards I felt at peace with the universe, although I was still interned and had to learn the lesson or the discipline of joy—how easy it is to forget God and all His benefits! I had known Him in a deeper way than I could ever have imagined, but God is to be found in the Resurrection, as well as in the Cross, and it is the Resurrection that has the final word.

God, in all His power and strength and comfort, is available to everyone of us today. He was revealed to me not because I was a special person but because I was willing *in faith* to accept what God gave. I know what I say is true, not just because the Bible says so, or because the Church has told us, but because I have experienced it myself; I know that whether you are despondent or in joy, whether you are apathetic or full of enthusiasm, there is available for you, *at this moment*, the whole life of God, with its victory over sin and pain and death. . . .

JOHN LEONARD WILSON (Bishop of Singapore, 1941-8)

V. GENTLENESS

151. St. Martin of Tours

A story of St. Martin of Tours who lived in the fourth century. Before becoming a Christian he was a Roman cavalry officer stationed in France.

It was winter, and Martin was riding with his regiment through the snow and slush into the city of Amiens. Crowds had gathered to watch the soldiers coming in, worn and weary, with sodden equipment, perishing with cold, in spite of thick, warm military cloaks and uniform. As they pass through the city gate a young officer dismounts. He has seen among the crowd a poor man, well-nigh naked, blue with cold, holding out a trembling hand for alms to buy bread. The officer flings off his cloak, and, having drawn his sword, he cut the cloak in two—gently and courteously he wraps one half of it round the shivering shoulders of the beggar. . . . Perhaps a great laugh goes up as the crowd see the surprised old beggar-man decked out in the smart purple-blue cloak, and Martin, laughing with the rest, wraps the other half round himself, remounts and rides on. That night, as he lay asleep in his billet, he saw a vision. He saw the half of a military cloak. And he heard a voice which bade him look well at it, and asked him if he had seen the cloak before. And as he looked upon it he expected to see beneath it the features of his shivering friend at the city gate, but he saw the figure of no beggar-man, but the strong and gracious face and form of Jesus Himself. And as in adoring silence Martin listened for the voice to speak again, the laughing crowd of peasants seemed changed into groups of the Heavenly Host. . . .

From *A Book of Saints*, by J. A. BOUQUET

152. George Herbert

A story of the seventeenth-century country parson and poet, George Herbert.

At which time of Mr. Herbert's coming alone to Bemerton, there came to him a poor old Woman, with an intent to acquaint him with her necessitous condition, as also, with some troubles of her mind; but after she had spoke some few words to him, she was surpriz'd with a fear, and that begot a shortness of breath, so that her spirits and speech fail'd her; which he perceiving, did so compassionate her, and was so humble, that he took her by the hand, and said, Speak good Mother, be not afraid to speak to me; for I am a man that will hear you with patience; and will relieve your necessities too, if I be able: and this I will do willingly, and therefore, Mother, be not afraid to acquaint me with what you desire. After which comfortable speech, he again took her by the hand, made her sit down by him, and understanding she was of his Parish, he told her, He would be acquainted with her, and take her into his care: And having with patience heard and understood her wants (and it is some relief for a poor body to be but hear'd with patience) he like a Christian Clergyman comforted her by his meek behaviour and counsel; but because that cost him nothing, he reliev'd her with money too, and so sent her home with a chearful heart, praising God, and praying for him. Thus worthy, and thus lowly, was Mr. George Herbert in his own eyes: and thus lovely in the eyes of others.

IZAAK WALTON (1593–1683), *Life of George Herbert*

153. St. Vincent de Paul (i)

Saint Vincent de Paul lived in seventeenth-century France. He dedicated his life to work amongst the poor and suffering.

Saint Vincent de Paul was chaplain to Gondi, Comte de
Joigny, the General of the Galleys, and so had access to
the various prisons in which the condemned men were
kept until they could be sent to the Mediterranean ports.
M. Vincent was appalled by the conditions in which he found
them.

It must be remembered that all prisons of the time were
extremely bad. . . . Gondi was a very good-natured man, but,
as he had not created the conditions, he . . . did not consider
that he was responsible. What is everybody's business is only
too likely to be treated as nobody's business. The situation
called for someone like Vincent de Paul who, so far from heav-
ing a sigh and shrugging his shoulders, would take upon himself what needed to be done. . . . [Prisoners] condemned to the
galleys were all poor and friendless and belonged to the most
desperate type of criminal. It never occurred to society to give
them any mercy—and they got none.

Vincent found them chained to the wall, in rags, with a little
black bread as their food, and for the only alleviation of the
monotony of their existence . . . branding and the lash. If ill
—and few escaped illness in such surroundings—no notice
was taken of them. They were covered with lice; rats scuttled
about the dark cells in which they were packed . . . while
waiting for the still worse fate of the galleys.

What Vincent did, as a start, was to get them transferred to
better quarters in a house in the Faubourg Saint Honoré.
There they had at least cleaner cells, more light and air and
some medical attention. They did not escape their chains,
but their new prison seemed to them a paradise after the
old. Above all, Vincent, by going among them with kindly

words, made them feel that there was somebody who cared for them.

THEODORE MAYNARD, *Apostle of Charity: The Life of St. Vincent de Paul*

154. St. Vincent de Paul (ii)

Another writer continues the story of St. Vincent de Paul which was begun in the previous reading.

Later (Vincent de Paul) visited the galleys with a view to procuring for them such relief as was possible. Pitiable beyond words was the state of things which he found there. . . . Touched with feelings of the deepest compassion for these miserable beings, Vincent set himself to comfort and assist them in all ways in his power. Above all, he tried by a loving tenderness towards them to soften their hearts and bring them to a state in which they might be susceptible of good. He listened patiently to their complaints, pitied their sufferings and did all he could to obtain some mitigation of the severity with which they were treated.

And the proofs of his tender compassion and brotherly love went further still, for, finding among the convicts a young man whose case was peculiarly hard, and who was broken-hearted at the thought of his wife and young children left destitute, Vincent prevailed with the officer in charge of the gang to let him take his place, and set the young man free to return to his family. In order to investigate more thoroughly the state of the galleys, Vincent had preserved a strict incognito, and neither the officer in charge, nor his fellow galley-slaves had any idea who it was that had made this strange request.

It appears that for several weeks he worked in chains with the rest of the gang until the Comte de Joigny, alarmed at hearing nothing from him, caused inquiries to be made which led to his release.

R. F. WILSON, *Life of St. Vincent de Paul*

155. *Pennsylvania, the Peaceful Colony*

William Penn, the Quaker, was granted land in the New World by King Charles II in return for a large sum of money which the King owed him. It was called Sylvania because of its forests and the King insisted on adding the name Penn. The Charter of Pennsylvania empowered Penn to make war on the Indian savages, but Penn refused to build any forts nor to have cannon or soldiers in his province.

It was prophesied that all his settlements would soon be destroyed. But Penn took no notice of these prophesies. He set about founding his capital city which he named Philadelphia, the City of Brotherly Love. He made friends with the Indians and they arranged that all quarrels should be settled by a meeting of six white men and six red men. The Indians enjoyed equal citizenship with the white men and an equal choice of land. When William Penn died they mourned him as their friend.

After Penn's death, while every other colony in the New World was constantly attacked by the Indians, Pennsylvania was perfectly free from attack as long as they refused to arm themselves. Many years later the Quakers were outvoted in the State and the colony gave way to pressure on them from the other States and began to spend money in building forts and to train soldiers against possible aggression. They were immediately attacked.

Compiled from *The Story of Quakerism*, by E. B. EMMOTT

156. *Mercy*

The quality of mercy is not strained,
It droppeth as the gentle rain from heaven
Upon the place beneath; it is twice blest;
It blesseth him that gives, and him that takes:

'Tis mightiest in the mightiest: it becomes
The thronèd monarch better than his crown;
His sceptre shows the force of temporal power,
The attribute to awe and majesty,
Wherein doth sit the dread and fear of kings;
But mercy is above this sceptred sway;
It is enthronèd in the hearts of kings,
It is an attribute to God Himself;
And earthly power doth then show likest God's
When mercy seasons justice. Therefore, Jew,
Though justice be thy plea, consider this,
That, in the course of justice, none of us
Should see salvation: we do pray for mercy;
And that same prayer doth teach us all to render
The deeds of mercy.

WILLIAM SHAKESPEARE (1564–1616), *The Merchant of Venice*

VI. GOODNESS

157. *The Two Hermits*

This is a story of two men who had gone away to live in the desert to devote themselves to holy living and prayer.

There were two old men living in one cell, and never had there risen even the paltriest contention between them. So the one said to the other 'Let us have one quarrel, the way other men do.' But the other said 'I do not know how one makes a quarrel.' The first said, 'Look, I set a tile between us and say "that is mine", and do thou say "it is not thine, it is mine," and thence arises contention and squabble.' So they set the tile between them; and the first one said 'That is mine,' and the second made reply: 'I hope that it is mine.' To which the first made answer 'If it is thine, take it.' After which they could find no way of quarrelling.

HELEN WADDELL, The Desert Fathers

158. Friar Juniper

Friar (that is, Brother) Juniper was one of the companions of St. Francis of Assisi, and thus one of the first Franciscans. This story is told of the time when the Franciscans had become a definite Order.

Friar Juniper, being on a time in Assisi, at the Nativity of Christ, engaged in deep meditation at the altar of the friary, which was richly decked and adorned, was asked by the sacristan to guard the said altar while he went to eat. And while he was in devout meditation, a poor little woman begged alms of him for love of God: to whom Friar Juniper thus answered, 'Tarry awhile and I will see if I can give thee aught from this altar so rich.' Now there was on that altar a hanging of gold, richly and sumptuously adorned with little silver bells of great worth. Saith Friar Juniper, 'These bells are a superfluity.' So he takes a knife and cuts them all from the hanging, and gives them out of compassion, to this poor little woman. No sooner had the sacristan eaten three or four mouthfuls than he remembered the ways of Friar Juniper, and was sore afraid lest out of his zealous charity he might work some mischief to the rich altar he had left in his charge. And straight way he rose from the table, in much dread, and went to the church and looked to see if any of the ornaments of the altar had been removed or taken away; and lo, he beheld the hanging hacked about and the bells cut off: whereat he was beyond all measure perturbed and scandalised. And Friar Juniper, beholding him thus agitated, saith, 'Be not troubled about those bells for I have given them to a poor woman that had very great need of them, and here they were of no use save that they made a show of worldly pomp.' . . .

This was reported to the Father-General, who was the head of the whole Order.

And having called all the friars together in Chapter, he bade call Friar Juniper, and in the presence of the whole house rebuked him very harshly because of the aforesaid little bells; and he waxed so furious in his wrath, that by raising his voice so high he grew quite hoarse. Friar Juniper heeded those words little or naught, for he rejoiced in contumely and when he was well abased; but returning good for evil, he began to think, only how he might find a remedy for his General's hoarseness. So having endured the General's scolding, Friar Juniper goes to the city and orders a good dish of porridge and butter; and a good part of the night being spent, he goes and lights a candle and comes back with his mess of porridge and takes it to the General's cell and knocks. The General opens to him, and beholding him with a lighted candle in one hand and a dish of porridge in the other, asks softly, 'What is this?' Friar Juniper answered, 'My father, to-day when you chid me for my faults, I perceived that your voice was growing hoarse, and, as I ween, from over-fatigue; and therefore I bethought me of a remedy, and I had this porridge made for thee; pray eat thereof, for I tell thee it will ease thy chest and throat.' Said the General, 'What hour is this for thee to go disturbing folk?' Friar Juniper answered, 'Look now, for thee 'tis made; prithee make no more ado, but eat thereof for 'twill do thee much good.' And the General, angry at the late hour and at his importunity, bade him begone, for at such an hour he had no desire to eat, and called him a base fellow and a caitiff. Friar Juniper, seeing that neither prayer nor coaxing was of any avail, spake thus, 'My father, since thou wilt not eat of this porridge that was made for thee, at least do me this favour; hold the candle for me, and I will eat of it.' And the pious and devout General, bearing in mind Friar Juniper's compassion and simplicity, and knowing that all this was done by him out of devotion, answered, 'Look now, since thou wilt have it so, let us eat, thou and I together.' And both ate of this dish of porridge, because of his importunate charity. And much more were they refreshed by their devotion than by the food.

Little Flowers of St. Francis, T. Okey's translation

159. Queen Philippa and the Prisoners

Edward III . . . was at war with France. For almost a year he had been trying to take the city of Calais. All that time the citizens had held out, hoping that the French King could save them. But at the end of eleven months the people were starving, and no hope was left.

So, when the people found that they must give up the city, they feared that all might have to die; and they sent to ask the English King for terms of mercy. Edward said he would spare their lives if they would give him six of their chief men to do with as he liked; and they were to come barefoot, each man in nothing but his shirt, and with a rope round his neck.

Now, when the people of Calais heard this news, there was great grief; and many wondered whether six men could be found willing to die for the rest.

But without waiting for names to be chosen, a great merchant named Eustace St. Pierre, the richest of all the men of Calais, offered to be the first. After him came five others. So these six men, amid the tears and blessings of the people they were now going to save, went out of the city, and were taken into the King's presence.

Then Eustace, speaking for the rest, knelt at the King's feet and offered their lives to his will, but begged him of his goodness to have mercy on them.

But King Edward III, full of wrath because the city had so long held out against him, refused their prayer, and gave word for them to be put to death. Then one of his own knights, Sir

Walter de Manny, pleaded for them, begging the King to do a gentle deed, and win honour and fame by granting pardon to men so noble and so brave.

But this only made the King more angry.

'Hold your peace, Sir Walter!' he cried.

'These men of Calais have killed many of mine, and they must die too.'

Then must it have seemed that their death was certain. But at the King's side sat his wife, Queen Philippa; and she, in spite of the King's wrath against his own good knight, took up the prayer and made it her own. Throwing herself at his feet, she begged him by the love he had for her, and for the many dangers and hardships she had borne in coming from England to be with him, and above all for the love of Christ, that he would now show mercy and spare these men their lives.

The King looked at her for awhile without speaking, for he was a man whose mind was always hard to change. Then said he: 'Lady, I would rather that you had not come here at all; for you know how to pray in such manner that I dare not refuse. But though I do it against my will, I put their lives in your hands.'

And so saying, he took the six men by the ropes which were round their necks, and gave them to the Queen.

Then, with tears of joy, Queen Philippa thanked the King for his mercy; and loosing them from their bonds, she gave orders for them to be well clothed and fed, and sent them back safe and alive to their own city.

LAURENCE HOUSMAN and C. H. K. MARTEN, *The Long Journey*

160. The Ideal Parish Priest

This is Chaucer's description of one of the pilgrims in his *Canterbury Tales*.

> A good man was ther of religioun,
> And was a poorë Parson of a town;

But riche he was of holy thought and werk.
He was also a lernèd man, a clerk
That Cristës gospel gladly woldë preach;
His parisshens devoutly wolde he teach.
Benigne he was, and wondrous diligent,
And in adversitee ful pacient;
And such he was i-proved ofte to be.
To cursen for his tithes ful lothe was he,
But rather wolde he given out of doute,
Unto his porë parisshens aboute,
Of his offrynge, and eek of his substaunce.
He coude in litel thing have suffisaunce.
Wyd was his parish, and houses far asonder,
But yet he laftë not for reyne or thonder,
In siknesse and in meschief to visite
The ferthest in his parisshe, smal and great,
Uppon his feet, and in his hand a staf.
This noble ensample unto his sheep he gaf,
That ferst he wroughte, and after that he taughte
Out of the gospel he those wordës caughte,
And this figure he addid yet therto,
That if gold rustë, what shulde iron do?
For if a priest be foul, on whom we truste,
No wonder if a lewèd man shulde ruste;
And shame it is, if that a priest take kepe,
A dirty shepperd and a clenë shepe;
Wel oughte a priest ensample for to give,
By his clennesse, how that his sheep shulde lyve. . . .
And though he holy were, and vertuous,
He was to sinful man ful piteous,
Nor of his spechë daungerous nor digne,
But in his teching discret and benigne.

Laftë not, ceased not; lewèd, ignorant; daungerous, difficult; digne, proud.

To drawë folk to heven by clenënesse,
By good ensample, was his busynesse:
But were it eny person obstinat,
What-so he were of high or lowe estat,
Him wolde he snubbë sharply for the nonce.
A bettre priest I trowe ther nowher non is.
He wayted after no pompe nor reverence,
Nor made himself spicëd in conscience,
But Chistës lore, and His apostles twelve,
He taught, and ferst he folwed it himselve.

GEOFFREY CHAUCER (1340?–1400), *The Canterbury Tales, Prologue*

161. *Robert Sanderson*

A story of a seventeenth-century country parson.

And that his practice was to do good, one Example may be,
That he met with a poor dejected Neighbour that complain'd
he had taken a Meadow, the Rent of which was nine pounds a
year; and when the Hay was made ready to be carried into his
Barn, several days constant rain had so raised the water, that
a sudden Flood carried all away, and his rich Landlord would
bate him no rent; and that unless he had half abated, he and
seven children were utterly undone. It may be noted, That in
this Age there are a sort of people so unlike the God of mercy,
. . . that they love only themselves and children; love them so,
as not to be concern'd, whether the rest of mankind waste
their days in sorrow or shame; People that are curst with
riches, and a mistake that nothing but riches can make them
and theirs happy. But 'twas not so with Dr. Sanderson; for
he was concern'd, and spoke comfortably to the poor dejected
man; bade him go home and pray, and not load himself with
sorrow, for he would go to his Landlord next morning, and
if his Landlord would not abate what he desired, he and a
Friend would pay it for him.

To the Landlord he went the next day; and in a conference,

the Doctor presented to him the sad condition of his poor dejected Tenant; telling him how much God is pleas'd when men compassionate the poor: and told him, That though God loves Sacrifice, yet he loves Mercy so much better, that he is pleas'd when call'd the God of mercy. And told him, the riches he was possest of were given him by that God of mercy, who would not be pleas'd, if he that had so much given, yea, and forgiven him too, should prove like the rich Steward in the Gospel, that took his fellow servant by the throat to make him pay the utmost farthing. This he told him. And told him, That the Law of this Nation (by which Law he claims his Rent) does not undertake to make men honest or merciful; but does what it can to restrain men from being dishonest or unmerciful, and yet was defective in both: and that taking any Rent from his poor Tenant, for what God sufferd him not to enjoy, though the Law allowed him to do so, yet if he did so, he was too like that rich Steward which he had mentioned to him; and told him that riches so gotten, and added to his great Estate, would, as Job says, prove like gravel in his teeth. These and other such reasons, were urg'd with so grave and so compassionate an earnestness, that the Landlord forgave his Tenant the whole Rent.

IZAAK WALTON (1593–1683), *Life of Sanderson*

162. Dr. Aggrey

Dr. Aggrey was a great African Christian educationist of the twentieth century who worked for understanding between the black and white races.

He was proud of his race, proud of being an African. He would say with his flashing smile: 'If I went to heaven and God asked me whether I would like to return to earth as a white man, I should reply: "I have work to do as a black man that no white man could do. Please send me back as black as You can make me."'

As he journeyed up and down Africa and to England and America on his great adventure of friendship, Aggrey was continually met by the unhappy prejudices of the white against the black. On one occasion when he travelled on a crowded British ship he was given a table to himself in the saloon because he was an African. Whenever he told his story Aggrey would end with his merry laugh which set all his listeners laughing with him and lifted race and colour out of tragedy into comedy. 'Don't you see the joke? The white people had to sit seven at one table, tightly wedged in and had only one steward between seven of them, while I had a whole table and a whole steward all to myself, so that of course I was much better looked after!'

His generous sense of humour always came to the rescue and took the sting from the wound. 'Laughing is the way to go through life,' he would say. But it was no easy thing to do. 'I need the prayers of the saints,' he said, 'to keep on seeing the joke as I travel from colony to colony.' It was only by the grace of God that his great jolly laugh could ring out and dissolve the bitterness of unfriendly thoughts and actions.

Aggrey never cherished any resentment for the insults he received, and he refused to judge the white race by the few who ill-treated him. He remembered too well his Cape Coast friends, the missionaries, and the many Europeans who had since welcomed him as a friend. He refused to take sides between African and European; with his passion for friendliness he sought always to build a bridge of understanding across the gulf which divided people. Being an African he put much of his teaching into the form of parables. When he wanted to picture the true relationship between black and white he spoke a parable of the piano keys. 'You can play a tune of sorts on the white keys, and you can play a tune of sorts on the black keys, but for harmony you must use both the black and the white.'

PHYLLIS GARLICK, *Pioneers of the Kingdom*

163. The Death of Oates

Captain Oates went with Scott on his last expedition to the Antarctic, and he was one of the five who reached the South Pole in January 1912. On the return journey all five were very weak. Oates was worst of all, and thought the others might have a chance without him. This is what Scott wrote in his diary.

Friday March 16 or 17. Lost track of dates, but think the last correct. Tragedy all along the line. At lunch, the day before yesterday, poor Titus Oates said he couldn't go on; he proposed we should leave him in his sleeping bag. That we could not do and we induced him to come on, on the afternoon march. In spite of its awful nature for him he struggled on and we made a few miles. At night he was worse and we knew the end had come.

Should this be found I want these facts recorded. Oates' last thoughts were of his Mother, and immediately before he took pride in thinking that his regiment would be pleased with the bold way in which he met his death. We can testify to his bravery. He has borne intense suffering for weeks without complaint, and to the very last was able and willing to discuss outside subjects. He did not—would not—give up hope till the very end. He was a brave soul. This was the end. He slept through the night before last, hoping not to wake; but he woke in the morning, yesterday. It was blowing a blizzard. He said, 'I am just going outside and may be some time.' He went out into the blizzard and we have not seen him since. . . .

We knew that poor Oates was walking to his death, but though we tried to dissuade him, we knew it was the act of a brave man and an English gentleman. We all hope to meet the end with a similar spirit, and assuredly the end is not far.

ROBERT FALCON SCOTT (1868–1912), *Diary*

164. How a Village dealt with the Plague

The story of how the Great Plague of London reached the village of Eyam in Derbyshire.

'This is a lovely place between Buxton and Chatsworth, perched high on a hill-side, and shut in by another high mountain. . . . At that time lead works were in operation in the mountains, and the village was thickly inhabited. Great was the dismay of the villagers when the family of a tailor, who had received some patterns of cloth from London, showed symptoms of the plague in its most virulent form, sickening and dying in one day.

'The rector of the parish, the Rev. William Mompesson, was still a young man, and had been married only a few years. . . . (He) wrote to London for the most approved medicines and prescriptions; and he likewise sent a letter to the Earl of Devonshire, at Chatsworth, to engage that his parishioners should exclude themselves from the whole neighbourhood, and thus confine the contagion within their own boundaries, provided the Earl would undertake that food, medicines, and other necessaries, should be placed at certain appointed spots, at regular times, upon the hills around, where the Eyamites might come, leave payment for them, and take them up, without holding any communication with the bringers, except by letters, which could be placed on a stone, and then fumigated, or passed through vinegar, before they were touched with the hand. To this the Earl consented, and for seven whole months the engagement was kept.

'Mr. Mompesson represented to his people that, with the plague once among them, it would be so unlikely that they should not carry infection about with them, that it would be selfish cruelty to other places to try to escape amongst them, and thus spread the danger. So rocky and wild was the ground around them, that, had they striven to escape, a regiment of soldiers could not have prevented them. But of their own free will they attended to their rector's remonstrance, and it was not known that one parishioner of Eyam passed the boundary all that time, nor was there a single case of plague in any of the villages around. . . .

'Day and night the rector and his wife were among the sick, nursing, feeding, and tending them with all that care and skill could do; but, in spite of all their endeavours' . . . 259 people, among them the Rector's wife, died of the plague but the infection did not spread to any other parish.

CHARLOTTE M. YONGE (1823-1901), from *A Book of Golden Deeds*

165. How a Russian Monastery fought Famine

This is a story of the monastery of Sarov, where St. Serafim was a deacon in the eighteenth century.

Russia is a country of extremes in all things. Years of abundance and years of famine constantly succeed each other. Towards the end of Serafim's diaconate, the governments of Penza, Tambov, and Ryazan were particularly hard hit. Pakhomius ordered the emergency barns to be flung open. For seven months, Sarov supplied grain to the famished population of the immediate neighbourhood. When the stocks were almost exhausted, the monks, fearing the agony of death by hunger, began to mutter. The monastery was like a ship on the eve of a mutiny. The abbot assembled all his men and spoke to them on compassion—the human link between good and evil. 'Does any one of us wish to outlive our brothers? If so, let him stand before us and say why. Of what avail is a life, preserved at the cost of another's death? No, we shall give away all, to the last bushel. Pray that our barns may be replenished, and prepare yourselves for death. What greater joy is there for a sinner than to die combating the death of his neighbour?'

IULIA DE BEAUSOBRE, *Flame in the Snow*

166. Values

Some words of Franklin D. Roosevelt, President of the U.S.A. from 1932 to 1945.

Life must be based on positive and permanent values.

The value of love will always be stronger than the value of hate; since any nation or group of nations which employs hatred eventually is torn to pieces by hatred within itself.

The value of a belief in humanity and justice is always stronger in any land than the value of belief in force, because force at last turns inward and if that occurs each man or group of men is finally compelled to measure his strength against his own brother.

The value of truth and sincerity is always stronger than the value of lies and cynicism. No process has yet been invented which can permanently separate men from their own hearts and consciences or prevent them from seeing the results of their own false ideas as time rolls by. You cannot make men believe that a way of life is good when it spreads poverty, misery, disease and death. Men cannot be everlastingly loyal unless they are free.

FRANKLIN D. ROOSEVELT (1882–1945), from his *Public Papers and Addresses*

VII. FAITH

167. What Faith is

Some words by a modern churchman and philosopher, Dean Inge.

Faith is a kind of climbing instinct, which draws us upward and onward. It is at first quite vague and undifferentiated, and partly subconscious. Then it takes shape as a homage to, and craving after, God, who shines as a triple constellation in the spiritual firmament, as the Source of the Good, the True and the Beautiful. . . . Whatever is real and permanent in the world that we know, partakes in these qualities.

. . . And let us note this—for it is very important. The normal movement of Faith is double, like the action of the valves of the heart. . . . In Jacob's vision . . . the angels were not only climbing up the ladder, they were also coming down it.

What does this mean? It means that we are not to run away from life even to find God, but that we are to come back with our treasure as soon as we have found it. . . . The Epistle to the Hebrews makes it clear that Faith is from first to last an *activity* of the soul. It is not a passive acceptance of dogmas or of a scheme of salvation. . . . This is the lesson which the writer (of the Epistle) draws from the roll-call of the Old Testament heroes.

The roll of honour is almost entirely of men of action, not of saints and prophets. He names the men who legislated and fought for Israel, her great patriots. And then he passes to the martyrs for their country. . . . Those of whom the world was not worthy were fugitives and vagabonds on the earth! And all alike, heroes and martyrs, having had a witness borne to them through their Faith, received *not* the promise. None of them! Nor was the promise ever fulfilled as they had pictured it themselves. God had provided some better thing, which He gave them instead. That, I think we may dare to say, is God's way. How seldom does the great man achieve what he meant to do. . . . It is the trials of Faith, its pains and disappointments, that are the sources of its real triumph, 'the victory that overcometh the world'.

W. R. INGE, *Personal Religion and the Life of Devotion*

168. St. Teresa's Victory of Faith

St. Teresa (1515–82) was an outstanding Christian woman who fought against ill health and other difficulties, and yet lived a life of prayer as well as being a great organizer. Like all her contemporaries she believed in devils, whereas we should speak of illness, fears, and worries.

'Well now,' I said to myself, 'if this Lord is so powerful, as I see He is, and if the devils are His slaves (and of that there can be no doubt . . .) what harm can they do me, who am a servant of this Lord and King? How can I fail to have fortitude enough to fight against all hell?' So I took a cross in my hand and it really seemed that God was giving me courage: in a short time I found I was another person and I should not have been afraid to wrestle with devils, for with the aid of that cross I believed I could easily vanquish them all. . . . 'Come on, now, all of you.' I said. 'I am a servant of the Lord and I want to see what you can do to me.' It certainly seemed as if I had frightened all these devils, for I became quite calm and had no more fear of them . . . they are no more trouble to me now than flies. They seem to me such cowards—as soon as they see that anyone despises them they have no strength left.

ST. TERESA (1515–82), *Life*, E. Allison Peers's translation

169. The Character of Edward Wilson

Edward Wilson went with Scott on his last expedition to the Antarctic as doctor and zoologist. He endured the terrible winter journey with Bowers and Cherry-Garrard when they went in search of Emperor Penguin eggs: and he was one of the five who reached the South Pole in January 1912.

Many of that band are now famous and dead—Pennell, who commanded the *Terra Nova* . . . and brought the survivors back a year after the tragedy and victory of the Pole: Atkinson, who commanded the Main Party during that last and most ghastly year: . . . Bowers, perhaps the hardest man who ever sledged: Oates, who walked out to try and save his friends. As time went on these men began to stand out and they with their companions agreed in an affection and admiration for Wilson which amounted to love.

What they did has become part of the history of England, perhaps of the human race, as much as Columbus or the Elizabethans, David, Hector or Ulysses. They are an epic.

What was it that gave Bill [as Wilson was called] such a position among such men? Looking back, I am sure it was character, combined with an immensely high standard of work, most unselfishly done; men such as I have named have an intuitive recognition that there is something good in a man like Bill. But at the time I had not the curiosity to inquire. During those two years, mostly sledging, when Bill and I lived in daily companionship I feel now that I wasted a lot of time. I knew him straight away as a famous explorer, tried naturalist and artist, and no doubt a skilled doctor, and accepted him as such. . . . If I had that time over again I should want to find out from Bill how he grew up, why he thought this and that, and I might have learned something of the great faith which I now believe was at the foundation of his greatness. . . .

Cowardice is catching; that is why men are down on cowards: they are frightened of them. But courage is catching too . . . it was easy to be brave when Bill was near; . . . we saw always his courage, his serenity and his sympathy. . . . Whatever was the matter you took your trouble to Bill and, immediately, he dropped what he was doing, gave you his complete attention, and all his help. . . .

How far was his courage based upon his faith? After all, courage alone will not take you far in the Antarctic . . . courage, as ambition, or love of notoriety, may take you to the Antarctic, or any other uncomfortable place in the world, but it won't take you far inside without being found out; it's courage: and unselfishness: and helping one another: . . . and good temper:

and tact: and good judgment: and faith. And the greatest of these is faith.

APSLEY CHERRY-GARRARD, Introduction to Edward Wilson of the Antarctic, by George Seaver

170. The Faith of Edward Wilson

Another impression of Edward Wilson the Antarctic explorer.

It was his steadfast and unalterable conviction that for a man who has wrapped his will in God's will, put his life consciously in the stream of the divine life, freed his soul from all personal ambitions, taken his life on trust as a divine gift—that for such a man there is an over-ruling Providence which guards and guides him in every incident of his life, from the greatest to the least. He held that all annoyances, frustrations, disappointments, mishaps, discomforts, hardships, sorrows, pains, and even final disaster itself, are simply God's ways of teaching us lessons that we could never else learn. That circumstances do not matter, are nothing; but that the response of the spirit that meets them is everything; that there is no situation in human life, however apparently adverse, nor any human relationship, however apparently uncongenial, that cannot be made, if God be in the heart, into a thing of perfect joy; that in order to attain this ultimate perfection, one must accept every experience and learn to love all persons; . . . that the worth of life is not to be measured by its results in achievement or success, but solely by the motive of one's heart and the effort of one's will.

GEORGE SEAVER, The Faith of Edward Wilson

171. Robert Morrison

When Robert Morrison set out in 1807 as the first Protestant missionary to China he had to travel by way of America as the East India Company, which had the monopoly of the trade with India and the East, refused to allow missionaries to travel to India or China in any British vessel.

His American host records this incident when they visited the captain of the ship on which he was to sail. . . .

'We set out together to the counting house of the ship owner previous to his embarkation. I cannot forget the air of suppressed ridicule on the merchant's face and in his speech and manner towards Morrison, whom he appeared to pity as a deluded enthusiast, while he could not but secretly respect his self-denial, devotion, courage and enterprise. When all business matters were arranged, he turned about from his desk and with a sardonic grin addressing Morrison said, "And so, Mr. Morrison, you really expect that you will make an impression on the idolatory of the great Chinese Empire?"

"NO, sir," said Morrison, with more than his usual sternness, "I expect God will."'

Compiled from PHYLLIS GARLICK, *Pioneers of the Kingdom*

172. St. Patrick

St Patrick was brought up in a Christian family in fourth-century Britain. When he was about sixteen he was captured by Irish raiders and sold as a slave to a heathen chief. He escaped but later returned to Ireland as a Christian missionary.

As he approached the palace of Loegaire, the High King of Ireland, he chanted the brave song which is called St. Patrick's Breastplate, or the Deer's Cry. For the king had caused men to lie in ambush on Patrick's road to destroy him and his followers, and Patrick, aware of danger, sought strength and courage from the thought of Christ's nearness. 'If Christ be with me,' he thought to himself, 'of whom shall I be afraid?' Tradition says that when Patrick and his monks passed by they appeared to the men in ambush as wild deer with a fawn following in the mist. And this was the brave and noble song

which Patrick chanted as he went on bravely to preach Christ
in the royal palace of Tara:—

> Christ with me, Christ before me, Christ behind me,
> Christ in me, Christ beneath me, Christ above me,
> Christ on my right, Christ on my left,
> Christ in breadth, Christ in length, Christ in height,
> Christ in the heart of every man who thinks of me,
> Christ in the mouth of everyone who speaks of me,
> Christ in every eye that sees me,
> Christ in every ear that hears me.

Though he failed to persuade the king to become a Christian,
Patrick received his permission to preach the Gospel in his
country.

PHYLLIS GARLICK, *Pioneers of the Kingdom*

173. *The Faith of St. Joan of Arc*

A speech of Joan of Arc to the King and nobles of France, as imagined
by the dramatist.

Where would you all have been now if I had heeded that sort
of truth? There is no help, no counsel, in any of you. Yes, I
am alone on earth: I have always been alone. My father told
my brothers to drown me if I would not stay to mind his sheep
while France was bleeding to death: France might perish if
only our lambs were safe. I thought France would have friends
at the court of the King of France, and I find only wolves
fighting for pieces of her poor torn body. I thought God would
have friends everywhere, because He is the friend of everyone;
and in my innocence I believed that you who now cast me out
would be like strong towers to keep harm from me. But I am
wiser now; and nobody is any the worse for being wiser. Do
not think you can frighten me by telling me that I am alone.
France is alone, and God is alone, and what is my loneliness
before the loneliness of my country and my God? I see now

that the loneliness of God is His strength; what would He be if He listened to your jealous little counsels? Well, my loneliness shall be my strength too: it is better to be alone with God: His friendship will not fail me, nor His counsel, nor His love. In His strength I will dare and dare and dare until I die.

G. B. SHAW (1856–1950), *St. Joan*

174. *Faith of the Quakers*

In 1775 in the State of New York a Quaker, or Friends' Meeting was being held. It was a troubled time because of the outbreak of the War of Independence and the Red Indians were taking advantage of the disturbance to attack the hated white men.

One of the Quakers had just spoken the words of the Psalmist, He shall cover thee with His feathers and under His wings shalt thou trust', when silently the meeting became aware of an Indian Chief staring in at the meeting-house window, showing his teeth in a cruel grin. In his hand he held a sheaf of poisoned arrows . . . the Friends were entirely unarmed. There was not a gun, or a rifle, or a sword to be found in any of their dwelling houses, so there could not be any in their peaceful meeting.

A minute later, a dozen other Redskins, equally terrible, stood beside the Chief. . . . Yet still the Friends sat on, without stirring, in complete silence . . . the patriarch of the Meeting gazing full at the Chief, who had first approached. . . . No word was spoken, but in silence two powers were measured against one another—the power of hate, and the power of love. . . . But at length the Indian's eyes fell . . . then signing to his followers . . . the bows were laid down and rested against the wall; many footsteps, lighter than falling snow, crossed the floor; the Indian Chief, unarmed, sat himself down in the nearest seat, with his followers . . . also unarmed, close round him.

The Meeting did not stop. The Meeting continued—one of

the strangest Quaker Meetings, surely, that ever was held. The Meeting not only continued, it increased in solemnity and power. . . . At last, when the accustomed hour of worship ended . . . (the Indian Chief spoke). . . .

'Indian come White Man House . . . Indian want kill white man . . . Indian come, See white man sit in house; no gun, no arrow, no knife; all quiet, all still, worshipping Great Spirit. Great Spirit inside Indian too;' he pointed to his breast; 'then Great Spirit say: "Indian. No kill them."'
. . . 'The Beloved of the Lord shall dwell in safety by Him. He shall cover him all the day long.'

LUCY HODGKIN, *A Book of Quaker Saints*

175. John Wesley

On a windy evening when the fires of the iron furnaces lit up the sky of the Black Country with a smoky glare, there rode over the moorland a small, slight figure, sitting with loosened rein on a tired horse. John Wesley was riding to Wednesbury, a town where the coal pits were opening out and the rough, untaught men and women were hard at work in the mines. In the guttering candle-light colliers swung their picks, and women in coarse sacking trousers crawled on all fours dragging behind them the little waggons full of coal. Children were working down there too, in the darkness of those little low underground passages.

There had been trouble in Wednesbury ever since Charles Wesley had first preached there in the midst of the flying stones of the mob, but some had listened to the message and in spite of persecution had stood firm. And now John Wesley was on his way to visit them.

That night a mob gathered round the house where he was staying. 'Bring out the minister!' they shouted. 'Away with him to the magistrate!'

'That I will with all my heart,' said Wesley, fearlessly facing the crowd. He was hurried along the streets to shouts of 'Down with him! Kill him at once!' The mob was like a raging sea. Some tore off some of his clothes; others smote him on the mouth, and a big fellow tried to strike him with a heavy, oaken club. At last Wesley managed to make his voice heard above the cries and shouts of the mob. 'What evil have I done? Which of you all have I wronged in thought or word or deed?' It was the voice of one who was master of himself because he was not afraid. Then Wesley began to pray aloud.

An amazing thing happened. The leader of the mob, a great, burly prize fighter known as 'honest Munchin', suddenly turned to him and said: 'Sir, I will spend my life for you! Follow me and not one soul here shall touch a hair of your head.' His example was followed by a butcher and some of the roughest of the mob. John Wesley, his clothes ragged and torn but his face shining, returned to his house under the safe escort of a group who a few minutes before had been his worst enemies.

From that day onwards 'honest Munchin' set out to follow Christ. A prize fighter turned preacher! It was a strange thing in those days to see a man of that type, and masons and cobblers and farmers, preaching the Christian message which it was the custom for only a clergyman in gown and bands to deliver in church.

PHYLLIS GARLICK, *Pioneers of the Kingdom*

176. Responsibility and Faith

God made man in His own image. Whatever that means, it means that man is important to God and is responsible to God. The Word became flesh and dwelt among us. God came to earth in the person of a humble carpenter, and thereby sanctified the individual. This means that what the individual believes, *is*, and does, counts. . . . We cannot foresee the results of our actions. It is our responsibility, not our helplessness, which appals me. . . . As each . . . goes out to industry . . . or university or family life, (his) influence, for good or bad, will radiate across the centuries. An act of kindness may help to mould a Gandhi, our failures may be creating a new Hitler. The progress of mankind has always depended upon those who, seemingly isolated and powerless in their own day, have seen their vision and remained true to it. In the darkening corridors of time they preserved integral their vision of the daylight at the end. This is a matter not of calculation but of faith. Our work may be small and its results invisible to us. But we may rest assured it will come to fruition in God's good time.

JOHN FERGUSON, The Enthronement of Love

VIII. MEEKNESS

177. *What Humility is*

The source of humility is the habit of realizing the presence of God. Humility does not mean thinking less of yourself than of other people, nor does it mean having a low opinion of your own gifts. It means freedom from thinking about yourself one way or the other at all. It may be quite right that a man conscious of certain powers given him by God should desire the opportunity to exercise these powers for God. It may be quite right that under certain circumstances a man should insist that he is more capable than another man of doing something that must be done. No one would select as an example of humility the elder Pitt; but there was nothing contrary to humility in his alleged declaration to the Duke of Devonshire: 'I know that I can save this country and I know that no one else can.' He knew the political life of the time pretty well; he was conscious of power in himself, and in a few years he showed he was right in what he said of himself; only if he set about his task in his own interest or for self-glorification did he fail in humility.

Humility means that you feel yourself, as a distinct person, out of count, and give your whole mind and thought to the object towards which they are directed, to God Himself in worship and to the fulfilment of His will in Christian love; and humility, in that sense, is quite plainly a source of effectiveness. The humility which consists in being a great deal occupied about yourself, and saying you are of little worth, is not Christian humility. It is one form of self-occupation and a very poor and futile one at that; but real humility makes for effectiveness because it delivers a man from anxiety, and we all know that in all undertakings, from the smallest to the greatest, the chief source of feebleness is anxiety. Even in a game we all know that nothing so much paralyses good play as anxiety. If you once begin to wonder whether you are going to catch the ball you will drop it, but if you just catch it without thinking about anything but catching it—not, above all, of what other people are going to think of you—probably you will hold it. That goes through everything from such a simple act to the greatest. But there is nothing big enough to hold a man's soul in detachment from the centre of himself through all the occupations of life except the majesty of God and His love; and it is in worship, worship given to God because He is God, that man will most learn the secret of real humility.

WILLIAM TEMPLE (1881–1944), *Christ in His Church*

178. 'Rights' that are Wrong

Fly a thousand leagues away from saying, 'I was in the *right*: it was not *right* for me to suffer this, they had no *right* to do such a thing to me.' Now God deliver us from such wrong rights! Do you think that there was any question of rights when Jesus suffered the injuries which were so unrighteously inflicted on Him. . . . When we receive honours or affection or kind treatment let us think what right have we to them—for certainly we have no *right* to them in this life.

ST. TERESA (1515–82), *The Way of Perfection*

179. The Humility of Mary

For He that is mighty hath done to me great things: and Holy is His name.

Behold, how completely Mary traces all to God, lays claim to no works, no honour, no fame. She conducts herself as before, when as yet she had naught of all this; she demands no higher honours than before. She is not puffed up, does not vaunt herself, nor proclaim with a loud voice that she is become the Mother of God. She seeks not any glory, but goes about her wonted household duties, milking the cows, cooking the meals, washing pots and kettles, sweeping out the rooms, and performing the work of maidservant or housemother in lowly and despised tasks, as though she cared naught for such exceeding great gifts and graces. She was esteemed among other women and her neighbours no more highly than before, nor desired to be, but remained a poor townswoman, one of the great multitude.

. . . When men accord us praise and honour, we ought to profit by the example of the Mother of God. . . . We ought neither to reject this praise and honour as though they were wrong, nor to despise them as though they were naught; but . . . ascribe them to Him in heaven to whom they belong.

MARTIN LUTHER (1483–1546), *The Magnificat*

180. Humility before the Truth

Sir Robert Boyle, born in 1627, is known as one of the first investigators into the physics of the atmosphere and the nature of heat, but his chief mission was to teach, by his example, the value of experiment in research, where he kept the humility of the true scientist always before him.

We are not always bound to reject everything as false, that we know not how to reconcile with something that is true. . . . I have sometimes thought God and men enjoy truth as differingly as they do time. For we men enjoy time but by parcels and always leave far the greatest part of it unreached by us; so we know but some particular truths, and are ignorant of far more than we attain to. Whereas God, as His eternity reaches to all the portions of time, so His omniscience gives Him at one view a prospect of the whole extent of truth; upon which account He sees all particular truths, not only distinct, but in their system and sees a connexion between those, that to us seemed the most distant ones. . . .

We ought not always to condemn the opinion which is liable to ill consequences, and incumbered with great inconveniences. . . . We must not expect to be able . . . to resolve all difficulties, and answer all objections, since we can never directly answer those, which require for their solution a perfect comprehension of what is infinite.

SIR ROBERT BOYLE (1627–91)

181. The Makers

The Architect stood forth and said:
'I am the master of the art:
I have a thought within my head
I have a dream within my heart.

Come now, good craftsman, ply your trade
With tool and stone obediently;
Behold the plan that I have made—
I am the master; serve you me.'

The Craftsman answered: 'Sir, I will
Yet look to it that this your draft
Be of a sort to serve my skill—
You are not master of the craft.

It is by me the towers grow tall,
I lay the course, I shape and hew;
You make a little inky scrawl,
And that is all that you can do.

Account me, then, the master man,
Laying my rigid rule upon
The plan, and that which serves the plan—
The uncomplaining, helpless stone.'

The Stone made answer: 'Masters mine,
Know this: that I can bless or damn
The thing that both of you design
By being but the thing I am;

For I am granite and not gold,
For I am marble and not clay,
You may not hammer me nor mould—
I am the master of the way.

Yet once that mastery bestowed
Then I will suffer patiently
The cleaving steel, the crushing load,
That make a calvary of me;

And you may carve me with your hand
To arch and buttress, roof and wall,
Until the dream rise up and stand—
Serve but the stone, the stone serves all.

Let each do well what each knows best,
Nothing refuse and nothing shirk,
Since none is master of the rest,
But all are servants of the work—

The work no master may subject
Save He to whom the whole is known,
Being Himself the Architect,
The Craftsman and the Corner-stone.

Then, when the greatest and the least
Have finished all their labouring
And sit together at the feast,
You shall behold a wonder thing:

The Maker of the men that make
Will stoop between the cherubim,
The towel and the basin take,
And serve the servants who serve Him.'[1]

The Architect and Craftsman both
Agreed, the Stone had spoken well;
Bound them to service by an oath
And each to his own labour fell.

DOROTHY SAYERS, from *The Man Born To Be King*

[1] St. John xiii. 1-17.

182. The Real Value of Money

In the fourth century many Christians left the cities for the desert to lead a life of meditation. This story tells of the experience of Melania, a young widow of a wealthy Roman, who went on pilgrimage to Egypt to visit the desert fathers. She came to a certain mountain called Mount Nitria.

The blessed Pambo was a dweller in this mountain. In many and diverse virtues he had the prerogative and palm, but was in this especially memorable, that he made so light of silver and gold that verily he seemed to have fulfilled the Lord's commandment. I had it myself from the worshipful lady Melania, that after she set out from Rome and first reached Alexandria, she heard much of his virtues from Isidore the priest and overseer of the church, and with him as guide came to him in the desert, and offered him three hundred pounds of silver, praying him to accept somewhat of her wealth. 'He was sitting there,' said she, 'and weaving a basket, and he blessed me with a single word saying, "May God reward thee." Then he said to his steward, "Take it carefully, and divide it among all the brethren that are in Libya and the islands, for these monasteries seem more needy than the others."' He also bade him give none of the money to those in Egypt, because he knew that these parts have abundance of food. So, as she herself told me, she stood on, waiting for some blessing on her gift or some praise; and hearing nothing from him, at last she spoke. 'I would have thee know, my lord,' says she, 'there are three hundred pounds in that casket.' But again without looking up he made answer, 'He to whom thou hast offered it, my daughter, has no need to learn its bulk from thee, for He who weighs the mountains in the balance knoweth far better than thou dost what the weight of this silver may be. If indeed it were to me thou didst offer it, thou didst well to tell me: but if not to me, but to that God who we know did not despise but gave most honour to the two mites,[1] hold thy peace and be still.'

HELEN WADDELL, from *The Desert Fathers*

183. King Oswin and St. Aidan's Horse

A story of an Anglo-Saxon king.

King Oswin was of a graceful aspect, and tall of stature, affable in discourse, and courteous in behaviour; and most bountiful, as well to the noble as the ignoble; so that he was beloved by all men for his qualities of body and mind, and persons of the first rank came from almost all the provinces to serve him. Among other virtues and rare endowments . . . humility is said to have been the greatest, which it will suffice to prove by one example.

He had given an extraordinarily fine horse to Bishop Aidan, which he might either use in crossing rivers, or in performing a journey upon any urgent necessity, though he was wont to travel ordinarily on foot. Some short time after, a poor man meeting him and asking alms, Aidan immediately dismounted, and ordered the horse, with all his royal furniture, to be given to the beggar; for he was very compassionate, a great friend to the poor, and, as it were, the father of the wretched. This being told to the King, when they were going in to dinner, he said to the bishop, 'Why would you, my lord bishop, give the poor man that royal horse which was so necessary for your use? Had we not many other horses of less value, and of other sorts, which would have been good enough to give to the poor, and not to give that horse, which I had particularly chosen for yourself?' To whom the bishop instantly answered, 'What is it you say, O King? Is that foal of a mare more dear to you than the Son of God?' Upon this they went in to dinner, and the bishop sat in his place; but the King, who had come from

[1] St. Mark xii. 41–44, St. Luke xxi. 1–4.

hunting, stood warming himself, with his attendants, at the fire. Then on a sudden, whilst he was warming himself, calling to mind what the bishop had said to him, he ungirt his sword, and gave it to a servant, and in a hasty manner fell down at the bishop's feet, beseeching him to forgive him; 'For from this time forward,' said he, 'I will never speak any more of this, nor will I judge of what, or how much of our money you shall give to the sons of God.'

BEDE (673–735), Ecclesiastical History of the English Nation

184. Advice to the Self-important

St. Teresa writes to her nuns:

It is very important for us to realize that God does not lead us all by the same road. . . . Remember that there must be someone to cook the meals and count yourselves happy in being able to serve like Martha. Reflect that true humility consists to a great extent in being ready for what the Lord desires to do with you.

Remember that the Lord walks among the pots and pans and that He will help you in the inward tasks and in the outward too.

ST. TERESA (1515–82), The Way of Perfection and The Foundations,
E. A. Peers's translation

185. St. Francis and Friar Masseo

A story of the famous St. Francis of Assisi, founder of the Franciscans.

St. Francis, desiring to humble Friar Masseo in order that by reason of the many gifts and graces God had bestowed on him he should not be puffed up with vainglory, but by virtue of humility should increase from virtue to virtue, said to him on a day when he was dwelling with his first companions in a solitary place—those truly holy companions whereof Friar

Masseo was one—'O Friar Masseo, all these thy companions have the gift of contemplation and of prayer; but thou hast the gift of preaching the word of God to the satisfaction of the people. Therefore I desire that thou take upon thee the offices of the door-keeper, the almoner, and the cook, in order that thy companions may give themselves up to contemplation; and when the other friars are eating thou shalt eat outside the door of the friary, so that thou mayest satisfy with some sweet words of God those who come to the convent, ere they knock; and so that no other friar than thou have need to go outside. And this do through the merit of holy obedience.' Then Friar Masseo drew back his cowl and inclined his head and humbly received and fulfilled his command, and for many days he discharged the offices of door-keeper and almoner and cook. Whereat his companions, even as men illumined by God, began to feel great remorse in their hearts, considering that Friar Masseo was a man of as great perfection as they were, or even greater; and yet on him was laid the whole burden of the convent, and not on them. Wherefore, moved by one desire, they went with one accord and entreated the holy father to be pleased to distribute those offices among them; for in no wise could they endure in their conscience that Friar Masseo should bear so many burdens. When St. Francis heard this he gave heed to their prayers and consented to their desire, and calling Friar Masseo he thus spake to him, 'Friar Masseo, thy companions would have a share in the offices wherewith I have charged thee: it is therefore my will that the said offices should be divided.' Says Friar Masseo with great humility and meekness, 'Father, whatsoever thou layest upon me, either all or part, that I hold to be wholly done by God.' Then St. Francis beholding the love of them and the humility of Friar Masseo, preached a wondrous sermon touching most holy humility, admonishing them that the greater the gifts and graces that God bestows upon us, the greater ought our

humility to be; for without humility no virtue is acceptable
to God.

And when he had made an end to his sermon he apportioned
the offices among them with the greatest loving-kindness.

The Little Flowers of St. Francis, T. Okey's translation

186. The Two Saint Johns

There were two nuns and, as I think, they are still living in the
convent of Luter in the diocese of Trèves, one of whom was
specially devoted to St. John the Baptist, but the other to St.
John the Evangelist. Now as often as they met, they used to
argue together as to which was the greater, so that sometimes
the abbess could scarcely restrain them. The one brought
forward all the privilege of her chosen saint, while the other
met them very effectively with the prerogatives of hers. One
night before matins St. John the Baptist appeared in a dream
to his worshipper, and said: 'Sister, you must know that St.
John the Evangelist is greater than I. Never was there a man
more pure than he; untouched both in mind and body, Christ
chose him to the apostolate and loved him more than all the
other apostles, and showed him the glory of His transfiguration.
He was most blessed that he was reclined on Jesus' breast at
the last supper; he was present at his death; to him . . . Christ
committed His . . . Mother. He soaring higher than the other
evangelists, and fixing more fully the eyes of his mind upon
the throne of God, thus began his gospel: "In the beginning
was the word" etc. He also wrote the Apocalypse, which
reveals the very deepest things in heavenly pictures. Also he
suffered very many tortures for Christ's sake. . . . See how for
these reasons and many other of his privileges he is greater
and worthier than I. In the morning therefore, ask your sister
to go with you before your abbess and falling before her feet

beseech her to pardon you, because you have so often exasperated her for my sake.'

At the bell for matins she awoke and began to meditate upon so clear a vision. Then after matins, when the other sister had returned to sleep, St. John the Evangelist appeared to her in a vision, and addressed his partisan in words which carried this meaning: 'Sister, you must know that the Blessed John the Baptist is a far greater saint than I. The Lord Himself bears witness that "among those born of women there has not risen one greater than he". He is a prophet and more than a prophet. His birth was announced by an angel, he was supernaturally sanctified when still unborn, he lived sinlessly in the desert. None of this can be said of me, for I was born of wealthy parents, and lived as a layman in worldly fashion among worldly people. . . . He recognised the Saviour when still unborn, among all the crowd He pointed Him out as He came to him, and in the Jordan He baptised him with His holy hands. He saw the heaven open, he heard the Father's voice, he looked upon the Son in the form of a man, and upon the Holy Spirit in the form of a dove. At last he was martyred because of his uprightness. Therefore he is greater than I. Now to-day you must call your sister into the presence of your abbess, and throwing yourself at her feet, you must beg her to pardon you, because you have so often exasperated her by contentiously preferring me to the Lord's Forerunner.' In the morning they both went to the abbess and told their visions. Then together they threw themselves down, and, as had been commanded them, sought pardon from each other, and were reconciled by the mediation of their spiritual Mother, who warned them never to contend in the future concerning the merits of the saints, which are known to God alone.

CAESARIUS OF HEISTERBACH (c. 1180–1240), *Dialogue on Miracles*,
H. von E. Scott and C. C. S. Bland's translation, 1929

187. God's Two Dwellings

Lord, Thou hast told us that there be
Two dwellings which belong to Thee,
   And those two—that's the wonder—
    Are far asunder.

The one the highest Heaven is,
The mansions of eternal bliss;
   The other's the contrite
    And humble sprite.

Not like the princes of the earth,
Who think it much below their birth
   To come within the door
    Of people poor;

No, such is Thy humility,
That though Thy dwelling be on high,
   Thou dost Thyself debase
    To the lowest place.

Where'er Thou seest a sinful soul
Deploring his offences foul,
   To him Thou wilt descend,
    And be his friend.

Thou wilt come in, and with him sup,
And from a low state raise him up,
   Till Thou hast made him eat
    Blest angels' meat.

Thus Thou wilt him with honour crown
Who in himself is first cast down,
   And humbled for his sins,
    That Thy love wins.

Though Heaven be high, the gate is low,
And he that comes in there must bow:
    The lofty looks shall ne'er
    Have entrance there.

O God! since Thou delight'st to rest
In the humble contrite breast,
    First make me so to be,
    Then dwell with me.

THOMAS WASHBOURNE (1606–87)

IX. TEMPERANCE

188. The Virtue St. Paul found Difficult

If now we consider how we ourselves stand in respect of this virtue of temperance, we discover that it must bring its sobering realisms into our social, personal and spiritual life. Its peaceful acceptance of facts must colour all our relations with others, all our dealings with ourselves, all our responses to God. . . . Those who come to the soul's house should find it nicely warmed all over; its inner chamber must not be like one of those rooms which have a fierce little gas-stove in one corner, and a deadly chill everywhere else. . . . Like Peter's wife's mother, while the fever is on us, we cannot really serve our fellow men. I often think that when St. Paul wrote his classic list of the fruits of the Spirit, he gave us unconsciously a wonderful account of his own growth in this spiritual realism. We should hardly think of the virtue of Temperance as specially characteristic of St. Paul, and even to the end of his days he probably found it difficult; yet in this he discovers the final proof of the working of Creative Spirit in his soul. He begins upon a note of convinced fervour. 'The fruit—the harvest—of the Spirit is love, joy, peace.' No three words could better express that rich beatitude which, in his holiest

moments, has flooded his soul. Then he pauses. We seem to
see him thinking: 'After all, I don't always feel like that.
Things are often very trying. I don't seem able to love; peace
and joy are unobtainable; I feel another law in my members
warring against the law of my mind. Yet the indwelling Spirit
is still there; to live *is* Christ. How does that Spirit act on my
troubled spirit in those less expansive moments? Surely in
long-suffering, gentleness and kindness which I know must
control all my reactions to the world of men.' They were not
the reactions which St. Paul found specially easy. . . . At last,
at the very end, we reach those unexpected characters which
are the earnest of his total transformation in the Spirit. Fidelity,
Meekness, Moderation: an unsensational but unbroken loyalty
to the infinite life and purpose which had made him its own,
an acceptance of its gradual pace, a refusal to hurry, a restrain-
ing of the impetuous desire to get everything possible out of
those new converts who were only babies still, and tell the
candid truth to those who had let him down—these are the
real fruits of his subjection to God. Paul, whose first idea had
been to breathe fire and slaughter upon the Christians, and
whose second idea had been to be 'all·out' for Christ—who was
quite as obsessed as we are by the vision of all that there was to
do, and the sense that he was called upon to do it—learns that
the final gift of the Spirit is not intensity of life, but Temperance.

EVELYN UNDERHILL (1875–1941), *The House of the Soul*

189. Erasmus

Amid the bitterness of the sixteenth-century controversy Erasmus
stood for moderation and tolerance. He tried to reconcile the followers
of Luther and the supporters of the Pope. Consequently he was
attacked by both sides and called a coward. In 1519 Erasmus wrote a
letter to Luther addressing him as a 'brother in Christ'.

He said he had not yet read the books (of Luther) which had
created so much clamour, and therefore could not judge of

them. . . . And it seemed to him, he said, that more good would come of courteous modesty than of impetuosity. It was by this that Christ drew the world under his influence. . . . It were better to exclaim against *abuses* of pontifical authority than against the Popes themselves. 'May the Lord Jesus "daily impart to you abundantly" (he concluded) "of His own Spirit to His own glory and the public good." . . .'

To the exasperated monks, who charged him with aiding and abetting Luther in writing the books which had caused such a tumult, he replied that, as he had not read them, he could not even express a decided opinion upon them.

To Cardinal Wolsey he wrote, that he had only read a few pages of Luther's books, not because he disliked them, but because he was so closely occupied with his own. Luther's life was such that even his enemies could not find anything to slander. Germany had young men of learning and eloquence who would, he foretold, bring her great glory. . . . If these German students were too free in their criticisms, it should be remembered to what constant exasperation they had been submitted in all manner of ways, both public and private.

To Hutten, who was perhaps the most hot-headed of these German young men, and whose satire had already proved itself more trenchant and bitter than any in which Erasmus had ever indulged, he urged moderation, and said that for himself he had rather spend a month in trying to explain St. Paul or the Gospels than waste a day in quarrelling.

FREDERIC SEEBOHM, *The Oxford Reformers*

190. *The Day of Liberation*

After fifty years of agitation against slavery Parliament passed a bill in 1833 ending slavery in the British colonies.

ow would the slaves take their freedom? There were gloomy prophecies of insurrection, unbridled license and drunkenness;

but the event falsified them. August 1st, 1834, was the day of liberation, and the news of what happened that day reached England in September and was received with profound thankfulness. Instead of breaking out into lawlessness the slaves spent the day quietly. On the evening of July 31st they crowded into their churches, and 'as the hour of midnight approached, they fell upon their knees and awaited the solemn moment, all hushed in silent prayer.' When midnight sounded they sprang to their feet and gave thanks to God for their deliverance.

JOHN A. PATTEN, These Remarkable Men

191. Virtue and Freedom

In 1644 an order had been made that no book should be printed unless approved and licensed by the government. This is part of Milton's great protest against trying to impose a censorship, instead of giving men freedom to choose.

Good and evil we know in the field of this world grow up together almost inseparably. . . . He that can apprehend and consider vice with all her baits and seeming pleasures, and yet abstain, and yet distinguish and yet prefer that which is truly better, he is the true warfaring Christian. I cannot praise a fugitive and cloistered virtue, unexercised and unbreathed, that never sallies out and sees her adversary, but slinks out of the race, where that immortal garland is to be run for not without dust and heat. Assuredly we bring not innocence into the world, we bring impurity much rather: that which purifies us is trial, and trial is by what is contrary. . . .

If every action, which is good or evil in man at ripe years, were to be under pittance and prescription and compulsion, what were virtue but a name, what praise would then be due to well-doing. . . ? Many there be that complain of Divine Providence for suffering Adam to transgress; foolish tongues! When God gave him reason, He gave him freedom to choose, for reason is but choosing. . . . We ourselves esteem not of that obedience or love, or gift, which is of force: God therefore left him free, set before him a provoking object, ever almost in his eyes; herein consisted his merit, herein the right of his reward, the praise of his abstinence. Wherefore did He create passions within us, pleasures round about us, but that these rightly tempered are the very ingredients of virtue?

JOHN MILTON (1608–74), *Areopagitica*

PART FOUR

SERVANTS OF THE KINGDOM

'*The best way of knowing God is to frequent the company of His friends.*'

ST. TERESA

'*To give our Lord a perfect hospitality, Mary and Martha must combine.*'

ST. TERESA

192. Prophets[1]

There have been few in all ages who have felt themselves irresistibly impelled to utter the truths of which they were persuaded; who have fought hopeless causes; who seem to have lost all feeling of themselves in their devotion to their country or to mankind. The term 'prophet' is no longer applied to them; they are not distinguished from their fellow-men by any external note in their way of life. We hardly recognise the analogy until after they are dead, and then we sometimes find that they have received a 'prophet's reward.' Such men have been the leaders of movements among ourselves, on behalf of the prisoner or of the slave, or the extension of education, or the spread of religious truth. They have been found equally among the clergy and the laity. The characteristic of them has been that in one direction at least they have seen further, and that their moral sense has been higher than that of the community at large.

The prophet lives with God rather than with his fellow-men; and he is confident that the word which he speaks is the Word of God.

BENJAMIN JOWETT (1817–93)

Always, soon or late, humanity turns to excellence as naturally as a flower turns to the sun: mankind crucifies Christ and executes Socrates, and they die amid derision and hatred; but in the end they receive the homage of the world.

SIR R. LIVINGSTONE

[1] Compare St. Mark vi. 1–5. 'A prophet is not without honour, but in his own country'—to which might be added 'and in his own generation'.

193. St. Ignatius of Antioch

St. Ignatius was Bishop of Antioch at the beginning of the second century. He was condemned to the wild beasts because of his faith, and travelled under guard from Antioch to Rome during the summer and autumn of A.D. 120. On this, his last journey, he wrote a number of letters to Christian communities, including one sent on ahead to the church in Rome. When he arrived in Rome he suffered death in the arena.

Ignatius . . . to the church which presides in the place of the region of the Romans. . . .

Only pray for me that God would give me strength both inwardly and outwardly, that I may not only say, but do; that I may not only be called a Christian, but be found one. . . .

I write to all the churches; and signify to them all that I am willing to die for God, unless you hinder me. I beseech you that your goodwill may not come unseasonably upon me. Suffer me to be the food of wild beasts; whereby I may attain unto God. I am the wheat of God, and I am to be ground by the teeth of the wild beasts, that I may be found the pure bread of God. . . .

Remember in your prayers the Church which is in Syria, which now enjoys the Lord for its shepherd, instead of me; the Lord who said, 'I am the Good Shepherd.' He alone, together with your love to Him, will be their Bishop. . . . My spirit salutes you, and the love of the churches which have received me, for the name of Jesus Christ, and not as a passenger only. For even those churches that did not belong to me, conducted me in the way from city to city.

These things I write to you from Smyrna, by the Ephesians, those most worthy and happy persons. . . . As for those that went before me from Syria to Rome; to the glory of God, I suppose you are not ignorant of them. Signify to them that I draw near. . . . This have I written to you the 9th before the Calends of September. Fare ye well, unto the end, in the Patience of Jesus Christ.

ST. IGNATIUS (*c.* 35–*c.* 107), *Epistle to the Romans,*
William Whiston's translation

194. Ulfilas the Goth

The pagan Goths in eastern Europe attacked the Roman Empire many times in the fourth century, and among the hostages sent to Constantinople was a young Goth named Ulfilas. He became a Christian and determined to return to his people as a missionary. He was the first person to translate the Bible into a language in which no literature existed.

. . . When he was thirty Ulfilas was made a bishop and was allowed to go back as a missionary to his own people. Perhaps some of the new friends he had made in Constantinople thought it was a pity he should give up his chance of becoming famous as a great scholar, choosing instead to live among the wild folk in the 'barbarian' land. We can picture them saying: 'You'll be nobody when you get back there; whereas here you are known to be clever and you can take part in all the learned debates and read all the books you like in the great libraries.' But Ulfilas knew he had found a great treasure in the imperial city, and he did not want to stay to enjoy it by himself but to share it with the people at home whom he loved.

The Goths could neither read nor write. Stories and songs lived on from generation to generation because they could be spoken or sung, but nothing could be written down. Of course they could not read the Greek Bible which belonged to Ulfilas, for they did not understand the foreign language which he had learnt in Constantinople. Yet Ulfilas knew that if they were to become strong and faithful Christians they must be able to read the Bible for themselves. 'Somehow I must translate the Bible into the language of my people,' he thought to himself. But there was not even a proper alphabet he could use. There was only a primitive one made from the Runic letters which he himself had learnt when he was a boy. . . . These 'runes' were strange letters formed from straight lines and angles, and Ulfilas knew that they were far too clumsy for his great work. So he set to work and made a new alphabet based chiefly on the Greek.

Having made the alphabet, Ulfilas began his long task of translating the Bible into Gothic. He was very thankful that he had learnt both Greek and Latin in Constantinople, for now he could use his knowledge to bring the good news of Christ right into the homes of his people. Ulfilas was the first missionary to translate the Bible into a language which had never been written down. It was a great task and he could only do it in his spare time, for most of his days were spent in teaching the people and in training Gothic missionaries. It was not at all an easy or straightforward piece of work to do. There were many words in the Bible for which there was no Gothic word because they stood for things or actions which belonged to civilized people, and so the savage Goths would not understand them. When he tried to think of a Gothic word for 'mammon' (St. Matthew vi. 24) he remembered that for his people wealth meant not money but cattle and made it form part of the word meaning 'hoard of treasure' or 'mammon'. As he thought of the Christian Goths who had only just learned to live at peace instead of constantly fighting, he decided to leave out of the Gothic Bible the books of Samuel and Kings with their love of stories of battle in case they should awaken the love of war among the Christians.

The new Bible grew bit by bit until at last it was finished. Then it was carried by Gothic missionaries, traders and warriors from village to village and from camp to camp of the Goths. Far and wide it spread into their homes in distant places which Ulfilas himself could never have reached with the message.

PHYLLIS GARLICK, *Pioneers of the Kingdom*

195. The Story of Rahere, the King's Jester

King Henry I had many gay courtiers, but Rahere was the merriest of them all. 'He was,' says the chronicler, 'a pleasant-witted gentleman.' By his jokes and flattery he made friends with everyone, and in pageants and gay feasts provided amusement for the Court. Wherever he went, laughter followed him.

But this life of pleasure did not long satisfy Rahere. A time came when, in the words of the chronicler, 'God converted this man from the error of youth, and added to him many gifts of virtue; for they are often lowly born whom our Lord chooses to confound the mighty.'. . .

Rahere quitted the court, became a monk, and left England on a pilgrimage to Rome. On the way he met with many perils, for at that time travelling in Europe was dangerous. The roads were haunted by fierce brigands, and hungry packs of wolves roamed through the countryside.

Escaping from these dangers, Rahere, when he got to Rome, fell a victim to the plague which was then raging, and nearly died of it. During his sickness he made a vow that, if his life were spared, he would go back to London and there build a hospital for the sick poor.

As soon as he was strong enough, he started to return home. On his way he had a dream, and that dream was the cause why the great Hospital, which he founded, stands where it does in London today, and why it is called St. Bartholomew's.

For during his stay in Rome, Rahere often went to pray in a church dedicated to St. Bartholomew. In his dream the Saint seemed to appear to him in a shining light; and he heard a voice saying, 'Go and build a house in my name at Smithfield, and I will be its master and patron, and watch over it.'

Rahere, awaking from his dream, renewed his vow, and continuing his journey in haste, arrived in London; and from

London, which then stood within walls, he went out into the open country of Smithfield beyond.

Now at that time Smithfield was all muddy swamp and marsh, and did not look like a fit place for building a hospital. But the land belonged to the King, and Rahere, because of his dream, went to the King and begged that it might be given him.

The King, touched by his zeal and devotion, granted his request; and for ten years, with the citizens of London to help him, Rahere worked at draining the marsh, laying foundations, and building walls. And now, on the very spot, where he and his fellow-citizens laboured eight hundred years ago, stands the great Hospital which is called 'Bart's.' It is very much bigger, and covers much more ground now, than the Hospital built by Rahere. But there in Smithfield was built London's first Hospital—the first, indeed, that had ever been built in England.

LAURENCE HOUSMAN and C. H. K. MARTEN, The Long Journey

196. William Tindale

The story of how Tindale set about translating the Bible so that it could be printed and circulated throughout England.

With the invention of printing, Tindale had an instrument put into his hands which he was eager to use. He made up his mind that the ploughboy should know more of the Scriptures than the learned ecclesiastic.

Despairing of being able to carry out the work in England, Tindale made his way to the Continent and found in the Low Countries and in Germany a larger measure of freedom than in his native land. . . . Even so he was spied upon, persecuted and driven from place to place. But he went on with his work. His New Testament was published in 1525; copies were smuggled over to England by friendly merchants; and the book was circulated far and wide, to the no small chagrin of the authorities. Cardinal Wolsey took immediate action. Orders were issued that all copies of the New Testament must be given up, and burnings of these and other heretical books took place outside St. Paul's on two occasions, the first in February 1526 and the second in October of the same year. Not many copies survived the flames: what did survive was the love of the Bible in the hearts of the English people and their determination to possess it for themselves.

Having completed the New Testament, Tindale addressed himself to the larger task of translating the Old; and he was still engaged upon it when he was arrested and thrown into prison. Even then he persevered with his sacred task, and did not desist from it until he was led to the stake to meet a martyr's death on October 6th, 1536. He was a martyr in freedom's cause and did not die in vain: a few years later his dying prayer, 'Lord, open the King of England's eyes,' was answered, and the English Bible was set up in every parish church throughout the land.

JOHN PATTEN, These Remarkable Men

197. John Colet and his School

The scholars of the Renaissance were anxious to reform the schools, universities, and Church of their day. In England Dean Colet, the friend of More and Erasmus, founded St. Paul's School in 1512.

After mature deliberation he resolved, whilst living and in health, to devote his patrimony to the foundation of a school in St. Paul's Churchyard, wherein 153 children, without any restriction as to nation or country, who could already read and write, and were of 'good parts and capacities,' should receive a sound Christian education. . . . The children should be taught good literature, both Latin and Greek, 'specially Christian authors who wrote their wisdom in clean and chaste Latin, whether in prose or verse; for,' said Colet, 'my intent is by this school specially to increase knowledge, and worshipping of God and Our Lord Jesus Christ, and good Christian life and manners in the children.'

And, as if to keep this end always prominently in view, he placed an image of the 'Child Jesus', to whom the school was dedicated, standing over the master's chair in the attitude of teaching, with the motto, 'Hear ye Him.'

FREDERIC SEEBOHM, *The Oxford Reformers*

Dean Colet wrote a catechism for the children, which contained these precepts for living:

> Love God.
> Thrust down pride.
> Forgive gladly.
> Be sober of meat and drink.
> Use honest company.
> Reverence thine elders.
> Trust in God's mercy.
> Be always well occupied.
> Lose no time.
> Falling down, despair not.
> Ever take a fresh, new, good purpose.
> Persevere constantly.
> Wash clean.
> Be no sluggard.
> Awake quickly.
> Enrich thee with virtue.
> Learn diligently.
> Teach that thou hast learned, lovingly.

JOHN COLET (1467?–1519)

198. The Death of Cranmer

The Archbishop of Canterbury, Thomas Cranmer, used his influence to make the English Bible available to the ordinary people. He also compiled a service book in English which is known as the Book of Common Prayer. In Queen Mary's reign he was condemned to death as a heretic, but before his execution he signed recantations of the beliefs which were really his. Then came the day of execution.

On 21st March, 1556, the day before Passion Sunday, Cranmer, with two friars walking beside him, was brought by the mayor to St. Mary's Church [in Oxford], where a stage had been erected for him opposite the pulpit; the incision into the pillar for the fastening of the stage is still visible. Confronted with the great congregation, this shy man turned his face to the pillar and secretly prayed until the preacher, Henry Cole, Provost of Eton, mounted the pulpit. . . . Cranmer listened while Cole justified his execution in spite of his recent confession of the Catholic faith. . . .

Cole then called upon Cranmer to proclaim his recovered faith. Cranmer began by humbly entreating God's forgiveness for all his sins, and at the point when he said, 'There is one offence which most of all at this time doth vex and trouble me,' there was the general expectation that he would read his latest recantation. Instead he drew from his bosom a beautiful prayer of his own composition which he then read, and a written exhortation. The latter was free from all controversial matter; he bid the people 'obey your King and Queen, willingly and gladly,' exhorted them to charity and 'to hurt no man, no more than you would hurt your own natural loving brother or sister.' It is characteristic of him that even in this hour of his own destruction he should commend the cause of the humble to the generosity of the more fortunate, 'for if they ever had occasion to show their charity, they have it now at this present, the poor people being so many, and victuals so dear.' After reciting the Apostles' Creed, he used these words, introducing

them with a sentence which must have led his hearers to
expect from him his latest recantation which would be so great
a triumph for his opponents:

'And now I come to the great thing, that so much troubleth
my conscience, more than any thing that ever I did or said
in my whole life; and this is the setting abroad of a writing
contrary to the Truth; which now here I renounce and refuse, as things written with my hand, contrary to the truth
which I thought in my heart, and written for fear of death,
and to save my life, if it might be. . . . And forasmuch as
my hand offended, writing contrary to my heart, my hand
shall first be punished therefore; for, may I come to the fire,
it shall be first burned.'

In two sentences that followed he abjured the Pope and
stood by his former book on the sacrament. There was an
immediate outcry at this unexpected recantation of his recantations, and he was pulled down from the stage and hustled
along the street to the ditch opposite Balliol College, where
Latimer and Ridley had been burned.

After kneeling in prayer he stripped himself of his shirt,
bared his head and feet, shook hands with some of the by-
standers . . . and so went to the stake.

'And when the wood was kindled, and the fire began to
burn near him, stretching out his arm, he put his right hand
into the flame, which he held so steadfast and immovable
(saving that once with the same hand he wiped his face) that
all men might see his hand burned before his body was
touched. His body did so abide the burning of the flame,
with such constancy and steadfastness, that standing always
in one place, without moving his body, he seemed to move
no more than the stake to which he was bound: his eyes were
lifted up unto heaven, and often times he repeated his
"unworthy right hand," so long as his voice would suffer

him: and using often the words of Stephen, "Lord Jesus receive my spirit"; in the greatness of the flame he gave up the ghost.'

F. E. HUTCHINSON, *Cranmer and the English Reformation*

199. William the Silent

William the Silent led the Netherlanders in their struggle for independence against Spain and was assassinated by a fanatic in 1584.

The work to which he had devoted his life and for which he had died was never to be accomplished. The Netherlands, as he had known them, were never to be one nation. . . . What he had done was to create a new State, the United Provinces of the coming century, the 'Holland' of the future. Even when it fell short of what he wanted, his achievement was very great. For it was a hard and desperate task, to restore the self-respect and freedom of a people borne down by apparently inescapable doom, to fight a great power with such small instruments and to fight it for five years without hope and alone. It was a strange, almost a unique, thing to be the idol of a nation and to remain uncorrupted, to be oneself the guardian of the people's rights sometimes against the emotional impulse of the people themselves. . . . Few statesmen in any period, none in his own, cared so deeply for the ordinary comfort and the trivial happiness of the thousands of individuals who are 'the people'. He neither idealised them, nor overestimated them and he knew they were often wrong. . . . But he believed in them, not merely as a theoretical concept but as individuals, as men. Therein lay the secret of the profound and enduring love between him and them. . . . He respected in all men what he wished to have respected in himself, the right to an opinion.

There have been politicians more successful, or more subtle; there have been none more tenacious or tolerant. 'The wisest, gentlest and bravest man who ever led a nation,' he is one of the small band of statesmen whose service to humanity is greater than their service to their time or their people. In spite of the differences of speech or political theory, the conventions and complexities which make one age incomprehensible to another, some men have a quality of greatness which gives their lives universal significance. Such men, in whatever walk of life, in whatever chapter of fame, mystic or saint, scientist or doctor, poet or philosopher, and even—but how rarely—soldier or statesman, exist to shame the cynic, and to renew faith in humanity itself.

Of this number was William of Nassau, Prince of Orange, called the Silent.

C. V. WEDGWOOD, *William the Silent*

200. *The Death of Sir Philip Sidney*

Sir Philip Sidney was a poet, scholar, soldier and statesman who lived in the reign of Queen Elizabeth. He was universally loved and admired and his early death at the age of thirty-two, fighting the Spaniards in the Netherlands, was mourned by the whole country.

At the battle of Zutphen Sir Philip was cutting his way through the Spaniards in the last charge of the day when he was severely wounded in the leg. He was slowly making his way back to camp when 'being thirsty with excess of bleeding, he called for drink, which was presently brought him; but, as he was putting the bottle to his mouth, he saw a poor soldier carried along, who had eaten his last at the same feast, ghastly casting up his eyes at the bottle, which Sir Philip perceiving, took it from his head before he drank and delivered it to the poor man with these words, "Thy necessity is yet greater than mine."'

Sir Philip told the surgeon at the camp not to spare him pain. . . . 'When they began to dress his wound he . . . told them that while his strength was still entire, his body free from

fever and his mind able to endure they might freely use their art ... that they should bear witness they had indeed a sensible natured man under their hands, yet one to whom a stronger Spirit had given power above himself, either to do or suffer.'
... Later, when hope of life was ended, 'I do,' said he, 'with trembling heart most humbly entreat the Lord that the pangs of death may not be so grievous as to take away my understanding.'

'It was proved to him,' says a friend who was present, 'that although his understanding and senses should fail, yet that faith, which he had now could not fail. ... At this he did with a cheerful and smiling countenance put forth his hand, and clapt me softly on the cheeks. Not long after he lift up his eyes and hands, uttering these words, "I would not change my joy for the empire of the world;" for the nearer he saw death approach, the more his comfort seemed to increase.'

Compiled from Fulke Greville's *Life of Sidney* (1652), and Gifford's account of the *Death of Sidney* (edited 1808)

201. John Howard

John Howard was the first Englishman to rouse the public conscience about the state of the prisons. As Sheriff of the County of Bedford he inspected the prisons in the county, and then travelled thousands of miles a year through Great Britain and Ireland collecting evidence which was published in his book *The State of the Prisons*. He next investigated the cause and treatment of the plague in France, Italy, Malta, Asia Minor, and Turkey. He published the results of his research and then set off in search of further information, but he caught an infectious fever in Russia and died near the Black Sea in 1790.

No one can read Howard's life and remain in any doubt as to the cause of his undertaking his mission. He believed God had called him to it. But assuming that Howard was right, and that Christ summoned His disciples then and now as surely as He did on the borders of Galilee, why should Howard have been chosen for the task, a middle-aged, ailing, ex-grocer's apprentice?

First, he was brave, and in one who had to visit pestilence-ridden dungeons that even doctors shrank from, courage was a first necessity. Such courage Howard showed almost every day of his life, and the one occasion upon which a rather more spectacular variety was needed, Howard met as he might have been expected to meet it. A vessel upon which he was travelling in the Mediterranean was surprised by a Tunisian privateer and was in danger of capture when Howard himself fired the solitary cannon his boat possessed, loaded to the muzzle with old nails, spikes, etc., into the enemy crew. As a result the enemy sheered off, and Howard, with the rest of his companions, escaped being butchered or sold into slavery, or more probably blown up, since Howard's captain, having decided that this was a more desirable fate than falling into the hands of the enemy, had made preparations accordingly.

Physical courage, however, is comparatively common; moral courage, of the type that Howard possessed, rare indeed. Every day of his life the comfort so well within his reach beckoned him from the hardships and dangers he had undertaken, and as he progressed along the narrow path he had chosen, the temptations that faced him did not lessen; his growing fame led kings and princes all over Europe to flatter and to seek to entertain. Howard's method was the same with all; if he felt their interest could further his work he agreed to see them, and then told them all the most unpalatable facts he knew about their prison administration. Otherwise he sent a message to say he was too busy.

Howard was also thorough. He was never content with a statement on hearsay when he could confirm it with a personal investigation .and did not care in the least what time and trouble he spent in the collection of his facts. In this connection a pregnant footnote to his *Remarks on the Gaol Fever* may be quoted.

'It may not be improper here to put persons on their guard against an artifice not infrequently practised by gaolers in order to prevent a proper examination of their prisons. When a gentleman, particularly a magistrate, has come with an intention to visit the gaol, the keeper has pretended the utmost willingness to accompany him, but at the same time has artfully dropped a hint that he fears there may be some danger in it, as he is apprehensive that *the fever* has made its appearance among them. The visitor, alarmed, returns thanks for the kind caution, and instantly leaves the house. On such occasions I have always the more insisted on the necessity of a close inspection; and have generally found the prison very dirty indeed, and out of order, but no *fever*.'

Howard was sane. His zeal never carried him into the fanaticism or sentimentality that so often ruins a good cause; his proposals were always sober and practical. In this respect his business apprenticeship at the grocer's store, no doubt, served him in good stead. . . .

Howard loved his fellow-men. One feels that a large part of the appeal of his prison mission was the scope it gave him for relieving the distresses of those most in need of comfort. Though there is little evidence in proof, for Howard was the last man to let his left hand know what his right was doing, there is every reason to believe he spent large sums in freeing the victims of misfortune and injustice among the debtors. And even when he was furthest from home, his letters were filled with the minutest directions to his steward for little kindnesses to his dependants, in which not even his horse was forgotten. Vast schemes of benevolence are well enough for staggering the imagination, but a faithfulness in these little kindnesses enriches humanity at least as much. One likes the story of the

Dutch prisoner of war, whose unselfish labours for the comfort of his fellow victims so impressed Howard that he asked whether there was any way in which he could serve him. The sailor at first steadfastly affirmed his content with his lot, but finally confessed that when at home his greatest enjoyment was in a dish of tea. A week later a small sugar loaf, a pound of tea and a tin kettle arrived at the prison. . . .

[Howard's] tolerance and large-mindedness were other characteristics which fitted him above other men for his task. By education and choice he belonged to the most unbending of the Puritan sects, the Independents, yet he was not one of those who thought he could best maintain his own beliefs by decrying those of others. When at home he frequently worshipped in his own parish church, and was fast friends with his vicar. When abroad, he was once asked if he was a Catholic, and replied, 'I love good people of all religions.' . . . In Rome he did not fear to speak with the man some of his fellow sectarians knew as Anti-Christ. The usual formalities were dispensed with at this visit, and, after they had spent some time together, the Pope, at parting, laid his hand on Howard's head saying, 'I know you Englishmen set no value on these things, but the blessing of an old man can do you no harm;' . . . The Spirit of Christ was in each of them, and transcended the forms of man-made religion.

And indeed any consideration of Howard's character must end where it began, with the recognition that it was above all his unceasing endeavour to live in the knowledge and love of God that enabled him to do and be what he was.

S. KENNETH RUCK, in *Christian Social Reformers of the Nineteenth Century* (ed. Hugh Martin)

202. John Wesley

In 1738, at the age of thirty-five, John Wesley, already an earnest clergyman of quiet and orderly habits, found himself converted to a new and living faith.

John Wesley had found his life work. He set himself to travel from one end of the land to the other with the great and glorious story of God's love. To the smugglers and the weather-beaten fishermen of Cornwall, the weavers of Lancashire, the grimy-faced miners of the Bristol and Staffordshire coal pits, the fashionable people of Bath, he carried the same glad message, speaking to crowds wherever he could gather them in church or market place, meadow or quarry. The ignorant, untaught masses of the working people of England, who were uncared for by the Church, found in Wesley's preaching a message they could understand and which altogether changed their lives.

Wesley was a scholar and was accustomed to using long words, but he had to make his sermons very simple for the humble folk to understand. Often he would read them over to an old maidservant called Betty, crossing out every phrase which was too difficult for her, and so he taught himself to use simple words and short, direct sentences. At first the idea of preaching in the open air rather horrified him. Wesley the missionary had quite a struggle with the old Wesley who had been a very dignified scholar and churchman. 'I could scarcely reconcile myself,' he wrote, 'to this strange way of preaching in the fields, having been all my life, till very lately, so tenacious of every point relating to decency and order, that I should have thought that saving of souls almost a sin, if it had not been done in church.' But Wesley soon forgot all about himself and his dignity in the joy of serving men for Christ's sake.

The three great comrades, John and Charles Wesley and George Whitefield, worked together, each bringing a special gift to this great religious movement which was to change the very heart of England. Charles, the poet, put new ideas into songs which were soon sung in nearly every town and village in the land, and which we still sing to-day. In those days, of course, nothing like our present-day hymn book existed. George Whitefield, the mighty preacher whose wonderful voice drew thousands of people to listen to his message, was the orator of the movement. And John Wesley, with his tireless energy, his cool judgment, his gifts of learning and his genius for organization, was the great leader. . . .

When Wesley was eighty-two he wrote in his journal: 'It is now eleven years since I felt any such thing as weariness.' That year he tramped the streets of London for nearly a week in January, ankle deep in snow, collecting £200 with which to provide clothes for the very poor. He was a missionary to the end, not from a sense of duty, but because it was the gladdest, most worthwhile life that he knew. Almost his last words were: 'The best of all is, God is with us.'

PHYLLIS GARLICK, *Pioneers of the Kingdom*

203. *William Wilberforce*

William Wilberforce was a north-country gentleman who entered Parliament in 1780. There he made friends with William Pitt, the younger, who soon became Prime Minister.

One never-to-be-forgotten day in the year 1786 Wilberforce and Pitt sat talking together under a gnarled old oak tree in the woods which surrounded Pitt's country home. They were discussing the evils of the slave trade, and Wilberforce was plying his friend with questions. Should he take up the question of slavery in Parliament? He was willing, but had he the power for so great a task in which there would be few friends and many enemies? The King and the aristocracy, lawyers and merchants, all would be against him, for the slave trade was a means of wealth to the nation.

Suddenly as they talked there came afresh to Wilberforce the cry of the slaves, toiling and sweating under the lash in the plantations of the West Indies. He could picture what it must mean for these men and women to be torn away from their native land and sold as cheap labour in the British colonies. First there was the raiding and burning of African villages by native warriors. As the men, women, and children rushed from their huts they were caught and bound and fastened together with ropes round their necks, or put in irons and marched in companies to the coast. And always there would walk beside them an armed guard ready to use whip, sword, or gun to hurry their stumbling footsteps through forest and swamps, over rocks and burning sand to the waiting slave ship, when the horrors of the long sea voyage began.

Through the cry of the slaves Wilberforce heard the call of God. He saw plainly the path that he must follow. But had he the courage? He sat with bowed head, counting the cost before taking up the challenge. He wrote later of his great decision: 'I resolved to give notice on a fit occasion in the House of Commons of my intention to bring forward the abolition of the slave trade.'

Wilberforce knew that feelings were not enough; he must have actual facts to put before Parliament. And he believed that when those facts were known the conscience of the English people would be stirred to put an end to the trade. So he began quietly and patiently to collect the facts. A committee was formed, of which Granville Sharp, who was always thinking of schemes for the uplift of the slaves, was chairman. Thomas Clarkson, a Quaker who had read and written a great deal about the slave trade, was specially chosen to collect all the facts he could.

Wilberforce kept open house for all his friends who were interested in the anti-slavery cause, and often talked with them long into the night. Once a week the members of the Slave Committee dined with him and told him of their progress. Clarkson, who frequently went on journeys to the chief ports concerned in the slave trade, had many stories to tell the others of what he had seen and heard. He brought with him from Liverpool specimens of handcuffs, thumbscrews, and leg shackles which he had seen in a shop window. He was able to describe to Wilberforce exactly what a slave ship looked like, for he had seen two in port and had taken careful measure-ments of the tiny space (two to four square feet) allowed to each slave on the long voyage through the tropics from Africa to the West Indies. The slaves, branded like sheep with the marks of their owners, were packed close together and could neither lie down nor change their position night or day. Throughout the voyage they were kept in irons and fed in groups on rice out of a tub, and always there was the lash and the thumbscrew for any who rebelled. The thought of the horrors of that voyage inspired Wilberforce to make his first great speech in Parliament proposing the abolition of the slave trade.

[But] by this time merchants, business men and planters were beginning to be alarmed at the attempt to overthrow their source of wealth. . . . They began to attack Wilberforce and his friends, and they tried to prove that not only did the development of our British colonies depend on slavery, but the slaves themselves benefited by being brought under the influence of civilisation. They made out that the voyage from Africa to the West Indies was a sort of pleasure cruise which the slaves thoroughly enjoyed. . . .

Just when the full tide of opposition was bearing down on the abolitionists Wilberforce received a letter from the aged John Wesley which must have been a special encouragement. 'If God be for you,' wrote the splendid old man, 'who can be against you? Go on in the name of God, and in the power of His might, till even American slavery, the vilest that ever saw the sun, shall vanish away from it.'

It meant a long, hard fight before freedom could be won for the slaves. But the leader of the cause had patience and pluck and grim determination. . . .

The great moment arrived on February 3, 1807, when the Bill which Wilberforce brought forward for the abolition of the slave trade passed the House of Commons. What a day that was! The House of Commons full and excited, the gallery crowded, Thornton and Sharp, Macaulay and Grant among the rest; all eyes turned on that slight, small, stooping figure, the hero of the hour, who sat with his head in his hands as they cheered him round after round. Through England and Scotland prayers of thanksgiving were being offered for him that day. Over the continent of Africa and the West Indian plantations thousands of slaves had learned to speak his name as their champion, 'the good Wilberforce.' From his place in the House of Commons he had changed the mind of England; he had broken the chains of slavery and set free thousands of slaves that they might become men in the world of men. This was his hour of triumph. But in the heart of this great little man there was no room for self glory, only a surge of praise to God Who had given him strength for the task.

PHYLLIS GARLICK, *Pioneers of the Kingdom*

204. Elizabeth Fry

Elizabeth Fry was born of a Quaker family at Norwich in 1780. From her earliest days she devoted an untiring energy to helping her poorer neighbours, the sick and the destitute. After her marriage she lived in London where she learnt of the terrible condition of the women prisoners in Newgate and she determined to make a human contact with them.

On a cold January day in 1817, in the gloomy vestibule outside the women's yard at Newgate, two turnkeys might have been seen arguing with a lady. The row inside the yard was as great as usual. Even while they talked a woman rushed wildly out of a doorway and, with shrieks of furious laughter, snatched off the caps and headgear of every woman that she could reach. 'And she wouldn't stop at doing that to you, ma'am. Tear off your things—scratch and claw you—that's what they'd do, ma'am.' The turnkeys felt that delicacy forbade telling all that could be done by these harridans to a lady who ventured alone into their midst. They themselves knew better than to go in alone; they always went in two together. The Governor himself went in guarded. But the lady was obstinate. She had in her hand a powerful permit from the prison Governor. She smiled. . . . 'I am not afraid! Open the gate for me, please!'

Reluctant, sullen, and very much alarmed as to results, the turnkeys pressed open the gate against the begging, scuffling crowd, and Elizabeth Fry went in. The gate clanged and locked behind her. There was an instantaneous silence of sheer astonishment. Then every woman in the yard surged forward. Curiosity can be as dangerous as violence in a rough crowd. The lady was surrounded—the turnkeys could only see the tip of her white cap. . . . Elizabeth was in great danger. If she should now show fear, or say or do the wrong thing—But she had never been less afraid in her life. . . . She has picked up a filthy little child, and it can be seen fingering her bright chain. She lifts her hand for attention. . . .

'Friends, many of you are mothers. I too am a mother. I am distressed for your children. Is there not something we can do for these innocent little ones? Do you want them to grow up to become real prisoners themselves? Are they to learn to be thieves and worse? . . .'

Ah, she has touched the spot. She has pierced their armour to their very heart. What, save their children? Sobs and tears answered her appeal. They gave her a chair, and brought their children to show her. What tales they told in their inarticulate way, of wickedness, remorse, injustice, and despair! She remained with them for hours. She tried to cheer them by mention of a mysterious person called Christ (some of them asked who He was) and by telling them a curious story about a man who owned a vineyard and hired labourers by the hour, and paid the people who came in at the eleventh hour as much as the people who came in at the first. But chiefly she was showing them how to do something that in former days had been the chief sign of their humanity and that had been crushed out of them by harsh bondage—she was making plans with them. And when at last she bade them farewell, and the barred gate opened for her civil egress, she left behind her an inhabitant very strange to Newgate, one usually as much abandoned at its doors as at the very gate of Hell, that revivifying spirit of human vitality called Hope.

What, then, was Elizabeth Fry's remarkable project? It was very simple. Hardly anyone could disagree with it. It required no Act of Parliament, nor any great outlay of money. In short, it was nothing more nor less than to establish a school, in Newgate, for the children of prisoners and for juvenile criminals.

This idea appeared to her so natural, so modest in its scope, that she did not think it necessary to invoke the aid of the noblemen's committee or of her stately brothers-in-law. By the genius of her common sense and practical simplicity she took the shortest way to her end.

But it was much more than the shortest way. By invoking the aid of the women themselves, she put herself more than a hundred years in advance of the most advanced thinkers of her time. She set going in that instant the most genuine 'reform' that any have been able to approach. It was a renaissance of soul.

So, casually and simply Elizabeth Fry began a work which within a few months had grown to a dimension which carried her name all over the country, within three years was to place her in correspondence, as prison adviser, with most of the crowned heads of Europe, and which since her death has given her a niche among the great women of history.

JANET WHITNEY, *Elizabeth Fry*

205. Lord Shaftesbury's Character

Lord Ashley, Earl of Shaftesbury, devoted his life to fighting the cruelty that existed in nineteenth-century England. He led the movements to help the weak and ill-treated—the women and children who worked in factories and mines, the climbing chimney sweeps, the insane, the paupers, and the animals who were tortured for sport.

Antony Ashley Cooper was the eldest son of the sixth Earl of Shaftesbury. . . . Fortune, kinder to the world than to him gave him an unhappy boyhood. His father, who was a very competent Chairman of Committees in the House of Lords, and a heartless and negligent landlord in the county of Dorset, was hard and cold to all his children, and his mother, a daughter of the fourth Duke of Marlborough, was a woman of fashion who took no interest in them. It was a nice question whether he hated his home, or his first school, the Manor House, Chiswick, to which he was sent when he was seven, with the greater bitterness. . . . His biographer tells us that he cried, when at home, at the thought of going back to school, and that he cried, when at school, at the thought of going back to his home. . . .

Of his school he wrote: 'At seven went to school—a very large one at Chiswick. Nothing could have surpassed it for filth, bullying, neglect and hard treatment of every sort; nor had it in any respect any one compensating advantage, except perhaps, it may have given me an early horror of oppression and cruelty. . . .'

This, if a bad beginning to a man's life, was not so bad a beginning for the kind of career that [Shaftesbury] was to pursue.

Melbourne could shut his eyes to the misery of children working in his mines for fourteen hours out of twenty-four, and persuade himself that there was nothing very wrong with the arrangement that gave England for her rulers the cultivated and gracious men with whom he mixed. [Shaftesbury's] sensibilities were quickened by memories of his own childhood. . . .

To the law of indifference and drift, taught by philosophers and accepted by politicians, he opposed the simple revelation of his Christian conscience. This was his service to England; not the service of a statesman with wide plan and commanding will, but the service of a prophet speaking truth to power in its selfishness and sloth. When silence falls on such a voice, some everlasting echo still haunts the world, to break its sleep of habit or despair.

J. L. and B. HAMMOND, *Lord Shaftesbury*

206. Lord Shaftesbury's Achievements

A hundred years ago very few children went to school at all, and as early as five years old they might have to work in the mines and factories for twelve or even fourteen hours a day, for only a few pence a week.

The children had no playtime. They were taught nothing. Some worked in factories. Others worked in the dark mines half-starved and half-naked, dragging loaded trucks like pit-ponies, and lifting heavy weights, which made them grow up twisted and deformed. In some of the coal-mines were children only four or five years old, doing various kinds of work with their tiny hands for as many hours a day as the men and women.

All that child-labour has gone now. The man more than all others who brought it to an end was Lord Shaftesbury, a land-owner of Dorset. He forced people to know what was going on in those factories and underground places, and made his country-men ashamed of it. First he got a law passed through Parliament forbidding children or women to go down and work in the mines at all. Then he got the hours of labour, in places where they still did work, shortened to ten hours a day.

From that he went on to make things better for the poor children living in the slums of our great cities. Of one of these children Lord Shaftesbury wrote:

'I recollect the case of a boy who, during last winter, passed the greater part of his nights in the iron roller of Regent's Park. He climbed every evening over the railings and slipped to his shelter, where he lay in some sort of comfort.'

Lord Shaftesbury and others took much interest in Ragged Schools where the very poorest could be taught free. These schools grew and grew until thousands came to them. Twenty years after they had been started, Lord Shaftesbury said: 'I would rather be Head of the Ragged Schools than have the command of armies.'

Such schools went on till better schools with free education were provided for all. But Lord Shaftesbury never stopped work; as soon as one good thing had been set going, he started on another. Nearly always he had against him people who made money out of the evils he was trying to get rid of; and nearly always he won. The people of this country began to know that any cause for which he spoke and worked was a cause which needed looking into.

One of the most cruel occupations for little boys at this time was to climb up narrow chimneys, sometimes only a foot wide, and sweep them. Lord Shaftesbury told Parliament that he himself knew of a child at that moment (1834) of four and a half years, and another of six years, employed in sweeping chimneys. But many laws had to be passed before that evil came to an end.

Lord Shaftesbury was also a friend of shoe-blacks and

street-costers; and in gratitude for what he had done for them the costers of London, when he was an old man, made him a member of their Union.

As [Shaftesbury] became known to the poor people in the slums, he was able to go where others dared not. He went and talked to burglars; they all welcomed him; for they knew that he was really their friend. Many of them he helped to go overseas and start a new life.

Even the thieves of London loved him; and here is a story of what once happened to him. Lord Shaftesbury had a gold watch which he valued very much, not because it was gold, but because it had been given to him by his old nurse whom he loved dearly when he was a child. One day he went into the East End of London and had his watch stolen. This made him very sorrowful. But two days later there came a ring at the bell of his house; and when the servant went and opened the door, he found no one there, but in the porch lay a sack; and in the sack was something that moved. When the sack was opened, inside was found a small boy bound with rope and gagged; and round his neck was tied the gold watch, and with it a scrap of paper, on which was written, 'This is the boy that stole your watch. You can do what you like with him.' Or, if those were not the very words, that is what they meant.

Lord Shaftesbury was very glad to have his watch back again; but he was still more glad to be given the boy who had stolen it. He did not punish him, nor get him sent to prison; he just took care of him himself, and had him trained so that he could make his living more honestly.

Not long after Lord Shaftesbury's death, a new street was being made in London; in his memory it was called Shaftesbury Avenue. At the end of it is Piccadilly Circus; and in the middle of the Circus is a fountain, which is also named after him. On the top of the fountain is a figure of Love, with great wings, flying swiftly, and in his outstretched hand he carries a bow. That figure was made to remind us of the good Lord Shaftesbury, who spent his life in doing service to his fellow men.

LAURENCE HOUSMAN and C. H. K. MARTEN, *The Long Journey*

207. Abraham Lincoln's Address at Gettysburg

Lincoln was President of the United States of America during the Civil War. As a Christian statesman he hated war but believed it necessary to defeat the Southern States which had left the Union. He made this speech at the dedication of a cemetery where those killed in the battle of Gettysburg were buried.

Fourscore and seven years ago our fathers brought forth upon this continent a new nation, conceived in liberty, and dedicated to the proposition that all men are created equal. Now we are engaged in a great civil war, testing whether that nation, or any nation so conceived and so dedicated, can long endure. We are met on a great battlefield of that war. We have come to dedicate a portion of that field as a final resting place of those who here gave their lives that that nation might live. It is altogether fitting and proper that we should do this.

But in a larger sense we cannot dedicate, we cannot consecrate, we cannot hallow this ground. The brave men, living and dead, who struggled here, have consecrated it far and above our power to add or detract. The world will little note, nor long remember, what we say here, but it can never forget what they did here. It is for us, the living, rather to be dedicated here to the unfinished work they have thus far so nobly advanced. It is rather for us to be here dedicated to the great task remaining before us, that from these honored dead we take increased devotion to that cause for which they here gave the last full measure of devotion; that we here highly resolve that the dead shall not have died in vain, that the nation shall, under God, have a new birth of freedom, and that the government of the people, by the people, and for the people, shall not perish from the earth.

ABRAHAM LINCOLN (1809–65), *Dedicatory Address at Gettysburg Cemetery*, 19 November 1863

208. Florence Nightingale

Florence Nightingale was convinced that God intended her to do some special work and in spite of many difficulties she trained herself to work as a nurse. In those days nursing was not considered suitable work for an educated lady and her family opposed her choice and made constant demands on her time. In December 1850 she wrote, 'O weary days, O evenings that never end! For how many long years I have watched that drawing-room clock and thought it would never reach the ten! . . . In my thirty-first year I see nothing desirable but death.'

Four years later her opportunity came. The Secretary at War, who was a friend of her family, asked her to take a group of nurses to work among the sick and wounded soldiers of the Crimean War.

Everything, as *The Times* correspondent had truly observed, was lacking, and the wards were filthy and verminous. There were no bedsteads, no blankets, no sheets, no chairs, no forks, no plates—indeed there did not appear to be even any medical equipment. The poor soldiers lay in their dirty blood-stained uniforms without even shirts and their wounds had perhaps not been dressed for several days. A few decrepit Chelsea pensioners were their only attendants except for some orderlies who were utterly incompetent. 'A man is selected for an orderly,' said a subsequent report, 'who does not fit well into the ranks, and who is an ugly or clumsy fellow.' The trouble, Florence quickly realized, had begun long before the men reached Scutari. In 1854 there were no air ambulances and even before arriving at the base hospitals the sick and wounded had had to endure a rough passage across the Black Sea lasting anything from six to eight days in an uncomfortable over-crowded boat. Sometimes there were not enough doctors or orderlies on board to attend to them and occasionally they had not even had enough food. In the four months since the beginning of the campaign, out of every thousand men that had embarked at Balaclava seventy-four had died on board. So they were often in a critical condition before they were disembarked, and the landing itself was difficult and very painful for men with severe wounds, as there was no proper pier at Scutari. The stretchers had to be brought down to where the transports were moored alongside a dilapidated landing-stage and from there the casualties were carried up the steep hill. When the weary stretcher-bearers did eventually reach the hospitals there were not enough beds to receive the patients and they were deposited on palliasses, a makeshift kind of mattress contrived by filling rough canvas bags with chopped straw. The climax of their misery was reached when it was found that there were not even bedsteads and that the palliasses had to be put straight down on to the cold floor.

On the very day after the nurses had arrived at Scutari, 5th November 1854, the battle of Inkerman was fought and she was warned that within a few days she might expect over five hundred more sick and wounded men to arrive in the already overcrowded hospital. This was a real challenge to her capacities, a challenge that was all the more rousing as the time for preparation was so short and there was so much to be done. It was then that her genius for organization asserted itself and her commanding spirit rose to meet this terrible emergency. All those years she had spent in studying hospitals and in training herself were now to bear fruit. . . .

Her nurses were set down to make more palliasses at once, and one of the Sellon sisters graphically records how hard they worked. Then the wards must be got clean—and how surprised the Purveyor must have been when he soon received a requisition for three hundred scrubbing brushes! This was only the first shock he had to endure, for Florence tells us: 'This morning I foraged in the Purveyor's store—a cruise I make almost daily, as the only way of getting things. No mops, no plates, no wooden trays (the engineer is having these made), no slippers, no shoe brushes, no blacking, no knives and forks, no spoons, no scissors (for cutting the men's hair which is literally alive), no basins, no towelling, no chloride of zinc.'. . .

She got two special kitchens established in different parts of the vast building in which extra diets and nourishing food could be prepared which the nurses could then take to those patients who needed them most. The ingredients of these delicacies she supplied from her own stores. . . .

Another very urgent need was to tackle the problem of providing clean linen, and Florence quickly got a laundry started for the hospital. Before she came only six shirts had been washed in a month by the fraudulent civilians who had contracted to perform this service, and even these could hardly be called 'washed', as all the 'washing' had been done in cold water and with scarcely any soap. One batch of linen handled in this way, although called 'clean' was so full of vermin that it had to be destroyed. So she took a house near by at her own expense, got the Royal Engineers to install a boiler and employed the soldiers' wives in this essential hospital service. . . .

Meanwhile, although these extraneous duties took up a disproportionate amount of her time and energy, Florence always worked her hardest at the task for which she had primarily come to Scutari, the nursing of the soldiers. This was the part of the work she preferred, she was never so happy as in the wards and it was as a nurse that most people admired her. . . . While the officials saw (and sometimes feared) the talented administrator, it was the sympathetic nurse that the soldiers loved, and her kindness was what they most vividly

remembered. The men idolized her and 'kissed her shadow'
as she passed along the wards.

LUCY SEYMER, *Florence Nightingale*

209. *A Letter from Florence Nightingale*

Florence Nightingale devoted most of her time at Scutari to trans-
forming the insanitary, filthy barracks into a clean and well organized
hospital. She had to fight the inertia and corruption of officials to
secure adequate supplies of medicine, food, and clothing. She wrote
long reports to the War Minister in London containing her criticisms
and recommendations. Yet she found time to give personal attention
and sympathy to her patients who regarded her as the personification
of kindness and gentleness. The letter that follows is typical of the
hundreds she wrote to the soldiers' families.

Barrack Hospital,
Scutari.
April 19 '55

I remember your poor brother, Alfred Knight's death on
the 30th December in this Hospital. We received above five
hundred Patients dying of dysentry in the week in which we
received him. He was admitted on the 22nd December, he was
ill but eight days—he was always quite sensible and talked
much about 'home', his home on earth and his home in heaven,
till within the last twelve hours when he became insensible to
all pain and anxiety—and the next morning was relieved from
suffering.

He prayed much—and saw the Clergyman the day before
he died. He was quite aware of his danger and quite resigned
to leave this world for a better.

He was much respected by his Regiment and his comrades
have told me that he was 'a very good liver.'

He was kept very clean and well cared for during his illness
and was constantly fed with Arrowroot and Port Wine and
attended by the best of surgeons.

He spoke much of a brother while he was ill.

He left nothing whatever which I could send you. For he had lost his kit, like thousands of others in the Crimea and had nothing. Hoping that I have been able to give you some comfort, with sincere sympathy for your grief, believe me

Yours truly,

FLORENCE NIGHTINGALE

210. Octavia Hill

Octavia Hill devoted her life to rousing public opinion about the slums and overcrowding of our cities. We owe a great debt to her for the improvement in housing standards in the last fifty years. She also worked hard to secure open spaces for people's enjoyment and was one of the founders of the National Trust.

She acquired a conviction, held with ever-deepening intensity, of the unique value of every individual, a value derived from the faith that each was the child of God and created to do His will. The importance of the individual in a democratic state is very generally conceded, and though probably most people would not be prepared to deny to him the status of a child of God, this has now come to be regarded as an academic question, irrelevant to practical policy. To Octavia it was the root of the matter. The material help she gave was merely a means to a spiritual end, and she judged any measure of reform by its effectiveness in promoting the growth of character. . . .

Her view of the relation of the individual to the State was equally based on her belief in the dignity of man. Being a member of a community confers certain rights and responsibilities; it is possible to stress either. Octavia always stressed the latter both for herself and for others. What one was able to contribute to the community always seemed to her more important than what one could get out of it. . . .

Octavia was an idealist, but not one of those who can believe comfortably that with a little good will all will come right. Her idealism was based on a realistic appreciation of the facts of human nature. She condemned alike the vague benevolence of the stupid and the complacency of the self-interested, knowing both to be equally dangerous and equally selfish. She distrusted improvised remedies and haphazard reforms; impulsive as she was by temperament she had learnt to curb her eagerness and to allow her reason to work on every problem presented to her before she took any action. She demanded of herself and of those who would work with her, all the intelligence and foresight that they could bring and the patience to look at every aspect of the matter in hand. If she was dealing with Open Spaces she must have a map of the whole district, and consider the rights of the owners, the needs of agriculture or industry, and the possibilities of recreation; if she was dealing with a poor family she must know all its commitments and responsibilities, all sources of relief, and as far as practicable all the possibilities open to each member. In things great or small, she demanded a plan, a really constructive effort based on the realities of the situation.

E. MOBERLY BELL, *Octavia Hill*

211. Kagawa

The rapid industrialization of Japan in the late nineteenth and early twentieth century created many problems for her people. Kagawa, a member of the small Christian community in Japan, has devoted his life to the poor and exploited. He has organized labour unions and roused public opinion to improve housing conditions in the slums of Japan's industrial cities.

To Kobe's worst slum, where 11,000 people were herded together in squalid, prison-like homes six feet square, where vice and disease were rampant, and light and air struggled for existence, came this young apostle aflame with the love of God. Amid all its poverty and wretchedness, its squalor and ugliness he made his home, for only in this way could he learn to understand the people he longed to help. He found an empty house where no one would live because a murder had taken place there. From the time that Kagawa came to live in it, in the Christmas of 1909, that hut was no longer shunned from fear, but was a home greatly sought after because love had come to dwell there. His six foot room became a heaven on earth to men and women who had never seen love like this in action. There the drunkard was tenderly nursed back to his senses, the blind beggar tapping his way in the dark along the narrow filthy streets found a roof for his head and warmth for his body under half a warm rug, and the children who knew so little of love found a friend.

At first his listeners did not understand much when he spoke of the love of a Person called Yaso (Jesus), but before long they began to wonder if this Yaso was not some relative of the speaker. For the love of Christ that Kagawa spoke of was made real to them by the acts of sympathy and kindness of this very human apostle, who dressed in working-men's clothes and spoke the simple language that they could understand.

To his work in the slums among the very poor and the overworked, Kagawa brought the sensitive heart of a poet and the keen mind of a scientist. While he poured out his life in loving service for the suffering folk around him, he also brought his mind to bear on the problems of poverty and the working conditions of the poor labourers and factory workers. In little more than a generation Japan had become a great industrial nation, but most people were blind to the suffering and the needs of the poor, and scarcely realized that in their very midst lived the victims of slum conditions and sweated labour.

The saint of the slums who would never hit back in his own defence, knew how to fight the cause of the weak. He fought ignorance with hard facts, and indifference with a burning indignation. By his work in the Shinkawa slums and the grim facts that he broadcast in his books and his preaching, Kagawa forced these evils on the attention of the nation. It was his courageous lead that eventually moved the Government to undertake a campaign for wiping out the slums in six of the largest cities of Japan, and to make improvements in the condition of Japanese workers. . . .

As a result of his work on behalf of the labouring folk of Japan Kagawa became a national figure. In the devastating earthquake of 1923, when the greater part of Tokyo was laid in ruins, he gave a lead in relief work which made him one of the heroes of the hour. . . . The Government was greatly impressed by his knowledge and devotion as well as his power of organizing, and for his part Kagawa found many new ways of serving his people through his responsible work as a kind of general adviser on social and economic questions. . . .

With all his passionate love for his own people Kagawa's vision travels far beyond Japan; he is a citizen of all the world. 'I love Japan very much,' he says, 'and for that reason I am serving the nation. But I never forget that I am a citizen of the kingdom of heaven first.' . . . He dreams of a world awakened to the love of God as the whole Christian Church throughout the world unites in showing forth the Gospel of Christ.

PHYLLIS GARLICK, *Pioneers of the Kingdom*

212. *Sir Ronald Ross and the Cause of Malaria*

If it is better to save life than to destroy it, then laud and honour should be given to those patient scientific investigators whose studies have shown how to lessen human suffering and prevent the spread of fatal diseases. Before a disease can be prevented it must be understood. . . .

No better examples could be found of the benefits of such work to the human race than are afforded by the studies of tropical and other diseases carried on in recent years. Perhaps the most important of these diseases is malarial fever, which causes the death of millions of people yearly in India alone. When Sir Ronald Ross was carrying out at Bangalore the intricate and minute researches required to determine the cause of malaria and its remedy, he wrote the pleading lines:

> The painful faces ask, can we not cure?
> We answer, No, not yet; we seek the laws.
> O God, reveal thro' all this thing obscure
> The unseen, small, but million-murdering cause.

At that time it was believed by most people that malaria was caused by some kind of vapour or 'miasma' which rose from swampy or marshy land. It is now known to be transmitted by certain mosquitoes which can harbour the germs of the disease and convey them from one person to another. . . .

The theory that mosquitoes are carriers of disease, and that malaria is transmitted by them or flies, was put forward fourteen centuries ago, and was revived in more modern times, but systematic practical study was necessary to establish it. . . .

To Sir Ronald Ross belongs the honour of tracing the various stages of the existence of the parasite in the body of the mosquito until it was ripe for injection into a human being by the bite of the insect. He proved by numerous experiments that the only means by which a healthy person can acquire malaria is by the bite of a mosquito which has previously bitten someone whose blood contains the particular organisms associated with the disease. . . . On the eve of this remarkable discovery, Ross offered up a prayer of thanks which makes a beautiful supplement to the lines written several years before:

> This day relenting God
> Hath placed within my hand
> A wondrous thing; and God
> Be praised. At His command,

Seeking His secret deeds,
With tears and toiling breath,
I find thy cunning seeds,
O million-murdering Death.

I know this little thing
A myriad men will save.
O Death, where is thy sting?
Thy victory, O Grave?

SIR RICHARD GREGORY, *Discovery*

213. *Albert Schweitzer*

Albert Schweitzer is probably the most gifted genius of our age, as well as its most prophetic thinker. A doctor four times over—in philosophy, in theology, in music and in medicine—he was earning three of these distinctions while in his twenties, at an age when most men are still serving their apprenticeship in one; and for him they are but incidental to the classic contributions which he has made to each of these subjects. What is rarer still, his practical achievements and manual skill have kept pace with his scholarship: a surgeon, a self-taught architect and builder, an agriculturalist, an organist and a consultant in organ-craft, he has further proved his ability as an administrator in founding, organizing and maintaining a hospital in the tropics.

In spite of much opposition from his friends Schweitzer gave up a brilliant career in Europe to become a medical missionary in West Africa. He and his wife left Günsbach in Alsace on Good Friday 1913 and reached Lambaréné in West Africa towards the end of April.

A disappointment awaited Schweitzer on his arrival at the Mission Station. The promised hospital was not in evidence: it had not been possible to recruit labour. Not to be outdone by any frustration, and anxious only to begin work without delay, he utilized a windowless broken-roofed fowl-house for his surgery, his bungalow for his dispensary, and the open sun-smitten courtyard for the treatment of his patients till the regular evening shower drove them for cover to his verandah. . . . From the very first he was besieged with patients who came to him upstream and downstream from distances of anything . . . up to two hundred miles. These conditions caused him needless fatigue and acute anxiety, since they involved the loss of much precious time. . . . In his first nine months he treated nearly two thousand patients. Malaria, leprosy, sleeping sickness, dysentery, tropical ulcers, . . . these were the commonest plagues.

It is not surprising that he is known all over the province of Gaboû as Oganga—Medicine-Man—or that the natives ascribe to him magical powers far beyond their own witch-doctors. What impressed them most of all was the use of anaesthetics, and they talked a great deal about this. As a little girl put it in a letter to one of her Sunday School correspondents in Alsace: 'Since Oganga came here wonderful things have happened. First of all he kills the sick people; then he cures them; and after that he wakes them up again.'

The right of the western nations to dominate peoples who stand on a lower cultural level is accepted by Schweitzer, but only on condition that there is a serious intention to educate those peoples morally and materially. For Schweitzer, missionary endeavour depends neither on dogma nor doctrine, but on the simple Gospel that teaches the liberation of the world through the Spirit of Jesus, as it went out to man in the Sermon on the Mount.

GEORGE SEAVER, *Albert Schweitzer. The Man and his Mind*

214. Schweitzer's Call to Service

Of his decision to give up a brilliant career in Europe to become a doctor in Equatorial Africa, Schweitzer writes:

The plan which I meant now to put into execution had been in my mind for a long time, having been conceived so long ago as my student days. It struck me as incomprehensible that I should be allowed to lead such a happy life, while I saw so many people around me wrestling with care and suffering. Even at school I had felt stirred whenever I got a glimpse of the miserable home surroundings of some of my schoolfellows and compared them with the absolutely ideal conditions in which we children of the parsonage at Günsbach lived. While at the University and enjoying the happiness of being able to study and even to produce some results in science and art, I could not help thinking continually of others who were denied that happiness by their material circumstances or their health. Then one brilliant summer morning at Günsbach, during the Whitsuntide holidays . . . there came to me, as I awoke, the thought that I must not accept this happiness as a matter of course, but must give something in return for it. Proceeding to think the matter out at once with calm deliberation, while the birds were singing outside, I settled with myself before I got up, that I would consider myself justified in living till I was thirty for science and art, in order to devote myself from that time forward to the direct service of humanity. Many a time already I had tried to settle what meaning lay hidden for me in the saying of Jesus 'Whosoever would save his life shall lose it, and whosoever shall lose his life for My sake and the Gospels shall save it.' Now the answer was found. In addition to the outward, I now had inward happiness.

ALBERT SCHWEITZER, *My Life and Thought*

215. Why Schweitzer went to Africa

Schweitzer writes:

I gave up my position of professor in the University of Strasbourg, my literary work, and my organ-playing, in order to go as a doctor to Equatorial Africa. How did that come about?

I had read about the physical miseries of the natives in the virgin forests; I had heard about them from missionaries, and the more I thought about it the stranger it seemed to me that we Europeans trouble ourselves so little about the great humanitarian task which offers itself to us in far off lands. The parable of Dives and Lazarus seemed to me to have been spoken directly of us! We are Dives, for, through the advances of medical science, we now know a great deal about disease and pain, and have innumerable means of fighting them: yet we take as a matter of course the incalculable advantages which this new wealth gives us! Out there in the colonies, however, sits wretched Lazarus, the coloured folk, who suffers from illness and pain just as much as we do, nay, much more, and has absolutely no means of fighting them. And just as Dives sinned against the poor man at his gate because for want of thought he never put himself in his place and let his heart and conscience tell him what he ought to do, so do we sin against the poor man at our gate.

ALBERT SCHWEITZER, *On the Edge of the Primeval Forest*

216. Elizabeth Pilenko

Elizabeth Pilenko came from a wealthy land-owning family in the south of Russia. She went to the Women's University of St. Petersburg and began at the age of eighteen, while still a student, to teach in the evening courses at the great Putilov factory. She published two books of poems and was a close friend of some of the best-known younger Russian poets.

She became a keen socialist revolutionary, and during the years 1914–1917 her life was taken up with revolutionary activities. After the October Revolution she worked with extraordinary skill and audacity in rescuing victims from the Terror. Later she became Mayor of her own home town, working for justice between the Whites and the Reds, both of whom had resorted to violence against their opponents. She was denounced as a Bolshevist, tried and acquitted.

In 1923 she came to Paris. The excesses of the Revolution as it developed revolted her, though she remained to her death a staunch advocate of its principles. She found her way back to religious faith largely under the influence of Serge Bulgakov, who had been a Marxist. She presented herself to the authorities of the Russian Church in Paris and announced that she wished to become a religious, 'beginning at once, to-day,' and to found a monastery. She had her way, but she was not the traditional Russian Orthodox religious. She was accused by some of neglecting the long services and the traditional contemplation. 'I must go my way,' she said. 'I am for the suffering people.' In the early morning she was at the markets buying cheap food for the people she fed, bringing it back in a sack on her back. She was a familiar figure in the slum, in her poor black habit and her worn-out men's shoes.

The many Russian refugees in France in those days were stateless persons, many of them poverty-stricken, without privilege, without claim on any of the services which the country provided for the poor. Mother Maria (as she was now called) worked among the poorest. She discovered that Russians who contracted tuberculosis were lying in a filthy hovel on the banks of the Seine. . . . With ten francs in her pocket she bought a château and opened a sanatorium.

Then she found that there were hundreds of Russians in lunatic asylums all over Europe. They had just 'disappeared' into these institutions, where no questions were asked about them. She raised a public outcry and got many of them released. . . .

When the German occupation took place Mother Maria summoned her chaplain and told him that she felt that her particular duty was to render all possible assistance to persecuted Jews. She knew that this would mean imprisonment and probably death, and she gave him the option of leaving. He refused. For a month the convent was a haven for Jews. Women and children were hidden within its walls. Money poured in to enable them to escape from France and hundreds were got away. At the end of a month the Gestapo came. Mother Maria was arrested and sent to the concentration camp at Ravensbruck. Her chaplain was sent to Buchenwald, where he died of starvation and overwork.

The story of her life in the camp is only now being pieced together. She was known even to the guards as 'that wonderful Russian nun,' and it is doubtful whether they had any intention of killing her. She had been there two and a half years when a new block of buildings [which consisted of gas chambers] was erected in the camp, and the prisoners were told that these were to be hot baths. A day came when a few dozen prisoners from the women's quarters were lined up outside the buildings. One girl became hysterical. Mother Maria, who had not been selected, came up to her. 'Don't be frightened,' she said. 'Look, I shall take your turn,' and in line with the rest, she passed through the doors. It was Good Friday, 1945.

The Christian News Letter, 17 April 1946

217. Light in Darkness

The light shineth in the darkness, and the darkness did not absorb it:[1] Imagine yourself standing on some headland in a dark night. At the foot of the headland is a lighthouse or beacon,

[1] St. John i. 5 (retranslated).

not casting rays on every side, but throwing one bar of light through the darkness. It is some such image that St. John had before his mind. The divine light shines through the darkness of the world, cleaving it, but neither dispelling it nor quenched by it. . . . Take any moment of history and you find light piercing unillumined darkness—now with reference to one phase of the purpose of God, now another. The company of those who stand in the beam of the light by which the path of true progress for that time is discerned is always small. Remember Wilberforce and the early Abolitionists; remember the twelve Apostles and the company gathered round them. What is seen conspicuously in these two examples is always true; and as we think of the spiritual progress of the race this truth finds a fresh illustration. As we look forwards, we peer into darkness, and none can say with certainty what course the true progress of the future should follow. But as we look back, the truth is marked by beacon-lights, which are the lives of saints and pioneers; and these in their turn are not originators of light, but rather reflectors which give light to us, because themselves they are turned to the source of light. . . . To St. John's deep spiritual insight it is apparent that the redemption of man is part, even if the crowning part, of a greater thing— the redemption, or conquest, of the universe. Till that be accomplished the darkness abides, pierced but unillumined by the beam of divine light. And the one great question for everyone is whether he will 'walk in darkness' or 'walk in light'.

WILLIAM TEMPLE (1881–1944), *Readings in St. John's Gospel*

218. By faith . . .

'Now faith is the substance of things hoped for, the evidence of things not seen.'[1] By faith the first Christians defied the Imperial Power of Rome 'and through great persecution, out

[1] Hebrews xi. 1 (see the whole chapter).

of weakness were made strong.' By faith when Rome was overthrown many strove to keep alive the Knowledge of the Kingdom through darkness and chaos. Of such were Augustine, Paulinus and Alcuin, and the Irish scholars.

By faith, when in time wealth and power had corrupted the Church, St. Francis and St. Teresa, Wycliff, More, Colet and Erasmus strove to establish a simpler and purer rule. By faith, through Luther and George Fox, Bunyan and John Wesley a fresh vision of truth was revealed. 'These all died in faith and confessed that they were strangers and pilgrims on the earth. For they that say such things declare plainly that they seek a country.'

By faith, having learnt from them the lessons of the Kingdom, a whole glorious company devoted their lives to the suffering and outcast so that the Kingdom might come on earth as it is in heaven.

Of these were Thomas Coram, Lord Shaftesbury and Dr. Barnardo who established the first schools and Homes and obtained the first legal protection for poor and friendless children. Of these, too, were John Woolman and William Wilberforce and in our own time Albert Schweitzer and Michael Scott, all of whom have given themselves to the service of the exploited African.

By faith too Elizabeth Fry brought comfort and hope to the miserable prisons and Florence Nightingale reformed the Hospitals. 'These chose rather to suffer affliction with the wretched' than to enjoy the position and privileges to which they were born.

All these by faith faced and overcame opposition and selfishness, apathy and stupidity and manifold disappointments and difficulties.

David Livingstone, Robert Morrison, Mary Slessor and William Carey are a few of the many who by faith 'wrought righteousness' in far countries and among strange peoples, leaving their homes to spread the knowledge of the Kingdom abroad.

By faith too lived and died those who 'had trial of cruel mockings and scourgings, yea moreover of bonds and imprisonment' from the early martyrs Ignatius and Perpetua and countless others and so through the ages, Joan of Arc, Latimer and Ridley, the seventeenth-century Quakers, the Covenanters down to those thousands of Catholics and Protestants alike who have suffered and are suffering today for their faith in Germany, Russia, in Eastern Europe and in China.

All these, prophets and teachers, helpers of the helpless, missionaries and martyrs by Faith served the Kingdom 'whose builder and maker is God'.

'Wherefore seeing we also are compassed about with so great a cloud of witnesses, let us lay aside every weight and the sin which doth so easily beset us and let us run with patience the race that is set before us.'

U. K. MOORE

PART FIVE

THE KINGDOM PERFECTED

I. THE CONQUEST OF DEATH

219. *Last Lines*

These were the last lines written by Emily Brontë before her death.

No coward soul is mine,
No trembler in the world's storm-troubled sphere:
I see Heaven's glories shine,
And faith shines equal, arming me from fear.

O God within my breast,
Almighty, ever-present Deity!
Life—that in me has rest,
As I—undying Life—have power in Thee!

Vain are the thousand creeds
That move men's hearts: unutterably vain;
Worthless as withered weeds,
Or idlest froth amid the boundless main,

To waken doubt in one
Holding so fast by Thine infinity;
So surely anchored on
The steadfast rock of immortality.

With wide-embracing love
Thy Spirit animates eternal years,
Pervades and broods above,
Changes, sustains, dissolves, creates and rears.

Though earth and man were gone,
And suns and universes cease to be,
And Thou wert left alone,
Every existence would exist in Thee.

There is not room for Death,
Nor atom that his might could render void;
Thou—Thou art Being and Breath,
And what Thou art may never be destroyed.

EMILY BRONTË (1818–48)

220. *The Dead and the Living*

He was but a Heathen that said, If God love a man, He takes him young out of this world; and they were but Heathens, that observed that custome, to put on mourning when their sons were born, and to feast and triumph when they dyed. But thus much we may learne from these Heathens, that if the dead, and we, be not upon one floore, nor under one story, yet we are under one roofe. We think not a friend lost, because he is gone into another roome, nor because he is gone into another Land; And into another world, no man is gone; for that Heaven, which God created, and this world, is all one world. If I had fixt a Son in Court, or married a daughter into a plentiful fortune, I were satisfied for that son and that daughter. Shall I not be so, when the King of Heaven hath taken that son to himselfe, and married himselfe to that daughter, for ever? I spend none of my Faith, I excercise none of my Hope, in this, that I shall have my dead raised to life againe.

This is the faith that sustains me, when I lose by the death of others, or when I suffer by living in misery myselfe. That the dead and we, are now all in one Church, and at the resurrection, shall be all in one Quire.

JOHN DONNE (*c.* 1571–1631); from one of his *Sermons*

221. *Death is the Gate of Life*

Death being the way and condition of life, we cannot love to live if we cannot bear to die. I have often wondered at the unaccountableness of man in this, among other things; that

tho' he loves changes so well, he should care so little to hear or
think of his last, great and best change too, if he pleases. The
truest end of Life, is, to know the Life that never ends. He
that lives to live ever, never fears dying. Nor can the Means
be terrible to him that heartily believes the End. For tho'
Death be a Dark Passage, it leads to Immortality, and that's
Recompense enough for suffering of it.

They that love *beyond the World* cannot be separated by it
(death).

Death cannot kill what never dies. Nor can Spirits ever be
divided that love and live in the same Divine Principle; the
Root and *Record* of their friendship.

If Absence be not Death, neither is theirs. Death is but the
Crossing the World, as friends do the Seas; They live in one
another still.

For they must needs be present, that love and live in that
which is *Omnipresent*.

In this Divine Glass they see Face to Face; and their converse is Free as well as Pure.

This is the comfort of Friends, that though they may be
said to Die, yet their Friendship and Society are, in the best
Sense, ever present, because *Immortal*.

WILLIAM PENN (1644–1718), *The Fruits of Solitude*

222. *Christian and Hopeful enter the Heavenly City*

A reading from *The Pilgrim's Progress*: the two pilgrims had now
reached the end of their dangerous journey, and had come to the gate
of the City.

Now while they were thus drawing towards the gate, behold a
company of the heavenly host came out to meet them; to whom
it was said by the other two Shining Ones, 'these are the men
that have loved our Lord when they were in the world, and

that have forsaken all for His Holy name; and He hath sent us to fetch them, and we have brought them thus far on their desired journey, that they may go in and look their Redeemer in the face with joy.'

Now when they were come up at the gate, there was written over it in letters of gold, 'Blessed are they that do His commandments, that they may have right to the tree of life, and may enter in through the gates into the city.' Then I saw in my dream that the Shining Men bid them call at the gate; the which when they did, some from above looked over the gate, to wit, Enoch, Moses and Elijah, etc.; to whom it was said, 'These pilgrims are come from the City of Destruction, for the love that they bear to the King of this place:' and then the pilgrims gave in unto them each man his certificate, which they had received in the beginning. Those therefore were carried in to the King, who, when he had read them, said 'Where are the men?' To whom it was answered, 'They are standing without the gate.' The King then commanded to open the gate, that the righteous nation, said He, that keepeth truth may enter in.

Now I saw in my dream that these two men went in at the gate; and lo! as they entered, they were transfigured; and they had raiment put on that shone like gold. . . . Then I heard in my dream that all the bells in the city rang again for joy; and that it was said unto them, 'Enter ye into the joy of your Lord.' I also heard the men themselves sing with a loud voice, saying, 'Blessing and honour and glory and power be unto Him that sitteth upon the throne, and unto the Lamb for ever and ever'.

JOHN BUNYAN (1628–88), *The Pilgrim's Progress*

223. Mr. Valiant-for-Truth crosses the River

At the end of *The Pilgrim's Progress*, Bunyan tells how other travellers, Mr. Honest and Mr. Valiant-for-Truth, were summoned to go across the river of death unto the Eternal City.

When the day that he was to be gone was come, he addressed himself to go over the river. Now the river at that time over-flowed its banks in some places; but Mr. Honest in his life-time had spoken to one Good-Conscience to meet him there; the which he also did, and lent him his hand and so helped him over. The last words of Mr. Honest were, 'Grace reigns:' so he left the world.

After this it was noised abroad that Mr. Valiant-for-Truth was taken with a summons by the same post as the other, and had this for a token that the summons was true, *That his pitcher was broken at the fountain*. When he understood it, he called for his friends and told them of it. Then said he, 'I am going to my Father's; and though with great difficulty I have got hither, yet now I do not repent me of all the trouble I have been at to arrive where I am. My sword I give to him who shall succeed me in my pilgrimage, and my courage and skill to him that can get it. My marks and scars I carry with me, to be a witness for me that I have fought his battles, who now will be my rewarder.' When the day that he must go hence was come, many accompanied him to the river-side; into which as he went, he said, *Death, where is thy sting?* And as he went deeper he said, *Grave, where is thy victory?* So he passed over, and all the trumpets sounded for him on the other side.

JOHN BUNYAN (1628–88), *The Pilgrim's Progress* (Part II)

II. GOD

224. 'The Word was made Flesh'

Oh, hearken, for this is wonder!
Light looked down and beheld Darkness;
'Thither will I go,' said Light.
Peace looked down and beheld war.
'Thither will I go,' said Peace.
Love looked down and beheld Hatred.
'Thither will I go,' said Love.
So came Light, and shone.
So came Peace, and gave rest.
So came Love, and brought life.
And the Word was made Flesh, and dwelt among us.

LAURENCE HOUSMAN; from 'Brother Sun', in
Little Plays of St. Francis

225. 'I believe in God'

Where is the emphasis in the Creed? Is it '*I* believe in God?'
Or is it 'I believe in *God*? There is no doubt where the answer
of all wholesome religion lies . . . the thing that is important is
that there is a God to believe in. There is a story of a young
lady who asked Dr. Jowett 'Oh Master, do tell me—what do
you think about God?' To which the Master replied 'That,
my dear young lady, is a very unimportant question; the only
thing that signifies is what He thinks about me.' In all our
efforts to study religious life, whether in our own or in other
forms of faith, and to build up our conscience, our character,
even to determine our form of service, if these things once get
into the first place, the whole religious life is wrecked; you
have got away from the one reality—God, and are centring

upon your own feelings and activities. . . . In the New Testament, if it is true at all, we are face to face with God; if that is not true, the New Testament is written under an illusion from end to end. It would be a very interesting illusion, and it would be thoroughly worth while to study it, for it has produced great effects in the history of the world, but an illusion all the same. The men who wrote the books of the New Testament believed that in Jesus Christ, God Himself lived and walked about among them. 'The Word was made flesh and dwelt among us.' They start from there.

WILLIAM TEMPLE (1881–1944), *The Universality of Christ*

226. 'God was in Christ'

In Jesus Christ, God was made visible to us. A modern Christian writer explains how this can be true.

First of all, Jesus Christ was a Man, in the full psychological sense, sharing truly and fully in the conditions of our humanity. The fact which confronts us in the New Testament in all the wonder of its perfection is an actual human life He was no phantom, archangel or demi-god.

It is vitally important that we do not in any way obscure the truth that Jesus was a Man. . . . He not only ate and drank; he knew hunger, thirst and weariness. Consider his bravery, his sense of humour, his severity, his tenderness. To use Pilate's words, 'Behold the Man'—poor, born in an outhouse, working, journeying, praying; tempted as we are tempted. Behold him, healing and teaching the pathetic multitudes, touched with the feeling of men's infirmities, himself a Man of sorrows and acquainted with grief. He was human enough to weep over the woes of those whom he was not ashamed to call his brethren. Bearing in his heart the burden and shame of their sin, he nevertheless stood in with them and loved them to the end. Utterly clear-sighted, he was the vigorous debater, ruthlessly exposing and fiercely denouncing the shams of much conventional religion. Without a trace of self-pity he went deliberately to Jerusalem to die. His was the highest, holiest Manhood which this world has seen or can see, and at the last—we men and women being what we are—he was nailed to a gallows to die with criminals, the innocent victim of fear, bigotry, jealous hatred, political opportunism and legalized murder. He was crucified, dead and buried. Here in this human life we meet the living God. It is God himself, personally present and redeemingly active, who comes to meet men in this Man of Nazareth. Jesus is more than a religious genius, such as George Fox, and more than a holy man, such as the lovable Lama in Kipling's *Kim*. He himself knows that he is more. The Gospel story is a tree rooted in the familiar soil of time and sense; but its roots go down into the Abyss and its branches fill the Heavens; given to us in terms of a country in the Eastern Mediterranean no bigger than Wales, during the Roman Principate of Tiberius Caesar in the first century of our era, its range is universal; it is on the scale of eternity. God's presence and his very Self were made manifest in the words and works of this Man.

In short, the Man Christ Jesus has the decisive place in man's ageless relationship with God. He is what God means by 'Man.' He is what man means by 'God.'

J. S. WHALE, *Christian Doctrine*

227. *The Life of Christ*

Jeremy Taylor, the seventeenth-century churchman, reminds us what sort of a life the Son of God lived on earth.

Christ entered into the world with all the circumstances of poverty. He had a star to illustrate His birth: but a stable for His bed-chamber, and a manger for His cradle. The angels sang hymns when He was born: but He was cold and cried, uneasy and unprovided. He lived long in the trade of a carpenter; He, by whom God made the world, had in His first years the business of a mean and an ignoble trade. He did good wherever He went: and almost wherever He went, was abused. He deserved heaven for His obedience, but found a cross in His way thither: and if ever any man had reason to expect fair usages from God, and to be dandled in the lap of ease, softness, and a prosperous fortune, He it was only that could deserve that, or any thing that can be good; but after He had chosen to live a life of virtue, of poverty, and labour, He entered into a state of death, whose shame and trouble was great enough to pay for the sins of the whole world. . . .

JEREMY TAYLOR (1613–67)

228. How Jesus Lived

We often hear of Jesus of Nazareth as a wandering teacher; and there is a vital truth in that view in so far as it emphasizes an attitude towards luxury and convention which most respectable people would still regard as that of a vagabond. It is expressed in his own great saying about the holes of the foxes and the nests of the birds.[1] . . . It is well to speak of his wanderings in this sense and in the sense that he shared the drifting life of the most homeless and hopeless of the poor. It is assuredly well to remember that he would quite certainly have been moved on by the police, and almost certainly arrested by the police, for having no visible means of subsistence.

G. K. CHESTERTON (1875–1936), *The Everlasting Man*

229. The Miracles of Jesus

The miracles of Jesus were the ordinary works of His Father, wrought small and swift that we might take them in. . . . In all His miracles Jesus did only in miniature what His Father does

[1] Matthew viii. 20.

ever in the great. Poor, indeed, was the making of the wine in the . . . pots of stone, compared with its making in the lovely growth of the vine with its clusters of swelling grapes—the live roots gathering from the earth the water that had to be borne in pitchers and poured into the great vases; but it is precious as the interpreter of the same, even in its being the outcome of Our Lord's sympathy with ordinary human rejoicing.

GEORGE MACDONALD (1824–1905)

230. The Call of Christ

He comes to us as One unknown, without a name, as of old, by the lake-side, He came to those men who knew Him not. He speaks to us the same words: 'Follow thou me!'[1] and sets us to the tasks which He has to fulfil for our time. He commands. And to those who obey Him, whether they be wise or simple, He will reveal Himself in the toils, the conflicts, the sufferings which they shall pass through in His fellowship, and, as an ineffable mystery, they shall learn in their own experience Who He is.

ALBERT SCHWEITZER, *The Quest of the Historical Jesus*

231. The Face of Christ

A famous Russian writer describes a dream which was full of meaning to him.

I saw myself, in dream, a youth, almost a boy, in a low-pitched wooden church. The slim wax candles gleamed, spots of red, before the old pictures of the saints.

A ring of coloured light encircled each tiny flame. Dark and dim it was in the church. . . . But there stood before me many people. All fair-haired, peasant heads. From time to time they

[1] Matthew iv. 19; John xxi. 22.

began swaying, falling, rising again, like the ripe ears of wheat, when the wind of summer passes in slow undulation over them.

All at once some man came up from behind and stood beside me.

I did not turn towards him; but at once I felt that this man was Christ.

Emotion, curiosity, awe overmastered me suddenly. I made an effort . . . and looked at my neighbour.

A face like every one's, a face like all men's faces. The eyes looked a little upwards, quietly and intently. The lips closed, but not compressed; the upper lip, as it were, resting on the lower; a small beard parted in two. The hands folded and still. And the clothes on him like every one's.

'What sort of Christ is this?' I thought. 'Such an ordinary, ordinary man! It can't be!'

I turned away. But I had hardly turned my eyes away from this ordinary man when I felt again that it really was none other than Christ standing beside me.

Again I made an effort over myself. . . . And again the same face, like all men's faces, the same everyday though unknown features.

And suddenly my heart sank, and I came to myself. Only then I realised that just such a face—a face like all men's faces —is the face of Christ.

IVAN TURGENEV (1818–83); from *Dream Tales and Prose Poems*,
Constance Garnett's translation

232. *The Kingdom of God*

O World invisible, we view thee,
O world intangible, we touch thee,
O world unknowable, we know thee,
Inapprehensible, we clutch thee!

Does the fish soar to find the ocean,
The eagle plunge to find the air—
That we ask of the stars in motion
If they have rumour of thee there?

Not where the wheeling systems darken,
And our benumbed conceiving soars!—
The drift of pinions, would we hearken,
Beats at our own clay-shuttered doors.

The angels keep their ancient places;—
Turn but a stone, and start a wing!
'Tis ye, 'tis your estrangèd faces,
That miss the many-splendoured thing.

But (when so sad thou canst not sadder)
Cry;—and upon thy so sore loss
Shall shine the traffic of Jacob's ladder
Pitched betwixt Heaven and Charing Cross.

Yes, in the night, my Soul, my daughter,
Cry,—clinging Heaven by the hems;
And lo, Christ walking on the water,
Not of Gennesareth, but Thames!

FRANCIS THOMPSON (1859–1907)

233. The Discovery of God

Once I remember I thus reasoned with myself, sitting in a little, obscure room, in my father's poor house: 'If there be a God, certainly He must be infinite in Goodness' (and that, I was prompted to, by a real, whispering instinct of Nature) 'And if He be infinite in Goodness, and a perfect Being in wisdom and love, certainly He must do most glorious things and give us infinite riches: how comes it to pass, therefore, that I am so poor? Of so scanty and narrow a fortune, enjoying few and obscure comforts? I thought I could not believe Him a God to me, unless all His power were employed to glorify me. I knew not then my soul or body; nor did I think of the heavens or the earth, the rivers or the stars, the sun or the seas; all those were lost and absent from me. But when I found them made out of nothing, for me, then I had a God indeed, whom I could praise and rejoice in.

THOMAS TRAHERNE (1634?–1704), *Centuries of Meditation*

234. *The Knowledge of God*

To know God is to know Goodness. It is to see the beauty of infinite Love: to see it attended with Almighty Power and Eternal Wisdom; and using both those in the magnifying of its object. It is to see the King of Heaven and Earth take infinite delight in giving. . . . He is not an object of terror but Delight. To know Him therefore as He is, is to frame the most beautiful idea in all worlds. He delighteth in our happiness more than we, and is of all other the most lovely object. An infinite Lord, who having all Riches, Honours and Pleasures in His own hand, is infinitely willing to give them unto me. Which is the fairest idea that can be devised.

THOMAS TRAHERNE (1634?–1704), *Centuries of Meditation*

235. *God's Forbearance*

When Abraham sat at his tent door, according to his custom, waiting to entertain strangers, he espied an old man, stooping and leaning on his staff, weary with age and travail, coming towards him, who was a hundred years of age; he received him kindly, washed his feet, provided supper, caused him to sit down; but observing that the old man ate and prayed not, nor begged a blessing on his meat, he asked him why he did not worship the God of heaven. The old man told him that he worshipped the fire only, and acknowledged no other God. At which answer Abraham grew so zealously angry, that he threw the old man out of his tent, and exposed him to all the evils of the night and an unguarded condition. When the old man was gone, God called to Abraham, and asked him where the stranger was. He replied, 'I thrust him away, because he did not worship thee.' God answered him, 'I have suffered him these hundred years, though he dishonoured me; and wouldst thou not endure him one night?'

JEREMY TAYLOR (1613–67), *The Liberty of Prophesying*

236. God's Goodness

God is unwearied patience, a meekness that cannot be provoked; He is an ever enduring mercifulness; He is unwearied goodness, impartial, universal love: He does everything that is good, righteous and lovely for its own sake, because it is good, righteous and lovely. He is the good from which nothing but good comes and resisteth all evil only with goodness. This is the nature and spirit of God.

WILLIAM LAW (1686–1781)

237. God's Mercy and Grace

John Bunyan, author of *The Pilgrim's Progress*, also wrote other books, from one of which these words are taken:

Mercy is that by which we are pardoned, even all the falls, faults, failings and weaknesses, that attend us, and that we are incident to, in this our day of temptation: and for this mercy we should pray, and say, 'Our Father, forgive us our trespasses.' For though mercy is free in the exercise of it to usward, yet God will have us ask, that we may have; as he also saith in the text, 'Let us come boldly unto the throne of grace, that we may obtain mercy.' That is what David means when he says, 'Surely goodness and mercy shall follow me all the days of my life, and I will dwell in the house of the Lord for ever.'

And again, 'When I say my foot slippeth; thy mercy, O Lord, held me up.'

This then is the conclusion, that as there is mercy to be obtained by us at the throne of grace, for the pardon of all our weaknesses; so there is also grace there to be found that will yet strengthen us more, to all good walking and living before him.

JOHN BUNYAN (1628–88), *The Saint's Privilege and Profit*

238. God's Compassion

Here is thy footstool and there rest thy feet where live the poorest, and lowliest, and lost.

When I try to bow to thee, my obeisance cannot reach down to the depth where thy feet rest among the poorest, and lowliest, and lost.

Pride can never approach to where thou walkest in the clothes of the humble among the poorest, and lowliest, and lost.

My heart can never find its way to where thou keepest company with the companionless among the poorest, the lowliest, and the lost.

RABINDRANATH TAGORE (1861–1941), *Gitanjali*

239. Immanence

I come in the little things,
Saith the Lord:
Not borne on the morning wings
Of majesty, but I have set My Feet
Amidst the delicate and bladed wheat
That springs triumphant in the furrowed sod.

There do I dwell, in weakness and in power;
Not broken or divided, saith our God!
In your strait garden plot I come to flower:
About your porch My Vine
Meek, fruitful, doth entwine;
Waits, at the threshold, Love's appointed hour.

I come in the little things,
Saith the Lord:
Yea! on the glancing wings
Of eager birds, the softly pattering feet
Of furred and gentle beasts, I come to meet
Your hard and wayward heart. In brown bright eyes
That peep from out the brake, I stand confest.
On every nest
Where feathery Patience is content to brood
And leaves her pleasure for the high emprize
Of motherhood—
There doth My Godhead rest.

I come in the little things,
Saith the Lord:
My starry wings
I do forsake,
Love's highway of humility to take:
Meekly I fit my stature to your need.
In beggar's part
About your gates I shall not cease to plead—
As man, to speak with man—
Till by such art
I shall achieve My Immemorial Plan,
Pass the low lintel of the human heart.

EVELYN UNDERHILL (1871–1941)

240. *All Times are God's Seasons*

God made sun and moon to distinguish seasons, and day and night, and we cannot have the fruits of the earth but in their seasons: but God hath made no decree to distinguish the seasons of his mercies; in paradise the fruits were ripe, the first minute, and in heaven it is always autumn, his mercies are ever in their maturity. We ask *panem quotidianum*, our daily bread, and God never says you should have come yesterday, he never says you must come again tomorrow, but 'today if you will hear his voice,' today he will hear you. If some king of the earth hath so large an extent of dominion in north and south, as that he hath winter and summer together in his dominions, so large an extent east and west, as that he hath day and night together in his dominions, much more hath God mercy and judgment together: . . . though . . . thou have been benighted till now, wintred and frozen, clouded and eclipsed, damped and benumbed, smothered and stupified till now, how God comes to thee, not as in the dawning of the day, not as in the bud of the spring, but as the sun at noon to illustrate all shadows, as the sheaves in harvest, to fill all penuries, all occasions invite his mercies, and all times are his seasons.

JOHN DONNE (*c.* 1571–1631)

241. *Love*

Love bade me welcome; yet my soul drew back,
    Guilty of dust and sin,
But quick-eyed Love, observing me grow slack
    From my first entrance in,
Drew nearer to me, sweetly questioning
    If I lacked anything.

'A guest,' I answered, 'worthy to be here':
  Love said, 'You shall be he.'
'I, the unkind, ungrateful? Ah, my dear,
  I cannot look on Thee.'
Love took my hand and smiling did reply,
  'Who made the eyes but I?'

'Truth, Lord; but I have marred them: let my shame
  Go where it doth deserve.'
'And know you not,' says Love, 'Who bore the blame?'
  'My dear, then I will serve.'
'You must sit down,' says Love, 'and taste my meat.'
  So I did sit and eat.

GEORGE HERBERT (1593–1633)

242. God's Providence

The Lady Juliana (or Julian) of Norwich was a woman hermit, or 'anchoress', and mystic.

As verily as we shall be in the bliss of God without end, Him praising and thanking, so verily we have been in the foresight of God, loved and known in His endless purpose from without beginning. In which beginning love He made us; and in the same love He keepeth us and never suffereth us to be hurt (in any way) by which our bliss might be lost. And therefore when the Doom is given and we be all brought up above, then (shall) we clearly see in God the privities which now be hidden to us. Then shall none of us be stirred to say in any wise: 'Lord, if it had been thus, then it had been full well;' but we shall say all with one voice: 'Lord, blessed mayst Thou be, for it is thus: it is well.'

JULIANA OF NORWICH (c. 1342–1413 or later),
Revelations of Divine Love

243. God

The Confessions of St. Augustine are in the form of a meditation in which the author speaks to God about himself, his doubts and sins, and how he was drawn to God.

But what do I love when I love Thee? Not grace of bodies, nor the beauty of the seasons, nor the brightness of the light, . . . nor inexhaustible melodies of sweet song, nor the fragrant smell of flowers, of ointments and spices. . . . None of these love I when I love my God: and yet I love a kind of light, and of melody and of fragrance . . . when I love my God. . . .

And what is this? I asked the earth and it said, 'I am not He:' and whatsoever is in it confessed the same. I asked the sea and the deeps, and all that swimming or creeping live therein, and they answered 'We are not thy God, seek above us.' I asked the wandering winds; and the whole air with his inhabitants spoke . . . 'I am not God.' I asked the heavens, sun, moon and stars, 'Nor (say they) are we the God whom thou seekest.' And I replied unto all those things which encompass the door of my flesh, 'Ye have told me of my God, that ye are not He: tell me something of Him.' And they cried all with a great voice, 'He made us.' My questioning them was my mind's desire, and their Beauty was their answer.

ST. AUGUSTINE (354–430), *Confessions*

INDEX

Names in CAPITALS are those of authors and others whose work is quoted. Numbers are those of the passages, not of pages.